Mark E. Sullivan

Client Letters for the Family Lawyer

Saving Time, Managing Relationships, and Practicing Preventive Law

16 15 14 13   5 4 3 2 1

Library of Congress Cataloging-in-Publication Data on file.

ISBN 978-1-62722-249-5

Discounts are available for books ordered in bulk. Special consideration is given to state bars, CLE programs, and other bar-related organizations. Inquire at Book Publishing, ABA Publishing, American Bar Association, 321 North Clark Street, Chicago, Illinois 60654-7598.

www.ShopABA.org

Contents

About the Author

Mark E. Sullivan is a partner in Sullivan and Tanner, P.A., a Raleigh, North Carolina firm specializing in family law. A board-certified specialist in family law since 1989, he has served as Chairman of the ABA Standing Committee on Legal Assistance for Military Personnel, as Vice-Chair of the North Carolina Bar Association's Family Law Section and as president of the state's chapter of the American Academy of Matrimonial Lawyers. Mr. Sullivan has written hundreds of articles on family law, military domestic issues, negotiations, mediation, family law arbitration, evidence, advocacy and persuasion. His book, *The Military Divorce Handbook* (ABA, 2nd Ed. 2011) has been a best-seller for the Section of Family Law, and he is a frequent speaker at CLE programs throughout the United States. He has authored over 80 info-letters for clients on various aspects of family law, trials, discovery and legal representation. Mr. Sullivan has also written dozens of client information letters for military personnel in North Carolina (TAKE-1) and around the world (Legal Eagle), as well as lawyers in North Carolina (Co-Counsel Bulletin) and worldwide (Silent Partner). His articles have been published in the AMERICAN JOURNAL OF FAMILY LAW, THE MILITARY LAW REVIEW, THE ARMY LAWYER, and dozens of state bar association family law journals.

Acknowledgments

I wish to thank my family and my law office staff for their support in my writing *Client Letters for the Family Lawyer*. Special thanks go to my wife, Teresa Sullivan, and my office manager, Donna Brickey, without whose help I couldn't have written this book.

Introduction

[Adapted from "A Handout Strategy for the General Practitioner," *The Practical Lawyer*, Vol. 43, No. 4, June 1997.]

It is well recognized by practitioners that an ounce of legal prevention is worth far more than a pound of cure. The avoidance of legal problems through education and publicity can go a long way toward reducing the time and expense of such problems for the client and prevent worrying about a car being repossessed, a credit problem, or a custody dispute. If a problem can be avoided or detected early, the time spent will be far less than if it is brought to the lawyer when it is really too late—the car has been towed away by the finance company, the credit rating is shot, or the child has just been snatched.

Lawyers prefer preventive law; it keeps the client caseload at a manageable level and reduces the incidence of schedule-crippling emergencies. Because of the substantial savings in time, money, and anxiety, preventive law and client education are favorites with the client as well. This being the case, why is it that the concepts of client education and preventive law are still vastly underused by lawyers? Why is it so difficult to create and sustain a client education program? The reason is that the program's best advocates are also its worst enemies.

The attorney who benefits tremendously from preventive law simply does not have the "down time" to devote to preparing speeches or writing pamphlets. Too often, lawyers get caught on a hopeless treadmill; they have to run so hard to catch up with today's problems, both emergency and routine, that they have no time to plan and prepare for prevention and education tomorrow. It is ironic that if someone *did* have the time to do substantial work in preventive law, it would very likely return an equivalent or greater net savings in time at the lawyer's office. Although empirical measurement is impossible, "time saved" should more than make up for "time spent" in a good preventive law and education program.

Once these handicaps are identified, it is easier to deal with them as obstacles to a preventive law and client education program. With persistence and organization, they can be overcome. This article covers the promise, problems, and practicalities of a sound preventive law and client education program for the general practitioner.

The Facts of Life

The general practitioner quickly learns "three facts of life" regarding clients' cases. These are common to all offices, regardless of location.

First, a high percentage of the office workload is composed of a half dozen or so key subjects. The best examples are:

1. Housing and real estate (evictions, security deposits, housing codes, leases, and home purchases);

2. Consumer protection (used cars and car repairs, freezer meat sales, interstate land contracts, door-to-door sales, mail-order offers, time-sharing agreements, and so-called "free gifts");

3. Criminal and traffic offenses (trespass, assault, speeding, driving while impaired, lack of proper registration or inspection); and

4. Family law (divorce, separation agreements, property division, custody and visitation, alimony, child support, adoption and paternity disputes).

Thorough knowledge of these key problem areas will inevitably expedite the intake and interview processes, as well as improve the ability of the attorney to render meaningful and effective aid to the client.

Second, there are certain key questions that continue to be asked in each subject area, such as:

1. "How do I get a divorce?"

2. "What do I have to pay when selling my house?"

3. "How can I get my child support on time?"

4. "What can I do to get back my rental security deposit?"

5. "What kind of insurance points will this ticket cost me?"

Third, the creation and avoidance of legal problems often depends on factors that can be taught as *basic skills* (e.g., how to read a contract, compare costs, or exercise sales resistance) that can be identified and publicized in advance and that are generic in nature, rather than specific to a certain client or location. A client who knows how to read a contract will usually avoid problems with separation agreements as well as with leases and credit applications. A client who can budget, plan ahead, and avoid impulse buying will usually avoid problems with repossessions and foreclosures as well as complaints regarding child support.

Key Questions and the Handout Strategy

So long as certain key questions continue to be asked by our clients, it will remain the responsibility of the general practitioner to devise ways to answer them. This can be done in the time-honored one-by-one method: *"Gee, Mr. Smith, you'll have to make an appointment to find out how you can get your car repaired/divorce finalized/security deposit back. I've got an opening two weeks from tomorrow—is that okay?"* Or, it can be handled on a broad but efficient basis with the use of client assistance fact sheets, handouts, and pamphlets. These can be made available at a rack in the waiting room of the lawyer's office, or the attorney can give each new client a list of the pamphlets that are available. The writer's list of pamphlets is too large for an office rack, so each new client is given a list titled, "Yours for the Asking . . . ," and is encouraged to request as many handouts as are needed.

Handouts are real "rainmakers" for the firm. They can be given or sent to potential clients who call or contact the attorney about a problem but have not yet been interviewed at the office and accepted as clients. They can also be used as interview tools so that the client is "introduced" to the answers through the pamphlet before meeting with the attorney; then the attorney can fill in the details in the client's case and prepare specific advice on the client's problem.

Handouts and info-letters are superior to larger printed manuals on state law for the client because they tend to be picked up, read, and used, rather than handed out, skimmed, and stored for future use. In addition, they are usually cheaper to reproduce and easier to amend as the law changes. Finally, they can speed up the interview process by providing concise and realistic answers to the most common questions in certain key legal areas.

Writing Your Own Info-Letters and Handouts for Family Law Clients

[Adapted from "A Handout Strategy for the General Practitioner," *The Practical Lawyer*, Vol. 43, No. 4, June 1997.]

The ABCs of Handouts

For handouts and info-letters, a catchy headline or logo is the first step. The fact sheet must first catch the eye of the client with a legal problem. Common examples might be "The Legal Eagle," "The Divorce Advisor," "Legal Hotline" or "The Consumer's Lawyer." A set of legal pamphlets labeled "**TAKE-1**," produced by this writer, is currently in use at the legal assistance offices at Fort Bragg, North Carolina, and other military bases in the state.

In addition to bold printing for the standard logo, the use of drawings at the top of the handout can be helpful. Some frequent examples include a gavel, an eagle, the scales of justice, or a judge dressed in black robe behind a bench. Illustrations may also be used throughout the text to keep the attention of the reader or to emphasize a point. Often the word-processing program used by the lawyer will have a good graphics package for use here; one can also get images from Google, Yahoo and other search engines.

When selecting the subjects for a pamphlet series to be developed, remember these rules:

1. *Each handout should cover a specific and well-defined subject.* The client should be able to recognize the subject from the title of the fact sheet, such as "Child Support and the Single Parent," "So Your Used Car Is a Lemon . . . ," or "The Case of the Missing Security Deposit."

2. *Don't make the subject too broad.* It is simply impossible to treat "Texas Family Law" or "Consumer Protection in California" in a single and simple handout. The more narrow and specific the topic, the better. This, of necessity, makes for short, easy-to-read pamphlets, with less strain on the attention span of the target population. In each case, keep it short and (if possible) sweet.

Packaging the Product

3. *Decide on your format.* Some authors use a "text box" on the first page to put an eye-catching box around the information there. Your word-processing software probably has this feature, located at "Insert" on the menu bar. You can choose a border with single or double lines, thick or thin, dotted or dashed.

Others use a tri-fold pamphlet similar to ones that are available at the bank for checking account information or other bank services. With most word processing programs, just click on "File," then on "New" or "Template," and you'll see a selection of brochures under "Publish" that are already formatted and ready to use.

Inquiries and Issues

4. *Make the questions and answers clear and readable.* It takes a conscious effort to write for the client and not for the judge. Where lawyers use words like "litigation," "marital dissolution," and "motor vehicle," the usual client would prefer "court fight" or "trial," "divorce," and "car." Keep most words at one to three syllables. Use common nouns and verbs. Write short, declarative sentences in the active voice whenever possible. A reading specialist at a local school can help in the editing process by performing readability studies to determine the reading level required for selected writing samples or pamphlets. You should be writing for a fifth-grade reading ability.

5. *Have a beginning and an ending.* A simple introduction is desirable for each pamphlet. Use it to explain the scope and purpose of the handout. Here's an example:

INTRODUCTION. This handout is about the process of divorce. It explains how to file for divorce and how a wife may request the resumption of her maiden name. It will also tell you the legal effects of obtaining a divorce, how the hearing is conducted and what your testimony should be.

Likewise, a standard ending belongs in each brochure. Use it to remind the client to ask the attorney if he or she has any questions and to reiterate that "we're here to help you!" Here's a sample ending:

CONCLUSION. This pamphlet has covered the basics of how a divorce is obtained and what the legal effects of divorce are. We recognize that all your questions cannot be answered in a single handout. If you have other questions about the process of separation and divorce, or about the issues of child support, custody, or alimony, please feel free to ask us. And if you have any comments, suggestions, or criticisms about this handout, let us know. We're here to help!

6. *Answers should usually be broader than the original question.* Too many single-line questions and answers will take up more space than necessary and provide less useful information than the format of a single-line question and full paragraph answer. The function of the question is to attract the reader's attention when the question is relevant, and to allow him or her to skip ahead when it is not. A paragraph-length answer can be helpful in addressing the follow-up inquiries gen-

erated by the answer to the initial question. For example, compare the following alternative answers for effectiveness:

Q. 1: Can't I get an annulment if I've only been married a very short time?

A. 1: No. A short-time marriage is not a ground for annulment.

A. 1A: Just because a marriage has lasted only a short time does not mean it can be ended by annulment instead of divorce. While annulment may sometimes be faster than divorce, it is used for a different reason than divorce. A divorce is the legal breakup of a valid and legal marriage. An annulment is a judge's ruling that a valid marriage, for some reason, has never existed. Some reasons may be that one of the parties is under the legal age of marriage, was already married at the time of the ceremony, or was forced to go through with the marriage by someone. If you want advice on the grounds for divorce or annulment, please ask one of our attorneys.

Q. 2: If I am not getting any child support from my ex-husband, I don't have to let him see the kids, right?

A. 2: Wrong—you cannot withhold visitation legally for this reason in North Carolina.

A. 2A: The law in North Carolina does not allow parents to use visitation or child support to punish each other. Even if you are not receiving enough or *any* child support, it is not a legal excuse for refusing to allow visitation. You should go to court or ask for help from an attorney to obtain child support. Similarly, if you cannot obtain visitation with your children, you should go to court for visitation rights rather than withholding needed child support from them.

What's the difference between the two types of answers? The second answer in each of the above examples is broad enough to cover two or three simple questions. Because these longer answers were used to answer anticipated follow-up questions, they provide a more comprehensive response than the shorter answers.

7. *Choose the text features you want.* Choose the right size typeface (or "font") for your opus. Most manuscripts and pleadings are done in 12-point size, but you can choose a slightly smaller one (say, 10-point) for your brochure and wind up saving a small amount of space (or getting more information in the same amount of space). Ten-point size for characters is approximately the size of newspaper print.

If you're using questions and answers, which is the best way of doing a client handout, make your life easier by choosing "Outline" or "Auto Paragraph Numbering" from "Tools" on the menu bar of WordPerfect (or "Bullets and Numbering" for MS Word). This will allow you to number your items automatically, and it will also renumber your questions if you decide to move or delete an item.

Want to save half the cost of reproducing the handouts? Think about front-and-back copying. Many copiers come equipped with this feature, and it will cut in half the number of pages you need to reproduce!

Name recognition is important. Use your letterhead at the top of the first page to tell the client who developed this wonderful handout! And don't feel you're stuck with plain paper; sometimes colored paper (gray or cream) is a better choice than plain white bond. Consider whether you want to print the pamphlets on a heavier stock than simple "typing paper" if the pamphlets are to be used and reused by your clients (or, better yet, passed on to others!).

Consider using "footers" for a copyright notice on the first page, as well as for reprint permission if that is to be given to others. A simple reprint notice might read, "Prepared and produced by Mark E. Sullivan, Attorney at Law, Raleigh, North Carolina. Reprint permission is hereby granted to other attorneys for this pamphlet so long as the preceding sentence is reproduced at the bottom of the first page of the handout." Both MS Word and WordPerfect have "footer" features.

Final Considerations

8. *Pace yourself and ask for input from others*. It is impossible to do an entire series in a month, or even a season, given the average attorney's schedule priorities and manpower constraints. Doing a fact sheet series in phases makes the project manageable and doesn't overwhelm the editor or author. It allows for ready revisions based on format modifications or changes in statutes or case law. It permits others to provide criticism, suggestions, questions, and other useful feedback. It may even be possible to obtain contributions from the local district attorney, motor vehicle department officials, consumer protection specialists, the state attorney general's office, Better Business Bureau or Chamber of Commerce, local housing or public health officials, any number of federal agencies and departments, and the federal government's Consumer Information Center in Pueblo, Colorado.

9. *Don't re-invent the wheel*. If it is possible to get permission to use and modify materials already developed by others, the resulting savings of time will allow more pamphlets in the series to be drafted or other projects to be started. Plagiarism is the sincerest form of flattery. In preparing the "TAKE-1" handout on wills currently in use at Fort Bragg, this author used and modified the questions and answers in two different will pamphlets, one from the North Carolina Bar Foundation and the other from the Naval Legal Services Office, Norfolk, Virginia. Because of the different approach in each handout, it was possible to generate about 17 different questions on matters such as interstate succession, executors, division of personal property, estate tax liability, trusts, and guardianship for minor children or incompetents. This was twice the number of questions in either individual pamphlet.

Conclusion

Handouts and fact sheets developed for clients by general practitioners can be helpful in preventing legal problems and useful in solving difficulties at an early stage. They can also reduce interview time because the client can obtain many answers before seeing the attorney. In considering the many advantages of using legal handouts with the time necessary for preparation and the cost of printing, it is clear that the handout strategy is an important phase of a serious preventive law and client education plan at the general practitioner's office. However, it is important to note that "one size fits all" does *not* apply here; you will need to adapt all material to conform to your own state laws and regulations.

Part I

Office Procedures

Section 1

Dispute Resolution

Checklist on Advantages of Arbitration

With mutual consent, arbitration can be used to settle disputes both big and small between the two parties to a domestic dispute. The parties usually split the cost of the arbitrator. Here are some pointers to remember about why arbitration is worth considering in your case.

- **ARBITRATE ANYTHING.** Other than the granting of a divorce, an arbitrator can do just about everything that a judge can do—custody, visitation, child support, alimony, and equitable distribution. We can even use arbitration for decisions in disputes that involve just a part of a case, such as decisions in a joint custody dispute or valuation of items of personal property.

- **NO COURTROOM.** The hearings are held outside the courthouse at a place of the parties' own choosing. Usually, this is in the conference room of one of the lawyers' offices. Privacy is ensured; there is no audience of onlookers, and the atmosphere is comfortable and less formal than a courtroom.

- **YOU PICK THE DECISION-MAKER.** Instead of having the court system pick the judge for you, as in many judicial districts, the parties and their lawyers can actually choose who will decide their case. They frequently will choose a Fellow of the American Academy of Matrimonial Lawyers or a Family Law Specialist who is certified as an arbitrator, giving them a "judge" with the knowledge and expertise—in family law *and* arbitration—to handle the case properly. In fact, the arbitrator doesn't even have to be a lawyer—you can choose an arbitrator whose background matches that of your case. If it's a visitation arbitration, why not try a psychologist or social worker? If the case involves a difficult business valuation, appoint a CPA or an economist.

- **EFFICIENCY.** Efficiency means saving time and money—and making smart use of the money and time you have. With arbitration, we don't have to wait for the calendar to be printed and the court administrator to set your case for a hearing several months down the line. We don't have to show up for calendar call and then sit around and wait for the case to be heard—assuming it isn't "bumped" by another case. Ours is the only case on the docket! We get to choose the date and the time with most arbitrators, and there isn't a 30–60 day wait to get on the docket, either. Most of the time, we can set a case for an arbitration within two to four weeks of the request. All of that translates into "money efficiency" for the client. It usually costs a client less money if the case is concluded promptly. That's just what arbitration can do. There are none of the delays associated with "going to court." You'll probably find that the money we save more than pays for the cost of the arbitrator, which is usually split 50-50 between the parties.

- **PREPARATION.** Preparation means we can take the case in stages if it's one with several issues, and set up separate hearings on different days. This gives us time to prepare separately for each one. In a custody case, we could deal with school issues on Monday, the psychologist's testimony on Wednesday, mom's issues on Friday, and dad's issues the following Tuesday. With an equitable distribution case, we can separately hear the issues of valuation, classification, and distribution at different times, or we can present evidence on separate dates as to the home, the spouse's business, the pension, and the personal property.

• FLEXIBILITY. There's much more flexibility available when the case is arbitrated instead of tried in court. You don't have to stop at 5 p.m., which is when the courtroom closes down. You can work through lunch if you want. In fact, with the agreement of the parties and the arbitrator, the case can be heard in the evenings so that the parties don't have to take off time from work, or even on a Saturday. Try doing that in district court!

■■■

Collaborative Family Law

What is "Collaborative Family Law"?

Collaborative Family Law is a process of resolving family law disputes without going to court. Attorneys and clients alike have long recognized the negative impact that litigation has on parties and their children. Studies have shown that the majority of parents going through a separation or divorce are unhappy with the court process and want a way to resolve disputes that is simpler, cheaper, less adversarial, and more attentive to their children's concerns about the events surrounding the divorce. Collaborative Family Law was developed to address these important concerns and to try to reduce the high emotional, psychological, and financial cost of the traditional adversarial litigation process.

Where did the idea come from?

Collaborative Law is the brain-child of Stuart Webb, a Minnesota family law attorney. After practicing family law for more than 20 years, Mr. Webb became disenchanted with the traditional litigation-based method of resolving family law disputes and its harmful effect on families. He invited his colleagues to join him in a dispute resolution process focused solely on creative settlements rather than on going to court. As Mr. Webb envisioned it, the attorneys involved in this new process would no longer go to court, but would instead represent clients through negotiations aimed at reaching practical, mutually agreeable settlements. If the process broke down and no settlement was reached, the attorneys would withdraw and refer the case to litigation counsel. From this beginning, the Collaborative Law model has grown in popularity and acceptance.

What are the features of Collaborative Family Law?

No Court. The primary feature of the Collaborative Law model is the limitation that the attorney will represent the client only in the negotiation process and will be disqualified from representing the client should the process break down and either side choose to go to court. This will be set out in the legal services contract that each party has with his or her attorney, as well as in the collaborative law participation agreement or pledge that all parties and their attorneys will sign. The "no court" approach motivates participants to approach negotiations without the litigation-based posturing which many times interferes with the settlement process. Instead, the collective problem-solving skills of both attorneys and both clients are focused on reaching an agreement rather than on preparing or building their case for court.

Full Disclosure. Another important feature of Collaborative Law is the agreement between all participants to provide full, open, and honest disclosure of all relevant information and documents. This approach helps minimize the game-playing and delay that sometimes accompanies the information-gathering process. It also enables the focus to quickly move toward negotiating an appropriate and realistic settlement based on a common understanding of the underlying facts.

JOINT NEUTRAL EXPERTS. In many cases, the assistance of other professionals, such as child psychologists, financial planners, tax specialists, real estate appraisers, business or pension valuators, etc., will be helpful to the parties as they work toward resolution. The Collaborative Law model requires that a neutral expert be hired jointly by the parties rather than having each party hire his or her own expert. This helps avoid the common problem in litigation of "the battle of the experts," which can be counterproductive and expensive.

FOUR-WAY CONFERENCES. The main method, although not the only method, of moving a Collaborative Family Law case forward through negotiations is by joint conferences with both parties and their attorneys. These four-way conferences allow the parties to work through the issues in their case in a time-efficient (and, therefore, cost-effective) way. There may be many four-way conferences or only a few, depending on the complexity of the issues involved and how effectively the parties are progressing toward a resolution.

How does it work?

Both parties must hire attorneys committed to handling the case under the Collaborative Law model. All participants involved in the process should sign a Collaborative Law participation agreement or pledge acknowledging their voluntary choice to use the Collaborative Law process and to adhere to the principles of that process. This is usually done at the first four-way conference. Also at the first four-way conference, the parties often develop a plan for exchanging necessary documents and information and discuss how the case will proceed. Through subsequent four-way conferences the parties discuss and work through all of the issues in the case until they have reached a resolution.

How do I know if Collaborative Family Law right for me?

Clients who want to use the legal process to punish the other party or insist on having court as a forum for telling their story are not good candidates for Collaborative Law. Likewise, clients who insist on taking unreasonable positions and are unwilling to compromise or whose motivation is to take advantage of the other party will not be compatible with the Collaborative Law process. On the other hand, clients who recognize that compromise is something that you do for yourself as much as for the other party will likely find the Collaborative Family Law process satisfying. Collaborative Law clients understand that reaching an agreement with which *both* parties can be satisfied is far better than investing the time, money, and emotional energy into going to court and letting a judge decide what will happen to your property or your children. A good Collaborative Law client must be willing to behave in a respectful and civil manner toward the other party as they work together to resolve the issues surrounding their separation or divorce. This does not mean that the clients must be the best of friends. In separation and divorce, it is unrealistic to expect there to be no anger, resentment, or hurt feelings. However, a Collaborative Law client must be willing to set those feelings aside and come to the settlement table with a good-faith commitment to work with the other party to reach a practical solution.

How do I let my spouse know about Collaborative Family Law?

Since *both* parties have to commit to the Collaborative Law process and retain attorneys who are also willing to commit to this process, it is important to share information about Collaborative Family Law with your spouse. Your attorney can provide you with copies of articles about Collaborative Family Law and the names of other attorneys in the area who understand and accept cases under the Collaborative Law model.

■■■

Section 2

Firm Procedures

Client Wish List

Now that you have hired a domestic lawyer, what next? *Tell your lawyer exactly what it is you want to get out of the divorce.* Give your lawyer a specific "wish list," detailing in writing everything you would like to have when your case is concluded: alimony, custody, visitation, property, etc.

The wish list should be as detailed and explicit as you can possibly make it. For example, don't say "household furniture," say "the bedroom suite in the master bedroom." Don't say "I'd like to get some alimony"; say "I'd like to receive at least $1,500 per month alimony for at least five years." The wish list should be built around specifics, not abstractions.

THE WISH LIST WILL HELP *YOU* identify your objectives. Rather than plunging forward haphazardly with only a vague idea as to what is important to you in the divorce case, the preparation of the wish list forces you to carefully identify the things that really matter to you.

THE WISH LIST WILL HELP *US* focus on "the prize"—the things that are important to you in your case. It is much easier to hit a target when you know what you are shooting at. The wish list also makes sure that we are *on the same wave-length*. This is critical, since we may otherwise have a very different set of goals and priorities. Left to our own devices, our natural tendency might be to think strictly in terms of dollars in a given case. Accordingly, unless you pinpoint exactly what you are hoping to accomplish in your case, we may mistakenly assume that all you care about is maximizing your financial outcome.

Once you have identified your specific goals, the final step is to prioritize the wish list so that you rank your goals in order from most important to least important. This process is uniquely personal, *and it may have little or nothing to do with money.*

For example, say you want both the master bedroom suite which you and your spouse recently purchased for $3,000, and the old dresser in the den worth $30. The old dresser is not going to be a priority item, *or is it?* What if that old dresser is a family heirloom, hand-made by your great-grandfather? That dresser may be a prized possession, one that you cannot replace. Although its dollar value is minimal, its sentimental value [to you] is priceless. Make sure you tell us this in writing.

Perhaps getting custody of your children is so vital to you that you are willing to sacrifice all other aspects of your divorce case. Tell us. We need to know that, from your perspective, custody is the Nobel Peace Prize, the "brass ring," and the Holy Grail all rolled into one.

Remember, we have no way of knowing the particular goals or possessions that you value. The wish list will keep us from guessing. It will also save you money, since we won't be spinning our wheels (and running up attorney fees) chasing after things that don't matter to you.

When you are preparing a first draft of your wish list, don't become consumed with doubts about what is possible or probable. Just decide what it is that you want. There will be plenty of time later for us to analyze the likelihood of achieving your desired goals. A form for you to use is found at the end of this handout.

After you have completed your wish list, do yourself (and us) a favor. Prepare a *second wish list*. This is a list of what you think are your spouse's goals and priorities. Why are your spouse's goals and priorities important to you? Once you have compared your wish list with your spouse's list, you will have identified the issues that are likely to be disputed in the divorce. Let's take an example. The most important thing to you is custody of your children, and this is also the number-one priority for your spouse. You can expect fireworks over the custody issue. On the other hand, if custody of the children is vital to you, but your spouse couldn't care less about spending time with the children, much less getting legal custody, then we can focus our time and energy on other issues that will be contested.

A final word on the subject of wish lists: Make sure your list reflects what you really want, not what you think you should want, or what you think sounds noble, or what your divorced friends tell you that you should "go for." This is not the time to examine your motives or question your desires. If your expectations are too high, or too low, we will discuss why, and what, if anything, you want to change.

The **Wish** _List_

CLIENT NAME: _____

Although there are many things which are important to me in my divorce case, I understand that I may not be able to get everything I want. Whatever else may happen in my divorce case, the **single most important thing** to me is:

_____

_____

The **second most important** thing to me in my divorce case is:

_____

_____

The **third most important** thing to me in my divorce case is:

_____

_____

The following things are important to me, but they are not essential. I am willing to negotiate about these things:

_____

_____

The following things are not important to me, but I would like to keep them in mind as part of my overall outcome:

_____

_____

The following things are of no consequence to me whatsoever:

_____

_____

_____   _____
CLIENT   **DATE**

CLIENT NAME: _____

SPOUSE'S WISH LIST

The **single most important thing** for my spouse is:

_____

_____

The **second most important** thing for my spouse is:

_____

_____

The **third most important** thing for my spouse is:

_____

_____

The following things will not be important to my spouse, and may be negotiable:

_____

_____

The following things will not be important to my spouse, but should be kept in mind as part of the outcome of the divorce:

_____

_____

The following things will be of no consequence whatsoever:

_____

_____

_____   _____
CLIENT   **DATE**

■ ■ ■

How Your Law Firm Operates

What you can expect when working with [name of law firm]

Introduction

We find that we can better serve our clients if we tell them what they can expect from their law firm. In return, we like to inform them of our office operating procedures. In this way a client can save money and time, as well as obtain maximum results from our office.

Your file is always open to you. The documents and folders that we keep are the property of our clients, held by us in trust for them. With reasonable advance notice, we can provide you with copies of any document in your file. We do ask that you let us know in advance if you wish to stop by and pick up copies of papers. If you will give us a telephone call, we will do the copying and mail the papers to you.

It is important to keep our files current. Accurate information is essential if we need to contact you at home or at work. Please be sure to let us know if there is a change in your telephone number, place of work, or home address.

Unless a flat fee is arranged, our firm bills on an hourly basis for the time spent on your case. Records are kept by each attorney for each tenth of an hour. Thus, a one-half hour interview will be listed as: "OV (*Office Visit*) with client—.5." We usually send our active clients an itemized billing at least once a month.

It is customary to arrange payment for the services of an attorney when the case is started. This is done by paying an initial deposit to our firm's trust account. When we receive your initial fee, along with a signed LEGAL SERVICES CONTRACT, we start working on your case.

Sometimes our attorneys will be very busy and unable to answer your telephone call immediately. If an attorney is not available, we specifically ask that you talk with the paralegal or one of our support staff and leave a message for the attorney as to what information you are requesting or what your question is.

Our office support personnel are listed on the back of this pamphlet. We ask that you talk with one of them to see if they can help you. While they cannot provide the legal advice that an attorney would, they can be very helpful in resolving routine inquiries that you may have.

We try to provide our clients with copies of all letters and pleadings that we prepare or receive. Feel free to ask for any document which may be involved in your case.

If we take your case, we will require certain things of you. First and foremost is a list of your goals and priorities. This will help us to organize our work to attain those goals for you.

Next we may require a "diary" or notebook from you telling us what facts we need to know. This will, of course, vary with the type of case. In a custody case, for example, you should tell us at least the following:

- Who has had primary responsibility for the child *before* the separation;

- Who has had primary responsibility for child *since* the separation;

- Information that might be used against you or the other parent at trial;

- Employment and income of the mother and father;

- Reasons why you should have custody;

- Reasons why the other party shouldn't have custody; and

- Witnesses you wish to call, including name, address, work and home telephone numbers, and a summary of what each would say.

We would request other kinds of information, for example, in a child support or alimony case. It is a more effective use of attorney time if you write these matters down at the earliest possible stage and go over them with us. We want to work together with our clients as a team.

No attorney can guarantee success in a particular case. It is our word and our promise to each individual client that we will work hard to attain the goals that the client has set for us. We will do no less for each client.

Fee Information

We believe in discussing fees early and openly with our clients. A client who knows about our fee structure will be better informed and more satisfied with the services we render. Such a client will also have a clear understanding of what our charges are and what we have done for the fee paid by a client.

Our attorneys keep time records in each case. Times are shown in tenths of an hour. We try hard to keep an accurate record of time spent drafting documents, preparing pleadings, or consulting in person or over the phone.

You should remember the following specific rules:

1. A telephone call by or to your attorney will be marked down on your files as at least one-tenth of an hour. This will be shown, for example, as follows: *"Telephone conference with client—.1"* on the ledger. You should realize that this is the minimum charge for a telephone call. Of course, if the telephone call lasts longer than one-tenth of an hour, we will enter the appropriate time notation in the file, rounded upwards to the nearest tenth of an hour.

2. A telephone call to an attorney at home during non-work hours will incur a surcharge of $50 in addition to the regular charge for the attorney's time. We understand that, in an emergency, it may be necessary for you to contact an attorney directly at his or her home. We want to be of assistance whether at the office or at home. At the same time, we believe that it is important for an attorney to have quality time to spend with his or her family. Therefore, we add an additional surcharge for a telephone call that reaches us when we are in our homes during the evening or on a weekend, rather than at the office during ordinary business hours.

Mr. Gray has limited his trial practice since 1981 to domestic cases. He charges $350 per hour for work done in his office and $375 per hour for work in court. His initial interview rate is a flat fee of $400 for up to the first hour. His minimum fee for handling a case is usually $10,000. It can, of course, be more than this, depending on the nature of the case. Ms. Wilson charges $250 per hour for work done in her office and $275 per hour for work in court. Her initial interview rate is a flat fee of $300 up to the first hour. Her minimum fee for handling a case is usually $7,500. Mr. Jackson charges

$200 per hour for work done in his office and for work in court. Mr. Jackson's initial interview rate is a flat fee of $200 up to the first hour. His minimum fee for handling a case is usually $5,000.

Contested court cases usually cost more than the above amounts. Court costs in a domestic case are $135 to file a new case (if that is necessary) and $15 for serving papers by an East Carolina Sheriff.

There are very few flat fees in domestic cases, for the simple reason that it is impossible to tell how difficult or complex a case may be. Fees will also vary according to which attorney you employ to work for you. For your information, however, we have set forth below four examples of initial fees we usually charge in three routine domestic areas. Your specific retainer may be higher. *Filing fees* and *initial consultations* are *not* included in these figures.

Name Change $250.00

Step-parent Adoption (consent) $600.00

Getting in Touch with Us

OFFICE HOURS:
Our office hours are 8:30 a.m.–5:30 p.m., Monday through Friday.

SWITCHBOARD HOURS:
We keep our phone lines open from 8:30 a.m.–5:30 p.m., Monday through Friday.

EVENING AUTO-ATTENDANT:
We utilize an evening auto-attendant whenever we are not in the office. Feel free to leave us a detailed message stating when you called, what you need, and when you need a response.

E-MAIL:
Our general office e-mail address is [e-mail address]. We check our e-mail account daily. In some cases, e-mail is a good way to contact us, but if your situation requires our immediate attention, please call our office.

YOUR LAW FIRM'S EMPLOYEES

Attorneys
[names]

Office Manager
[name]

Paralegals
[names]

Administrative Staff
[names]

Wrapping Up Your Divorce

Name and Address Changes

If you are resuming a former name and/or changing addresses, confirm changes in writing to:

1. Local U.S. Post Office;

2. Social Security Administration and other government benefits programs;

3. Internal Revenue Service, state and local tax authorities. See Treasury Form 8822;

4. Department of Motor Vehicles;

5. Insurers, including medical, dental, disability, life, automobile, homeowners, tenants;

6. Banks and other financial institutions;

7. Credit and charge account issuers.

Payroll and Benefits

If you are employed outside the home, you should notify your payroll or personnel department of this change in your marital status. Be sure to notify your benefits department of any changes or requirements relating to the divorce. Obtain written confirmation of current status or required changes to the following:

8. Life insurance. If you are not the owner of the policy, find out whether there is a written procedure for notifying the insurer of any future claims applicable under the divorce judgment;

9. Medical and dental insurance;

10. Note deadlines for the election of COBRA;

11. Obtain cards and claims forms;

12. Retirement benefits. Follow up with QDRO or other appropriate domestic relations order;

13. Other work-related benefits.

Property Transfers

Call our office, if necessary, to transfer title to property in accordance with your agreement or court order:

14. Motor vehicles (cars, trucks, motorcycles, boats);

15. Stocks, options, bonds, and mutual funds;

16. Retirement benefits;

17. Life insurance policies;

18. Real estate; and

19. Bank accounts.

Debts and Liabilities

Handle in accordance with your divorce papers:

20. Obtain an updated credit report from a national credit bureau. Continue to do so every six months if your former spouse is responsible for paying down joint debt.

21. Close joint credit and charge accounts.

22. Mortgages. Generally, mortgage lenders do not remove a co-borrower's name unless the mortgage is refinanced. If your former spouse is responsible for making mortgage payments, get confirmation of timely compliance and review your credit report every six months.

23. If your former spouse files a bankruptcy petition, consult our office immediately.

Taxes

24. Joint returns may be filed if you and your spouse are still married on December 31 of the tax year in question.

25. Separate returns may be preferable in certain cases; consult your tax advisor on this.

26. Dependency exemptions and tax credits may be transferred to the noncustodial parent. See Treasury Form 8332. Otherwise, the custodial parent claims the children.

27. Keep copies of old tax returns for future reference. Also keep documents confirming the *cost basis* of your real estate, stocks, and other assets. Enlist the help of your stock broker or investment advisor.

28. Maintain up-to-date records on capital improvements (installing a new furnace, adding on a back deck, etc.) to real estate for future reporting of capital gain or loss.

29. Some or all of your legal fees may be deductible. Check with your tax advisor.

30. Alimony is ordinarily deductible by the payor and taxable to the recipient.

31. Child support and lump-sum payments are nondeductible and nontaxable.

Custody and Visitation

32. Be flexible. Do not use the children to retaliate or to spy on the other parent.

33. Inform schools, health and care providers, and day care centers of both parents' names, addresses, and telephone numbers. Certain abuse prevention orders prohibit disclosure to an abusive parent of the address and telephone number of the child and other parent; if you have such orders, tell the above places to keep this information *separate*.

34. Custody and visitation may be changed to reflect a substantial change in circumstances which has affected or will affect a child adversely.

35. Consult with counsel at least once a year on custody and visitation (unless there are no changes to report).

36. Consult with your attorney if the children are in danger.

37. Moving out of state with a minor child may require prior approval of the other parent or the court if your decree or parenting agreement says so. Consult with counsel as soon as there is talk about an out-of-state move. If you move, consult with out-of-state counsel about registering alimony and support orders to facilitate collection.

Alimony

38. Alimony terminates upon death, and possibly the remarriage or cohabitation by the recipient, depending on the order or agreement. Consult with counsel for details.

39. Alimony is usually deductible by the payor and taxable to the recipient. Keep accurate records of payments made/received for tax purposes. Never pay in cash. Consult with your tax advisor about the tax aspect of alimony.

40. If a party's financial circumstances change, consult with counsel about a possible adjustment to alimony.

Child Support

41. Unless your agreement or court order says otherwise, child support is payable until a child turns 18 or leaves high school, whichever comes later. Refer to your divorce papers for other terms.

42. If child support is late at least 20 days, consult with counsel to implement a wage assignment and a possible contempt action.

43. If financial circumstances of a parent or child change for better or worse, consult with counsel about a possible adjustment to child support.

44. Never deduct from or withhold child support without a formal written document, signed by both parties, or a court order. Child support is never reduced for long periods of visitation unless the agreement or order says so. A parent cannot deduct from child support any sums that he or she has spent on gifts, clothes for the children, etc.

Extraordinary Expenses, Uncovered Health Care Expenses, College, and Other Expenses

45. Do not incur any non-emergency expense without prior agreement if you expect a contribution from your former spouse.

46. Send copies of all bills to your former spouse or former partner. Keep copies for your files. Consider filing a contempt action if you do not receive reimbursement after 30 days.

47. Pay your share on receipt of agreed-upon bills.

48. Give your former spouse the appropriate share of medical insurance proceeds on receipt.

49. Cooperate with your former spouse in seeking financial aid for education.

Updating Wills and Trusts

Now is the time to update your will and any trust agreements. These documents should be reviewed every two years or upon remarriage, birth or adoption of a child, or material change in financial circumstances. Be sure you've changed the beneficiaries for your life insurance, retirement plans, IRA, financial accounts, and your will.

■■■

You and Your Case

Introduction

Thank you for coming to our office for help and advice concerning family law. It is the aim of this pamphlet to give you important facts and goals which will help you and us in resolving your case. Please take the time to read it completely, and feel free to ask any questions you wish about the information in this brochure.

Quite often the domestic case is the first time that a person will ever come to an attorney. This occasion may be marked by confusion, anger, frustration, and many questions. It is important to find out the facts as well as the law at the earliest possible stage. We want you to know what your rights are and what alternatives you may have. We want to outline choices and suggestions for you. For this reason, our firm has prepared this pamphlet for your information and use.

"Who's in Charge Here?"

The client is, in a very real sense, the boss in the law office. It is the client who must make the major decisions in his or her case. This is so for two reasons.

First, the Rules of Professional Conduct require the lawyer to leave these to the client. The ethical duty of a lawyer is to inform a client of the important issues and consequences and then let the client make the major choices in his or her case. The canons of ethics under which lawyers operate impose this duty on us.

The second reason is that, in reality, it is your case and not the attorney's. It is your obligation to decide these matters which so vitally involve you. Strictly speaking, the lawyer has no business in telling you, for instance, what is "enough child support" for you to receive or whether you should pay alimony or not. It is you (in these examples) who would be receiving the child support or paying the alimony, not the lawyer. While the lawyer's guidance is important, it is you who must make such major decisions as these.

At the same time, there are other matters which the lawyer must decide in your case. These are not major policy decisions, but rather tactical decisions that our training in the law helps us to make. Issues such as how to question a witness, what approach to use in the argument to the judge or jury, or what motions to present to the court ought to be made by your lawyer. You are free, of course, to ask us about these matters or to give suggestions or offer criticisms. In the final analysis, these tactical decisions should be made by the lawyer using his best judgment, just as the major policy decisions ought to be made by you with the guidance and information provided by us.

Openness and Honesty

One of the most important duties of your lawyer is a frank and honest discussion of the facts and issues in your case. This duty of openness and honesty to you involves the following items:

1. We will advise you about the positive and negative aspects of your case. You need frank and honest information on the difficulties that may be present in your case as well as the advantages you may have. No purpose is served in your lawyer telling you only the "bright side" of things. This will only lead to unmet

expectations and dissatisfaction if the outcome is not exactly as you wish. It is our obligation to be candid and honest with you in evaluating all sides of your case.

Although we can provide clients with some comfort through an understanding of the laws pertaining to divorce, support, and custody, it is important to remember that the legal counselor cannot act as a family counselor. If a client feels the need for non-legal guidance, counseling, therapy, or just a shoulder to lean on, he or she should seek that type of help separately. There are many psychologists, psychiatrists, and other professionals in this field.

2. *Money and time* are important factors for a client to consider.

Lawsuits can be complex, time-consuming, and quite often very frustrating for the parties, the lawyers, or the judge. We believe in discussing with our clients at the initial interview such matters as the firm's hourly rates, the amount of the initial fee that you pay our firm for services to be rendered, the approximate time we expect your case will take, and the possibility of requesting an award of attorney's fees as reimbursement to you. It is our belief that our client will be better informed and more satisfied with our services if we discuss these early and openly. You will find in the pamphlet "HOW YOUR LAW FIRM OPERATES" fees and further information about office procedures, specific fees for services, and costs for typical cases. You should realize, of course, that no case is exactly like another. Cases which appear to be simple often turn out to be very complex. No good lawyer in most cases will tell you that your case is "easy" or "no problem." Many cases which appear to be routine at first glance can later be found to involve problems in areas such as jurisdiction, default, Fifth Amendment privilege, merger, and tax liability, for example.

Absent a specific agreement otherwise, our clients are entirely responsible for the fee for professional services charged by our firm. After payment of the fee, it is customary to bill the client at regular intervals, to inform him or her of work done in the case, and to request, if necessary, additional funds to continue work on the case.

We maintain records of the time we have spent on your case. Our files, including these records, are open to you at any time with reasonable advance notice. A good lawyer should have nothing to hide from a client, and we want our clients to know the time and nature of the work we are doing for them.

3. Our clients are entitled to know the law in their particular case. We believe in discussing cases and statutes openly with our clients. A good lawyer will not put off a client requesting legal information about his or her case by claiming that it might be too difficult or complex for the client. We believe that our clients want to know about the statutes and court decisions that might affect their position. This is one way that we try to keep our clients satisfied and aware of current legal developments and cases.

Your Confidential Information

What you say to us in confidence remains that way. Whatever you wish to reveal to your lawyer is "privileged"—that is, the lawyer is forbidden to repeat or discuss what you have told him without your permission. What you say in our office remains here unless you allow us to discuss these matters with someone. No judge or court can order a lawyer to disclose the confidential matters you bring to your attorney's office (outside of unusual circumstances, such as the intention to commit a crime in the future or to commit perjury on the witness stand).

The purpose for this rule is to ensure that you will be frank and candid in your discussion of facts with us. We need to get the full facts directly from you. A lawyer should not have to wonder if his client is telling the whole truth.

Even if you believe that there is some fact that may be harmful to you, it is better to discuss this openly with the attorney in the first place. It is far better that the attorney be confronted with this fact at an early stage rather than learn about it in the courtroom, when the other attorney and that lawyer's client have known about it all along. Surprises of this kind can only harm your case.

With advance knowledge of problems or difficulties, the lawyer can often suggest courses of action that can avoid exploitation of the problem by the other side. You can trust us to keep your confidential information to ourselves and not reveal it, without your permission, to people outside our law firm.

Your Attorney's Loyalty

An attorney has an obligation of loyalty to the client. Especially in domestic cases, this is very important for the client to remember.

Some clients believe that the lawyer's friendship or contacts with the attorney on the other side of the case is a sign of disloyalty or inability to represent aggressively the client's position. This is not so. It is the sworn duty of the attorney to represent fully, zealously, and competently the lawful needs and legitimate goals of the client.

Your Attorney's Duties

One of the best summaries of your attorney's duties to you is contained in a "Declaration of Commitment" published by the American Bar Association, which asks that all lawyers live by these principles and provide copies of them to their clients.

OUR DECLARATION OF COMMITMENT TO CLIENTS

To treat you with respect and courtesy.

To handle your legal matter competently and diligently in accordance with the highest standards of the profession.

To exercise independent professional judgment on your behalf.

To charge a reasonable fee and to explain in advance how that fee will be computed and billed.

To return telephone calls promptly.

To keep you informed and provide you with copies of important papers.

To respect your decisions on the objectives to be pursued in your case, as permitted by law and the rules of professional conduct, including whether or not to settle your case.

To work with other participants in the legal system to make our legal system more accessible and responsive.

To preserve the client confidences learned during our lawyer-client relationship.

To exhibit the highest degree of ethical conduct in accordance with the Code of Professional Responsibility/Model Rules of Professional Conduct.

A good attorney can have no divided loyalty. We cannot and will not settle your case without your permission. When you hire our law firm to represent you, your case demands undivided loyalty.

Summary

Thank you for reading this information. Lawyers can do a better job for a client who is satisfied with their services and knows of their obligations as lawyers. Feel free to ask during your initial interview, or at any time afterwards, any questions you might have based on this information.

■■■

Section 3

Legal Fees

How Much Will My Case Cost?

Some clients want to know how much their case will cost. The total cost of your case cannot be predicted. It's sometimes hard to make even a rough guess, because the cost will depend on a number of factors.

One of these is *the nature and complexity of your case*. Most of the time the attorney you see can give you an idea of these issues during an interview. Please keep in mind, however, that sometimes even these will change in midstream if a new issue comes up while the case is proceeding.

A second factor is *settlement vs. trial*. Many factors are involved in reaching a compromise, a negotiated settlement:

- If you and the other party try to negotiate a settlement, how long will it take to reach an agreement?

- How much time will be spent drafting the initial proposal? How much time will be spent before the response?

- How close will the response be to the first proposal? Or how far off?

- Will negotiations be in person or in writing (letter, fax, or e-mail)?

- Does the other party want to settle? Does she want to hold out for a better deal? Does he want to dig in his heels and get you to make more concessions? Or does the other side just want to delay a trial?

- How many drafts will it take to prepare the final agreement?

If the case is *tried in court* (or submitted to *binding arbitration*), an entirely different set of factors will be involved:

- How long will it take to prepare for the hearing?

- How long will it take to conduct "discovery," that is, to obtain documents and answers to written questions from the other side? Will you need to take the deposition of the other side and their witnesses, that is, ask questions in person under oath in front of a court reporter? Will the other side cooperate in discovery or engage in "stonewalling" to resist disclosure? Will you have to go to court for an order compelling responses?

- Will you have to hire expert witnesses (such as a CPA or appraiser) to testify?

- How long will it take to schedule a trial? Once again, will the other side cooperate or make choosing a trial date difficult?

- Will there be lots of cases ahead of yours, which might result in your being "bumped" off the trial calendar for that day? Will your case start on time—or at 3 p.m. on the day of trial because several other cases were ahead of it on the calendar? [Note: These don't apply to arbitrations, which almost always go forward at the date and time specified and usually take less time than a trial in court.]

- Will it take three hours or three days for the trial?

- How long will it take for the judge or arbitrator to make a decision?

- Once the decision is made, how long will it take to draft the order? How long will it take for the attorneys to agree on its terms (or for the judge to determine the wording if there is a disagreement)?

These—and many other factors—are what determine your attorney's charges. As you can see, there's *no way* that we can tell you in advance what you'll spend, since *we* don't even know that. We can, however, give you several pointers to remember about your attorney's fees.

First of all, remember that no case we handle is *simple* or *easy*, other than a name change, an uncontested divorce, or a basic will.

- If you *think* your case is simple, please talk this over with your attorney at the outset so that she or he can correct this misconception. None of the cases we handle are simple or easy.

- If you still *believe* your case is easy or simple after this discussion, please take it to some other lawyer. We want to work with clients who have a clear and honest understanding of the problems and challenges we encounter in settling or trying a case. We don't want clients who think their cases are simple, that "most of the work was already done" when we got the case, or that we spent too much time and effort on "an easy case." Give another lawyer the opportunity to work on your case if you truly believe it's "simple."

If you'd like to see some tips on how to reduce your legal fees, ask for a copy of our handout, "Tips for Clients on Reducing Legal Fees."

∎∎∎

Client Information Letter #15

Subject: Initial Information on Fees

Because we want our clients to understand fully the fees and costs paid for services rendered, we ask each client to read the following and sign this letter at the bottom.

1. We charge our clients as follows:

   a. *Initial interview.* Mr. Grant's rate is $400 (flat fee) up to the first hour and pro-rated after the first hour at his regular hourly charge of $350 for office work. His hourly charge for in-court is $375. Mr. Brown's rate is $300 (flat fee) up to the first hour and prorated after the first hour at his regular hourly charge of $250 for office work. His hourly charge for in-court is $275. Mr. Green's rate is $165 (flat fee) for up to the first hour and prorated after the first hour at his regular hourly charge of $165 for office work. His hour charge for in-court is $165. These rates also apply to follow-up phone calls and other work. **The client is expected to pay for the initial interview at the time it is concluded.**

   b. *Other costs.* Postage, parking, fax, copying (@ .25 per page in-office), and long-distance telephone calls are charged to the client. Filing a divorce complaint in Wake County District Court costs $165, and the fee for service by the sheriff is $15 within North Carolina. N.C. Certified Paralegal charges are $95 per hour. Paralegal and Law Clerk charges are $90 per hour. Non-paralegal charges are $75 per hour. Certain work is performed on a job or task basis, and the service charges are contained in our standard written contract. One example is:

      - *Advanced Document review*—Mr. Grant charges a flat fee of $400 for review of any agreement not prepared in our office (without opinion letter), separate from the interview fee. Mr. Brown and Mr. Green charge a flat fee of $300.

2. We bill on a bi-weekly basis, and you are expected to pay the balance shown and any additional fees shown upon receipt of the statement. If suit is necessary to recover attorney's fees due to us, the client agrees to pay fifteen percent (15%) of the amount claimed as additional attorney's fees in such action. Mr. Grant charges a flat reservation fee ($1,000) in most cases, and this is shown on the face of the contract that you will sign.

3. Please read our client brochure, "**You and Your Case—Family Law**," for further information.

I HAVE READ THIS LETTER AND AGREE TO BE RESPONSIBLE FOR THE ABOVE CHARGES.

_____ (SEAL)   DATE: _____

SIGNATURE OF CLIENT

_____

PRINT NAME HERE   *Rev. 3/10*

When Money Runs Low

Options for Our Clients

1. Q. HELP! I'm not even near the end of my case, but I'm at the end of my money! My mom says that she won't finance my divorce case any more, and I have no money of my own—my husband took it all.

A. First of all, before we talk about letting the law firm withdraw or other options, let's see if there's really no money. Are there any credit cards available? Other family members who might help out? Funds in the house equity which can be "pulled out" through a refinance or a home equity line?

2. Q. But if I try to get money out of the house equity, won't my spouse have to sign? Can the court order him to do so? Are there other options?

A. Sometimes the court can enter an order for "interim distribution." This would free up some of your marital funds when they're in the hands of the other side. You first locate funds that are marital. That means, in general, that they were earned during the marriage, such as a savings account, investments (stocks, bonds, mutual funds), CD's, or, if you're willing to take a hit on taxes and penalties, retirement assets (e.g., 401(k) account, IRA). Equity in the home might also qualify. Next, you file a motion for interim distribution, asking that the court award you all or part of the asset containing the money. Then you calendar a hearing and, when the case is called, you make your case. If the judge grants the relief you've requested, then you'll be able to spend your own money, not your mother's, on your divorce case. Of course, the judge will require that you be credited with those funds when the final hearing on property division (or settlement) takes place. In effect, you've just gotten "an advance" on your final settlement.

3. Q. What if there are no liquid assets lying around—just a house, the land, and the furniture and vehicles? There's just too much case for the money! I have no credit cards and I can't get a loan.

A. In that case, the option that most of our clients choose is a consent for the firm's withdrawal. This might be called the **Clean Break Option**, since it allows you to let our firm go before the account goes into the red; the last thing you need is to owe money to one more person or business.

4. Q. Please explain about the **Clean Break Option**. What does withdrawal involve?

A. In a case that is not in litigation—one that's only at the negotiation stage, with no lawsuit filed—then you can write to your attorney and instruct him to stop work on the case and that you no longer wish to employ him to assist you on your case. That's all it takes. If, on the other hand, you have a case that is pending in the courts, you'll need to sign a withdrawal consent so that your attorney can file a motion to withdraw. The withdrawal consent merely states that you agree with the attorney's petitioning the court for withdrawal. The withdrawal is complete upon the judge's signing an order allowing withdrawal.

5. **Q.** Are there any complicating factors?
   A. Here are two:

   - If the motion to withdraw is done shortly before the trial, the judge might not allow withdrawal, since it's so "late in the game."
   - And, of course, one big complicating factor is that you'll be representing yourself from now on. This can be a very unpleasant experience if you have skilled counsel on the other side. Judges are not permitted to "help you out" when you have no attorney. A *pro se* litigant—one with no attorney—is treated the same as one with an attorney.

6. **Q.** Can't the firm keep working on my case? I know that I'll eventually get some money!
   A. While some firms may extend credit to their clients, that's not our practice. As a small firm, we have to rely on every case paying its own way to allow our employees, creditors, and landlord to be paid each month. Even one case falling behind can create problems. Our firm's lawyers are not permitted to tell clients that we will continue to work on the case although the client has no funds left. How would you feel if your boss told you to keep working every day, but your paycheck would not be there for a couple of weeks (or months)? The lawyer's responsibility is to work hard, competently, and diligently for the client. The client's responsibility is to cooperate in preparing the case, in providing funds, and in locating witnesses. Both sides—attorney and client—have to meet their respective obligations. We ordinarily expect that our trust account balance for each client will have sufficient funds for at least two months' anticipated work.

7. **Q.** Well, let's talk about other options. My account has at least $5,000 in it. Can I get some help from the firm, but not at the "full-bore" litigation rate?
   A. Yes, there's another way that the firm could help by withdrawing from the litigation case and then helping you "on the sidelines." This might be called the **Coaching Option**.

8. **Q.** How does the **Coaching Option** work?
   A. Once we're "off the case" (no longer appearing as your attorney of record in the litigation), we can assist by providing you information on how you can handle the case yourself. For example, we can:

   - Advise on responding to motions that the other side files;
   - Suggest ways to obtain information (such as documents) from the other side through a "document request";
   - Tell you what to do when the other side serves interrogatories on you, demanding that you reply with the answers under oath;
   - Give you information on how to conduct a hearing or trial;
   - Outline the questions you might want to serve as interrogatories on the other side;
   - Provide information on what to do if the other side refuses to answer your questions or turn over documents; and
   - Give you advice on what the law requires and how the courts operate, especially regarding the Local Rules for Wake County, which have extensive requirements for disclosure of documents and production of information in financial cases.

9. Q. But you don't understand! I just want my case *over with*! I want it done. I don't want to be in court any more, and I definitely don't want a "do-it-yourself" solution.
    A. Well, the final option that we could discuss is called the **Quick Conclusion Option**.

10. Q. How does the **Quick Conclusion Option** work?
    A. When there are sufficient funds in the account (and we're not talking about only $1,000!), then the firm can try—and the emphasis is on TRY—to get the other side to agree to a quick settlement of the outstanding issues.

11. Q. OK—tell me more. It sounds simple and easy!
    A. It can be relatively easy if there is only one issue on the table, such as a motion for increased visitation. Whether you're asking for it or resisting it, there are probably some compromises that can be worked out. We've learned that it's a lot easier if both of the parties meet at the same time (but not necessarily in the same room) to work things out and to print and sign a settlement, whether it's an amendment to the separation agreement or a consent order for the judge. Instead of phone calls, letters, and e-mails, do it all at once.

12. Q. Can it get complicated?
    A. Yes, it can—either when there are multiple issues at stake or when the issues are few but complex. It can also be difficult when the client is very attached to a particular outcome, such as:

    - *First Example*: Sally wants the house, but her husband, Bert, demands that it be put on the market and sold immediately so that he can pull out his one-half share of the money and use it to buy a new home. Unless Sally has the financial resources to refinance the house, there is NO simple answer which will come close to pleasing both sides. Someone will have to back down! If *your* funds are about to dry up, then *you* will probably have to be the one to give in and allow the other side what he or she wants.
    - *Second Example*: Bert demands joint and equal custody of the child, Johnnie. Sally is adamantly opposed to this. "He doesn't deserve it" is her first response. "He didn't lift a finger to help with caring for our son during the marriage, and he shouldn't be rewarded now, after the separation, when he's finally decided to step up to the plate and *be a good dad*." In addition, Sally feels strongly that it will be confusing and harmful for Johnnie to spend half of every week or every month in two different homes. Bert is just as insistent that they ought to give it a try, and that it will be the best solution for Johnnie, who can have *two* involved parents instead of just one. Once again, there's no good answer to this. You cannot make both parties happy with any solution that is proposed. Someone will have to sacrifice. If you're coming to the end of the funds, then that will probably be *you*.

13. Q. But that's just awful. That's not fair. Why should I have to give in?
    A. That's the main problem with the **Quick Conclusion Option**—it often involves a "quick and dirty" solution to a complex problem, and that usually requires the one who is out of money—our client—to make sacrificial concessions to obtain an end to the dispute.

14. Q. Are there other problems with the **Quick Conclusion Option**?
 A. Yes—there are several:
- First of all, there must be enough money in the trust account to enable your attorney to conduct the negotiations and quickly wind down the dispute. This is, unfortunately, neither easy nor fast. Once the other side realizes that you are desperate, it'll be like a shark that smells blood in the water. The other side will realize that the longer it's dragged out, the better chance for more sacrifices by you! Rather than proceeding to a quick resolution, sometimes this approach just winds up prolonging the dispute and placing other demands for concessions on the table.
- We often need to hire a mediator to bring the parties together and bring the case to a conclusion. That can be very beneficial in "attitude adjustment" for the parties, in calming them down, and in pushing them and nudging them to a conclusion that is quick and complete, even though they might feel it is a "cut and run" solution that is totally unfair. However, engaging a mediator takes time and costs money.

15. Q. Are there any other options available to me when the money is about to run out?
 A. Not that we've been able to discover. If there are no funds available through interim distribution, then the client ordinarily selects the **Clean Break Option** and consents to the withdrawal of the attorney from the case. If there is sufficient money left, we can always assist on the side with the **Coaching Option**. If the client is willing to make major concessions in order to finish the case, then we can attempt to negotiate a settlement through the **Quick Conclusion Option**.

■■■

Tips for Clients on Reducing Legal Fees

Here are some ways that will help you save money on attorney's fees:

1. **PREPARE FOR YOUR PHONE CALLS.** You are charged for every phone call with your lawyer or paralegal. Call only when necessary. Before calling, make a list of topics you want to discuss. When you have questions about your case, consider "saving them up" so you can ask them in one phone call or interview, rather than making a call or an appointment for each single question or concern.

2. **BE HONEST.** Your lawyer needs to know the good and bad points of your case. The opposition will find out the bad points against you and exploit them. If you do not tell your lawyer the bad points, it will be more expensive for him or her to protect your rights and defend you.

3. **IF YOU THINK THERE IS A BILLING ERROR . . .** If you believe there is an error on your bill, contact our office manager immediately. If you believe you have been overcharged, make an appointment to discuss it with your lawyer.

4. **CALL FOR APPOINTMENTS.** When you need to discuss your case in person, schedule an appointment. You are bound to be disappointed if you "drop in for a few minutes" because your lawyer more than likely will be busy with other clients.

5. **WRITE DOWN QUESTIONS.** If you have questions for an appointment, write them down so you'll remember what to ask (and so we can make sure we have addressed every issue).

6. **MAKE AN EXTRA COPY.** If you have documents in your case that we need, make an extra copy for us at the outset.

7. **YOUR AFFIDAVITS.** Spend some extra time finishing your financial affidavit or equitable distribution inventory affidavit, if those apply in your case. We wind up spending a lot of time with these affidavits when clients don't come up with the figures and the calculations or provide detailed notes and documents showing how they arrived at the numbers. Provide sorted, organized, and summarized backup documents along with your affidavits to avoid having to pay the attorney or paralegal to organize and summarize these for you.

8. **DEAL WITH THE OTHER SIDE.** Do as much as possible in dealing with the other side. When we have to do everything by contacting the other attorney, rather than you contacting your spouse or ex-spouse, for example, it takes a lot of additional time and effort. If there's a straightforward matter, such as weekend visitation or signing off on medical insurance forms, see if you can undertake that yourself.

9. **HELP WITH WITNESSES.** Ask if you can help with interviewing witnesses or preparing summaries of their statements. This can save time and effort in trial preparation on the part of your attorney or paralegal.

10. **COPYING.** Do your own copying. It takes a lot of work to do all the copying in a lawsuit; ask us if there's some copying that you can do for your case.

11. **ARBITRATION.** Opt for arbitration. Under the Family Law Arbitration Act, all cases that can be tried in front of a judge can also be arbitrated. We find that this results in substantial savings for our clients. We get a certain date for the hearing, there's no danger of being "bumped" in favor of another case on the docket, and we get 100% of the arbitrator's attention for as long as the case takes to conclude.

12. **AVOID "PHONE TAG."** To make sure you connect with your attorney by phone, ask our receptionist about your attorney's schedule. Make a telephone appointment with the receptionist for a mutually convenient time for you and your attorney to talk.

13. **DATES AND DEADLINES.** Cooperate with your attorney and keep records of dates and deadlines given to you. Make sure you do not miss any deadlines on projects assigned to you to complete.

14. **FOCUS.** We know this is a difficult time in your life and understand you may have anger or resentment concerning your situation. To avoid having to pay us for "emotional consultations," please keep your discussions focused on the legal issues at hand. We understand that lawsuits are stressful and emotionally draining. However, your lawyer is not your psychologist or psychiatrist. It is less expensive to handle your stress by regular exercise, a healthy diet, and companionship with good friends. If your condition is serious, seek professional help. Your lawyer can provide a referral.

15. **HOME CALLS.** When you call lawyers at home, remember that there is an additional charge of $50 over and above the hourly fee. These calls should only be made regarding emergencies that must be handled immediately and cannot wait until the next business day.

16. **HOW TO COMMUNICATE.** Communicate or send information to us via e-mail. This saves you on fax costs and it is faster. E-mail is checked several times during the day.

17. **MESSAGES.** Leave detailed messages with staff or use our office voice mail. If the attorney or paralegal you call is not available and you cannot set up a call through the staff that is convenient for you and the attorney's schedule, you should leave a detailed message with specific questions or instructions with our receptionist or through the company's voice-mail system. This allows the attorney or paralegal to respond more quickly to specific information, saving you time and money. This will also allow them to respond to you by e-mail when appropriate instead of playing "phone tag."

18. **BE SELECTIVE.** As parents quickly learn in dealing with child discipline issues, "Pick Your Fights" is a good motto. If you cannot afford to contest every little detail, you must be willing to forgo some smaller items for larger ones. You need to be able to trade matters of lesser importance for ones that mean a lot more to you. Make sure you plan and prioritize your goals. Keep your eye on the ball. Be willing to make concessions. Help your attorney by making a list of goals and priorities in a trial or settlement, listing them as "Must Have," "Nice to Have," and "Can Give Up."

19. **Billing questions.** When you have a question about attorney's fees, call our office manager, Gladys C. Hughes, to make your initial inquiry. You will have the chance to review in detail how your money has been used in each billing statement. We typically send out billing statements twice each month. When you receive your statement, review it carefully. If you have any questions or concerns, please call our office manager first. If she can't help you, she'll pass it on to the attorney or paralegal whose work is involved and you'll get an answer. We do not charge to discuss billing errors with you. It is important to address billing issues at the time you receive the bill and notice a problem. If we need to set up a consultation about some questions you have regarding your bill, we'll set that up for you. We are always willing to discuss billing issues, and we want you to feel free to ask about your attorney's fees and how you can save money.

20. **Keep your sense of humor.** Lawsuits are expensive. Sometimes the results are unfair. Seldom does anyone get everything they want in a lawsuit. Just the same, keep your sense of humor. Put things in perspective. It will save you money by preventing you from litigating non-essential points.

■■■

Part II

Discovery and Trial Procedures

Section 1

Discovery

Discovery

Introduction

Requests for information in a lawsuit are called DISCOVERY. Whenever we are sent discovery papers from the opposing side in your lawsuit, we will need your help to complete our response on time.

Interrogatories

The most common type of discovery is called INTERROGATORIES. These are typed questions with sufficient space provided for an answer to be inserted (typed) below the question. These must be answered within 30 days of their being served on us. We ask that you send them back (answered in pencil) to us 10 DAYS AFTER YOU RECEIVE THEM. This will give us enough time to review your answers, type each response, and set aside time for you to come in and read the final document before signing it under oath in front of a notary public.

Helpful Hints

A. If you don't know the answer and can't find out, answer *I DON'T KNOW.*

B. If you can find out the answer with a reasonable amount of effort, do so. The rules require us to use *due diligence* in obtaining information. Thus, if the question demands your mortgage balance three years ago, the name of the hospital where you were born, or the serial number on your truck—information that can be obtained without undue effort—you should obtain the information and set it out where the answer belongs.

C. If you object to answering a question, set out (in your own words) the nature of the objection *and then answer the inquiry* as best you can directly below your objection. Some examples of objections might be "Self-Incrimination" (when you're asked to confess to adultery or assault), "Irrelevant" (when your ex-spouse asks about your new spouse's salary), or "Burdensome and Oppressive" (when they ask you to name all companies that have ever extended you credit or provided you with a charge card). By answering the question directly below, you help us make the legal judgment on whether to stick with the objection (and move for a protective order) or answer the question as best we can without an objection.

D. We want to go over your answers with you—in person or, if you wish, by phone. You should read everything printed as answers before signing the Interrogatories. *Don't wait until the last minute—30 days after service is the outside limit,* and we like to review, refine, and revise your answers in most cases before we submit a final, signed response.

E. Call us promptly when questions arise. Frequently our administrative staff can put you through to us (or take a message) to speed up the process of replying to questions. You will help us greatly if you ask us *all the questions* you have when you phone us, rather than calling several times with different questions on each occasion. If we are not available, please speak with our administrative staff and leave a specific message or question; this will help us get back to you promptly. You may also e-mail us when questions arise.

Request for Production of Documents

This discovery document specifies a date, time, and place for you to produce certain papers, records or objects. You may produce copies of any documents (unless specified otherwise in the Request), and we will take care of transmitting them to the other side. The same rules as set out under *Helpful Hints* apply to Request for Production of Documents. Please let us have your records or documents WITHIN 10 DAYS after you get a copy of the Request from our office. This also applies to those cases where we have agreed to accept a subpoena for documents on your behalf (instead of having a deputy deliver this to you).

You cannot refuse to produce documents because you don't want to do so. When and if you object, we will need a specific reason for each objection. The questions we ask are:

- Does the document exist?

- Is it in your possession or within your control (this means you can get it from someone who's your agent, such as your banker, your lawyer, or your accountant)?

- Is it protected by privilege (such as the Fifth Amendment privilege against self-incrimination, the lawyer-client privilege, or the privilege for doctor-patient communications)?

- Is the production going to be burdensome, time-consuming, and expensive (such as producing cancelled checks from 14 years ago)?

If any of these applies, then you'll need to let us know with detailed objections and reasons so we can talk to you and jointly decide about producing or the alternative, which is objecting, filing a motion, and going to a hearing on the motion (all of which costs a lot more money than just producing the documents most of the time).

Request for Admissions

This is a series of statements that you are asked to *admit or deny*. This type of discovery can be a TIME BOMB because

A. Any statements that we don't answer within 30 days are *deemed to be admitted*. These admissions can and *will be used against you* in a court of law.

B. If we deny something that should have been admitted, the other side can ask the judge to tax us with the costs incurred in their proving the statement to be true. This can make your lawsuit doubly expensive!

Please make sure that you answer any Requests for Admission promptly and correctly; we will need your response *10* days after you get the Request for Admissions from our office. The suggestions shown at *Helpful Hints* also apply here.

Conclusion

Please read these paragraphs closely and follow our advice. We want to help you give prompt, fair, and accurate answers to any discovery sent by the opposing party in your lawsuit. Please keep us informed if any answers given by you should change in the future. Let us know if there is any discovery you want to do regarding information, documents, or admissions from the other side, so that we can decide whether to serve a similar discovery request on opposing counsel.

■■■

What Happens at a Deposition and

How to Prepare for It

Procedure—What Will Happen

Under the law, the opposing lawyer has a right to take your "deposition." This means that you will be put under oath, just as you would be in court, and he or she will ask you questions relating to this case. The questions and your answers will be taken down word-for-word by a court reporter. Of course, your lawyer will be present.

No judge or jury will be present. After the deposition, the court reporter will type the questions and answers.

If your case goes to a trial and you are present, this deposition can be used by the other lawyer in cross-examining you if your testimony at trial differs from your testimony at the time of the deposition. Furthermore, any part of your deposition can be read out loud to the court by the opposing attorney at trial. So it is important to be careful of everything you say.

It is essential that you have as many facts in mind as possible about the case at the time of the deposition (and there is nothing wrong in doing so), but it is helpful if you refresh your recollection before you meet with us.

The other lawyer in this deposition can ask you questions that are admissible in court under the rules of evidence. In addition, he can ask questions that may seem as if they are none of his business and would not be admissible in court. The courts allow broad "discovery" in these depositions. You may be asked for "hearsay" and other things that will enable the other side to make further investigation into the case. Do not be surprised if we do not object to questions that seem to you to be out of line, but be assured that if the opposing attorney questions you on any subject that is not proper, we will object to the question. If we object to the question and instruct you not to answer it, then you should refuse to answer the question. Please do not refuse to answer any question that we have not instructed you to refuse to answer.

The rules of procedure provide that when the court reporter types your testimony, it will be submitted to you for review. That means you will have an opportunity to make corrections.

Rarely will we ask you questions during a deposition taken by the opposing attorney. Sometimes, however, we may find it advantageous to ask some leading questions, to which your answers should be very brief. If we don't ask any questions, don't be surprised or disappointed; but if we do, keep your answers short.

If you are not a party but only a witness, we may not be your attorney, so we can suggest, but not instruct you. It is always a good idea to bring your own attorney.

Reasons for Taking This Deposition

The opposing side is taking your deposition for at least three reasons:

1. They want to find out what facts you actually have regarding the issues in the case. In other words, they are interested in what your story is now and what it is going to be at trial.

2. They want to pin you down to a specific story, so that you will have to tell the same story at the trial and they will know in advance what your story is going to be. The other lawyer will seek to commit you under oath to all the facts about your side of the case so that you cannot say anything different at trial without being subject to impeachment with the deposition on cross-examination.

3. They hope to catch you in a discrepancy. They may be looking for an inconsistency between your sworn statements at trial and at the deposition. If that happens, they hope to show that you are not a truthful person and that your testimony should not be believed on any of the points—particularly the crucial ones.

Those objectives all point directly toward trial. However, a deposition will also assist the other side in evaluating their case for settlement purposes. This is often the first and only opportunity the other lawyer has to see you before the case comes to trial. You should answer the questions in an honest and straightforward manner so that the other lawyer will be convinced that if the case is tried, the judge will believe that you are completely honest and sincere.

Your Conduct in the Deposition

We know that you would not deliberately lie, but it is important that you not be misled into stating something that is not true. For this reason, listen to each question carefully and be sure that you understand it before answering.

Sometimes the other lawyer will be friendly and will not "bully" you in any manner. His theory may be that the more he can get you to say, the more apt you are to "put your foot in your mouth." Telling the truth means more than simply refraining from telling a deliberate falsehood. Telling the truth requires that you testify accurately about what you know. If you tell the truth and tell it accurately, nobody can confuse you.

1. UNDERSTAND THE QUESTION BEFORE YOU ATTEMPT TO ANSWER. You can't possibly give a truthful and accurate response unless you understand the question. If you don't understand it, ask the lawyer to repeat it. He will probably ask the court reporter to read it back. Keep a sharp lookout for questions with a double meaning and questions that assume you have testified to a fact when you have not done so.

2. TAKE YOUR TIME. Do not hurry. Give the question the thought required to understand it, formulate your answer, and then give the answer. Do not give a quick answer without allowing time for your lawyer to understand the question and object, if necessary.

3. DO NOT VOLUNTEER INFORMATION. Listen very carefully to the question that is asked, answer only the question asked of you, and then stop. Give direct answers. If counsel wants any elaboration, he'll ask for it. If we want you to explain further, we'll ask you when it is our turn to ask questions. Don't try to assist your attorney, as it may turn out to be harmful to you.

4. SPEAK SLOWLY AND CLEARLY. Do not nod your head in response to a question. You must answer audibly. If you point or indicate, try to describe what you are

pointing to or indicating. Do not be too concerned about this; if you do not, it is up to opposing counsel to describe for the record how you are pointing or indicating.

5. **DON'T LOOK AT YOUR LAWYER FOR HELP WHEN YOU ARE BEING QUESTIONED.** You are on your own. It is you that must answer the questions.

6. **BEWARE OF QUESTIONS INVOLVING DISTANCES AND TIME.** Make sure that everyone understands that you are estimating. Think clearly about distances and intervals of time. Be sure your estimates are accurate and reasonable.

7. **NEVER ATTEMPT TO EXPLAIN OR JUSTIFY YOUR ANSWER.** You are there to give the facts as you know them. You are not supposed to apologize or attempt to justify those facts. Any such attempt would make it appear as if you doubt the accuracy of your own testimony.

8. **ONLY GIVE THE INFORMATION WHICH YOU HAVE READILY AVAILABLE.** If you do not know certain information, do not give it. Do not turn to your counsel and ask him for the information. (On occasion, to save time, your attorney may volunteer information, but let him make the decision.) Do not promise to get information that you do not have readily at hand unless your attorney advises it. Do not agree to look up anything in the future to supplement the answer unless your counsel advises you to do so.

9. **DO NOT, UNLESS YOUR COUNSEL REQUESTS, REACH IN YOUR POCKET FOR A DRIVER'S LICENSE, SOCIAL SECURITY CARD, OR OTHER DOCUMENT.** The deposition is to elicit facts which you know and have in your mind. It is not for the production of documents. If the opposing side is interested in obtaining documents from you, there are other legal procedures with which to obtain them.

10. **NEVER JOKE IN A DEPOSITION.** The humor may not be apparent in the printed transcript and may make you look crude or cavalier about the truth.

11. **DON'T VOLUNTEER ANY FACTS NOT REQUESTED BY A QUESTION.** Such information cannot help you and may hurt you.

12. **AFTER THE DEPOSITION IS OVER, DO NOT CHAT WITH THE OPPONENTS OR THEIR ATTORNEYS.** Remember, the other attorney is your legal opponent. Do not let his friendly manner cause you to drop your guard and convey information that he has failed to request in the deposition.

13. **DO NOT TRY TO FIGURE OUT BEFORE YOU ANSWER WHETHER A TRUTHFUL ANSWER WILL HELP OR HINDER YOUR CASE.** Always answer truthfully. Your lawyer can deal with the truth effectively. He is handicapped when you answer any other way.

14. **DO NOT ARGUE WITH THE LAWYER ON THE OTHER SIDE.** He has a right to question you, and is probably more skilled at give-and-take than you are. Don't answer a question with a question unless the question you are asked is not clear.

15. **DO NOT LOSE YOUR TEMPER NO MATTER HOW HARD YOU ARE PRESSED.** If you lose your temper, you have played right into the hands of the other side.

16. IF ASKED WHETHER YOU HAVE TALKED TO THE LAWYER ON YOUR SIDE, OR TO AN INVESTIGATOR, ADMIT IT FREELY. It is quite normal and proper to do so.

17. DO NOT GUESS. If you do know the answer, say so. If not, say you don't.

18. IF COUNSEL INSISTS THAT YOU ESTIMATE IN YOUR ANSWERS, BE SURE THAT YOU MAKE IT CLEAR THAT IT IS AN ESTIMATE.

19. IF YOUR COUNSEL MAKES AN OBJECTION, WAIT FOR HIM TO ADVISE YOU WHETHER TO PROCEED WITH YOUR ANSWER OR NOT TO ANSWER THE QUESTION.

20. LIMIT YOUR TESTIMONY TO FACTS WITHIN YOUR KNOWLEDGE AND EXCLUDE ANY OPINIONS THAT YOU MAY HAVE FORMED, UNLESS SPECIFICALLY ASKED FOR SUCH AN OPINION.

21. DON'T MEMORIZE ANY STATEMENT YOU'VE GIVEN OR ANYTHING THAT YOU ARE GOING TO SAY IN ANSWER TO QUESTIONS. You should simply visualize what happened and, in your own words, answer any questions concerning it.

Please follow our recommendations at the deposition. However, **do not watch us** as we will not "signal" you how to answer.

Additional Suggestions

1. BE ON TIME AND BE MODESTLY AND CONSERVATIVELY DRESSED AND GROOMED.

2. TREAT ALL PERSONS IN THE DEPOSITION ROOM WITH RESPECT.

3. IT IS IMPERATIVE THAT YOU ARRANGE TO DISCUSS YOUR DEPOSITION WITH YOUR ATTORNEY IN ADVANCE. You should prepare a list of questions or concerns about how you can truthfully respond to certain lines of inquiry that concern you.

4. YOU SHOULD FEEL FREE TO REQUEST A CUP OF COFFEE OR TEA, A COLD DRINK, OR WATER.

■■■

Section 2

Trial

Testimony of Your Child

Preface

The purpose of this pamphlet is to assist you in answering questions that you may have regarding the testimony of your child in a custody or visitation case and the law in North Carolina. It is, of course, impossible to answer all of your questions in a short brochure such as this, so we want to encourage you to ask other questions of your lawyer at the appropriate time. If you have any comments or suggestions for improving this handout, please do not hesitate to let us know.

1. **Q.** I'VE HEARD MY DAUGHTER CAN TELL THE JUDGE WHERE SHE'S GOING TO LIVE WHEN SHE BECOMES 12 YEARS OLD. IS THAT RIGHT?

   A. Not quite. Nobody can tell the judge in a custody or visitation case what to do—not you, not your lawyer, and certainly not your child. Not even at 17½ years old, just six months from the age of majority in this state, can your child tell the judge what arrangements may be made for custody or visitation. The judge decides these issues based on the *best interest of the child*, whether or not the child agrees with the decision.

2. **Q.** CAN MY DAUGHTER EVER TELL THE JUDGE WHERE SHE WANTS TO LIVE AND WITH WHOM?

   A. Of course. Children often testify during custody and visitation trials. The cases in North Carolina state that it is *very important* for the judge in such a hearing to listen closely to the wishes of the child of the plaintiff and defendant (the parties to the lawsuit). But the cases also emphasize that the judge should only give strong weight to the preference of a child *of suitable age, discretion, and maturity.* That means, basically, that if your child is really *old enough* and *grown-up enough* (and these are two different things!) to know with whom she wants to live, along with some good reasons for the decision, then the judge should be willing to listen to her explain her preferences. Also, you should understand that the younger the child is, the less the judge will likely consider her testimony.

3. **Q.** ARE THERE ANY AGE LIMITS FOR TESTIMONY? HOW YOUNG CAN A CHILD BE? CAN I ALSO HAVE MY THREE-YEAR-OLD SON TESTIFY THAT HE HATES HIS FATHER AND WANTS TO STAY LIVING WITH ME?

   A. Not so fast! There are limits to everything. The youngest age of a child that testified in a court case that we've been able to uncover is *six years old.* It would be pretty hard for a judge to give "considerable weight" to the testimony of a child who is younger than six (and, in many cases, to children who are between six and nine but are simply not mature enough). The older a child is, the more weight will be given to her testimony. At age 16, for example, a child's testimony—if straightforward, believable, and honest (not subject to bribes or promises of rewards)—would be very helpful to the judge and would probably be followed most of the time if the rest of the case also supports the child's preference. Also, you should understand that the younger the child is, the less the judge will likely consider his/her testimony.

4. Q. CAN THE JUDGE DISREGARD MY CHILD'S WISHES ENTIRELY?

A. Yes, indeed. There's no rule of law that says the judge must follow the child's preferences. In a 1966 case, the North Carolina Supreme Court stated that a child's wishes are not controlling in a custody dispute but must yield to the standard of the *best interest of the child*. And in a 1993 case, the Court of Appeals upheld a trial judge in Wake County who ordered visitation rights for a father over the strong objections of the teenage daughter, stating that visitation in such cases is "the father's right," which cannot be undone by the wishes of the child.

5. Q. DOES MY SON TESTIFY IN THE JUDGE'S OFFICE OR ON THE WITNESS STAND?

A. Unless the parties agree otherwise, the child testifies in open court like any other witness. If your lawyer cannot get the other attorney to agree to the son's meeting with the judge "in chambers" (i.e., the judge's office), your attorney may at least make a motion to clear the courtroom, as would be the case in a juvenile court hearing, but whether this motion is granted depends on the judge. There is no doubt, of course, that testimony in chamber is the most comfortable way of presenting testimony, not only for the son but also *for the judge*, and most judges will do a little "jawboning" of their own if it looks like the child is going to testify to see if the attorneys will agree to the "in chambers" approach to this important testimony.

6. Q. SUPPOSE WE AGREE TO LET MY SON TESTIFY IN CHAMBERS, AND SO DOES THE OTHER SIDE. IS IT JUST JOHNNY AND THE JUDGE IN THERE? HOW WILL I KNOW WHAT HE SAYS? WHAT IF HE *GOES OFF THE DEEP END* AND STARTS SAYING UNTRUE THINGS ABOUT ME?

A. The judge can hear the child in chambers without the parties present, assuming that they consent to be absent. The judge can also exclude the attorneys if the parties consent. But the judge is not allowed to speak alone with the child with *no record at all* of what was said. A custody or visitation trial, after all, is supposed to be *on the record*, meaning that everything is taken down and recorded (either by court reporter or by tape recorder). Without any record of the conversation, there is no end to the mischief that could occur based on the child's comments, well-intentioned or otherwise. So the judge will usually make arrangements for one of the above two methods of memorializing the meeting in chambers with the child when the parties and the attorneys are not present.

7. Q. SHOULD I BE AT ALL CONCERNED ABOUT HOW TESTIFYING COULD AFFECT MY CHILD?

A. Absolutely! Remember that your child has a relationship with you and the other parent. It is often very difficult for children to "take sides" with one parent over another. Indeed, while a child may say to Dad, "I want to live with you," he/she may also be saying that same thing to Mom. Children who testify usually feel as though they are betraying one of their parents. If you have any question in your mind as to how or if this will adversely affect your child, we suggest taking your child to a psychologist who can make a recommendation for you. Please let us know if you need a referral for this purpose.

■■■

Custody Witness Summary

[To our clients: Use this to summarize information for the witnesses you'd like to call in your custody/visitation trial.]

CASE: _____

* *

NAME OF WITNESS: _____

ADDRESS: _____

_____

PHONE #: _____

BUSINESS: _____

ADDRESS: _____

_____

PHONE #: _____

KNOWN MOTHER/FATHER/CHILD HOW LONG? _____

NATURE/ORIGIN OF CONTACT OR KNOWLEDGE: _____

_____

FREQUENCY OF CONTACT WITH MOTHER/FATHER/CHILD: _____

_____

_____

MAIN TOPIC(S) FOR TESTIMONY: _____

_____

_____

_____

SUMMARY OF TESTIMONY: _____

_____

_____

_____

_____

(Use reverse for additional space for answers to above.)

■ ■ ■

Worksheets to Use in Child Custody

Preface

This "Client Custody Worksheet" is intended as a supplement to the "Journal" which is described in the Guidelines we have provided to you. If you review the various categories listed on the Worksheet, they may give you ideas as to subject matters and events to write about in your Journal.

In addition, we ask that you provide us with an outline listing (preferably in the same sequence as the categories on the Worksheet) your comments as to each of these categories.

Remember, this Worksheet, as well as the Journal, will be very helpful to your attorney in preparing your case. Therefore, it cannot be emphasized strongly enough that you provide as much detail as possible, give examples of both past and present events, both routine and special, and include dates, where possible.

Finally, please ask any questions you may have about it.

A. DAILY/WEEKLY SCHEDULES

1. days and hours of work of parent(s)
2. travel and absence from home
3. any unusual (emergency) time requirements due to work
4. children's school schedules
5. when children go to bed, wake up, leave for school, arrive home from school
6. how schedule will change (if needed) to accommodate custody
7. weekend schedules/activities

B. FOOD AND FEEDING

8. meals as a family
9. meal preparation/children's involvement
10. shopping—when? children's involvement
11. nutrition
12. special dietary requirements
13. table manners
14. meals outside the home

C. PERSONAL HYGIENE/HABITS

15. bathing, showering, washing
16. toilet training
17. nails, hair, etc.
18. acne
19. cosmetics
20. adolescent/puberty questions
21. drugs, cigarettes, alcohol

D. HOUSEHOLD DUTIES/JOBS

22. house and rooms—who cleans? children's involvement
23. dishes, take out trash, etc.
24. jobs of children outside of home—paper route, babysitting, lawn work, etc.

E. MEDICAL/HEALTH

25. visits to pediatrician
26. special problems surgeries/treatments
27. prescriptions
28. during illness—attention to children/care
29. mental health—counseling
30. advised other parent
31. visits to dentist
32. teeth brushing
33. flossing/Waterpik®
34. braces/orthodontia

F. CLOTHING

35. purchases/acquisition of clothing
36. dress them or help them dress
37. laundry
38. mending/sewing

G. RECREATION

39. books, magazines, etc.
40. television (choices and limitations)
41. movies
42. crossword puzzles, board games, etc.
43. sporting events
44. outdoor recreation/play
45. organized events
46. video games
47. music
48. computers

H. EDUCATION

49. what schools?—private/public? which district?
50. how children go, or will go, to school
51. visits to school
52. conferences with teacher
53. help with homework

I. RELATIONS

54. relations with father/mother
55. relations and activities with other parent and family
56. relations between siblings
57. birthdays
58. association with other children
59. cooperation with therapist, counselor, school or other psychologist

J. DISCIPLINE OF CHILDREN

60. manners, politeness—how taught
61. punishment—when and how
62. speech problems

K. RELIGION OF CHILDREN

    63. Christening
    64. Sunday school
    65. religious school/instruction
    66. prayers
    67. symbolism in home
    68. attendance at house of worship
    69. respect for other faiths
    70. religious books
    71. confirmation/first communion
    72. Bar Mitzvah/Bat Mitzvah

L. HEALTH OF CLIENT AND OTHER PARENT

    73. physical
    74. psychological
    75. drugs
    76. alcohol

M. EVALUATION OF CLIENT AND OTHER PARENT

    77. gentle
    78. kind
    79. patient
    80. attentive
    81. caring
    82. intelligent
    83. careful
    84. trustworthy

N. AFFECTION—DEMONSTRATION

    85. words of love/expression by parent
    86. words of love/expression by children
    87. laugh together
    88. cuddling
    89. kissing
    90. hugging

O. NEGATIVE ACTIONS

    91. mistreat
    92. neglect
    93. beat
    94. abuse
    95. yell and scream
    96. inattentive
    97. rude
    98. improper

P. FINAL QUESTIONS

■■■

Help Us With Your Testimony

When we are preparing a case for trial, it is helpful for you to draft the questions you'd like us to ask about a specific incident or topic in the hearing. You often know best what you need to say or what your witness will state. Thus getting your suggested wording for the questions and answers makes our job easier and our questions more accurate. It helps save *our* time and *your* money. Here's how to do it:

First, write a sentence or two about what the testimony (yours or that of your witness) is supposed to prove. For example:

My testimony will show that I was having supper at a restaurant and then shopping at Arcadia Shoe World getting a pair of bedroom slippers between 6 and 9 p.m. on Tuesday, March 30. I was not at the house of Larry Corbett.

Next, write a summary paragraph as to what you or the witness would say.

I left our house on March 30 at 6 p.m. and drove to Sam's Steak Villa, where I ate supper between 6:30 and 7:45 p.m. Then I drove on Page Blvd. to Oakmont Shopping Center, parked the car and went into Arcadia Shoe World. It was about 8 p.m. I went into the store, looked over the slippers, and chose a pink pair with bunnies. Then I paid for them. I even have the receipt. I left the store and drove home, arriving about 9 p.m.

Finally, write the questions that will prompt the answers corresponding to the summary paragraph.

Q. WHEN DID YOU LEAVE THE HOUSE ON MARCH 30?
A. I left our house on March 30 at 6:00 p.m.

Q. WHERE DID YOU GO?
A. I drove to Sam's Steak Villa.

Q. WHAT TIME DID YOU ARRIVE THERE?
A. I got there about 6:30 p.m.

Q. WHAT DID YOU DO THERE?
A. I had supper there.

Q. WHEN DID YOU LEAVE SAM'S STEAK VILLA?
A. I left around 7:45 p.m.

Q. THEN WHERE DID YOU GO?
A. Then I drove on Page Blvd. to Oakmont Shopping Center, parked the car and went into Arcadia Shoe World.

Q. WHAT TIME WAS IT WHEN YOU ARRIVED?
A. It was about 8:00 p.m.

Q. WHAT DID YOU DO THERE?
A. I went into the store, looked over the slippers, and chose a pink pair with bunnies. Then I paid for them.

Q. DO YOU HAVE ANY PROOF?
A. I have the receipt.

[Note to attorney: introduce exhibit (my receipt from the store) into evidence.]

Q. Then what did you do?
A. I left the store and drove home.

Q. When did you arrive home?
A. I got home around 9:00 p.m.

Here's another example:

1. Write a paragraph about what the testimony will show or prove.
   My testimony will show that I owned the 120 shares of IBM stock before I was married, and I did nothing to alter its value during the marriage.

2. Next, write a summary paragraph as to what the supporting testimony would be.
   I bought 120 shares of IBM stock for my IRA three years before my marriage to Jane Doe. I left it in the USAA account, which I opened in 1999, from then until our separation, when I cashed it in to help pay for my increasing attorney fees. I didn't do anything regarding the investment while we were married.

3. Finally, write the questions that will prompt the answers corresponding to the summary paragraph.

Q. When did you purchase the stock in IBM?
A. I bought it in January 2002. That was three years before our marriage.

Q. Where did you put it?
A. I put it into my IRA, which is managed by USAA and which I had opened in 1999.

Q. What did you do with it during the marriage?
A. Nothing.

Q. Did you move the funds around or invest in other assets?
A. No.

Q. What eventually happened to it?
A. I liquidated it in 2008 to pay your attorney fees in this case.

That's all there is to it!

■■■

Preparation for Cross-Examination

1. WHAT IS CROSS-EXAMINATION?
   A. It is an opportunity to question the other party under oath for the purposes set out below.

2. PURPOSES OF CROSS-EXAMINATION:
   A. To test the credibility of the witness.
   B. To *impeach* (discredit or challenge) the testimony of the witness.
   C. To bring out additional facts not given by the witness on direct examination.
   D. To catch the witness in a lie. (NOTE: This is seldom possible.)
   E. To show bias, prejudice, or interest on the part of the witness (i.e., the witness is related to someone in the lawsuit, has an unreasonable or unfounded prejudice, or has a financial interest in the outcome of the case).
   F. To make the witness sound unbelievable—to "paint him into an illogical corner."

3. RULES OF THE CROSS-EXAMINER:
   A. When in doubt, do not cross-examine.
   B. "Always ask leading questions."
      1. Leading questions are ones that suggest a particular response.
      2. Examples of leading questions:
         a. "Aren't you the mother of the plaintiff?"
         b. "You hope to get custody in this case, right?"
         c. "You didn't see the stop sign, did you?"
         d. "Isn't it a fact that the knife was nine inches long?"
   C. Always ask questions that require a YES or NO answer (see examples above).
   D. Never ask *open-ended* questions; these will let the witness do too much explaining (i.e., "Why do you want custody?" or "When did you see the stop sign?").

4. RULES FOR THE WITNESS ON CROSS-EXAMINATION:
   A. Answer only the question asked.
   B. Do not evade or try to dodge questions—meet them *head-on*.
   C. If a leading question can be answered properly with only a YES or NO, do so (i.e., "You are 40 years old?" or "You have brown hair?" or "You were in the Army in 1981?").
   D. If a leading question cannot be answered properly with YES or NO, do not try to do so.
      1. "I don't know" or "I can't remember."
      2. "I'll answer YES [or NO], but I have to explain . . ."
      3. "The answer is MAYBE . . . could I explain?"
      4. When the question is "Have you stopped beating your wife?" (or something similar), the answer might be "I can't answer that with a YES or NO . . . can I explain that, please?"

E. Always look to the judge in answering.
   1. If you want to persuade or convince someone, the judge is the one!
   2. If you want to ask to explain, the judge is the one who can let you do this.
F. Hold a card up your sleeve—see if you can give additional facts (outside of your direct examination) to support your position and upset the questioning of the cross-examiner.

■■■

Quick Tips for Witnesses in Domestic Cases

1. Look at the judge while you are speaking. He or she is the most important person in the room. You don't need to convince <u>ME</u> when you talk, and you probably won't succeed in convincing the other side. But you do need to convince the judge and the best way to do this is to make eye contact!! If the judge does not look back at you, then swivel your chair toward him or her and, if necessary, intersperse "Your Honor" throughout your testimony.

2. Use open gestures and body language to convey to the judge an impression of honesty and straightforward explanations. Don't cross your legs or arms while testifying.

3. Speak slowly and clearly. Be serious. Don't raise your voice and don't be angry. Try not to "run your mouth" on the witness stand.

4. When referring to children, always say "<u>**OUR**</u> children," "<u>**OUR**</u> son," or "<u>**OUR**</u> daughter." Kids don't just happen—two parents (not one) make them happen. "<u>**OUR**</u>" recognizes the existence of the other party. "<u>**OUR**</u>" is not greedy or grabby. Don't ever say "<u>**MY**</u> child"!

5. Be humble. Be sorry for **anything** you might have done to scare, hurt, or offend the other side. Don't be afraid to say "<u>I was wrong</u>."

6. Don't get into an argument with the opposing counsel; you won't win and it will hurt your case in the process. Always call the other attorney "sir" or "ma'am."

7. Give details, if appropriate, concerning any incident or transaction that is involved in your court case. **DETAILED TESTIMONY** is generally more credible than vague, general or conclusory statements.

■■■

Suggestions to Witnesses

You may be called to testify in court. Here are some practical suggestions on what to do and how to do it well when you are asked to serve as a witness.

Before You Testify

1. If you are going to testify concerning records, become familiar with them. You should know what the records contain and be able to refer to them easily if you must do so while you are on the witness stand.

2. If you are going to testify concerning some event that happened months or years before, try to refresh your recollection. You may wish to return at least once to the place where the event occurred. Close your eyes and try to picture the exact scene; note the location of physical objects and approximate distances, for you may be asked about these things. If you gave a written statement, ask to see it. Talking with friends or co-workers who were there may help to recall details that you had forgotten. But do not try to develop a common story. Remember, your testimony must state what you recall, not what someone else told you.

On Your Day in Court

1. Dress neatly, but don't overdress. Your normal business attire is probably about right.

2. If you have received a subpoena, take it with you. It may prove to be useful, for example, if you are not sure in which courtroom the trial is being held.

3. When you arrive at the courtroom, if you do not know the attorney who has subpoenaed you, ask for him or her and introduce yourself. If the trial is in progress and you must wait for a recess, you may sit in court or remain outside the courtroom.

4. The attorney will probably want to discuss your testimony with you, which is a proper thing to do. If you are producing records, however, do not turn them over to the attorney until the judge orders you to do so.

5. Avoid any undignified behavior, such as loud laughter or talking, from the moment you enter the courtroom. Smoking and gum-chewing are permitted in the corridors but not in the courtroom itself.

When You Are on the Stand

1. When you are called as a witness, stand upright while taking the oath. Pay attention and say "I do" clearly, so that all can hear. Try not to be nervous; there is no reason to be.

2. While you are on the witness stand, you are sworn to tell the truth. Tell it! In testifying, the first rule is to tell the truth. Don't answer questions with half-truths. Don't try to judge whether an answer is going to help or hurt one side

or the other. Don't let your personal feelings of who should win or lose color your testimony. Avoid giving your opinion about the guilt or innocence of the people involved. That is the job of the court. As a witness, your only duty is to tell it like you saw it, nothing more, nothing less.

3. Talk to the members of the jury, if there is one, or to the judge. Speak frankly and openly as you would to a friend or neighbor. Do not cover your mouth with your hand. Speak clearly and loudly enough so that everyone can hear you easily.

4. Speak in your own words. There is no need to memorize your testimony beforehand; in fact, doing so is likely to make your testimony sound "pat" and unconvincing. Be yourself.

5. Listen carefully to each question and make sure that you understand it before you start to answer. Have the question repeated if necessary. If you still do not understand it, say so. Never answer a question that you do not fully comprehend or before you have thought your answer through.

6. Answer directly and simply, with "yes" or "no" if possible, only the questions asked; then stop. Do not volunteer additional information that is not requested. If, however, an explanation is required, say so. Sometimes an attorney will try to limit you to a "yes" or "no" answer. If that happens, simply say that you cannot answer the question "yes" or "no." Usually the judge will let you explain, but in any event, everyone will get the point.

7. The court only wants the facts that you yourself have observed, not what someone else told you. Nor is the court interested in your conclusions or opinions. Usually you will be unable to testify about what someone else told you, and only "expert" witnesses are allowed to give their conclusions and opinions.

8. When at all possible, give positive, definite answers. Avoid saying "I think," "I believe," or "In my opinion" when you actually know the facts. But if you do not know or are not sure of the answer, say so. There is absolutely nothing wrong with saying "I don't know." You can be positive about the important things without remembering all the details. If you are asked about little details that you do not remember, just answer that you do not recall.

9. Do not exaggerate. Be wary of overbroad generalizations that you may have to retract. Be particularly careful in responding to a question that begins, "Wouldn't you agree that . . .?" or "Isn't it a fact that . . .?"

10. If your answer was wrong or unclear, correct it immediately. It is better to correct a mistake yourself than to have the opposing attorney discover an error in your testimony. If you realize that you have answered incorrectly, say "May I correct something I said earlier?" or "I realize now that something I said earlier should be corrected."

11. Stop instantly when the judge interrupts you or when the other attorney objects to what you say. Do not try to sneak in an answer.

12. Usually, a witness should not ask the judge for advice; it is your attorney's job to object to any improper questions.

13. Always be polite, even if the opposing attorney is not. Use "ma'am," "sir," and "your honor." Be serious at all times. The courtroom is not the place to be cute or humorous. Do not be an argumentative or sarcastic witness. Remember, the attorney has a big advantage—he or she can ask the questions.

14. The honest witness has nothing to fear on cross-examination. Some of these rules may make more sense, however, if you understand what an attorney tries to do on cross-examination. If your testimony has not been harmful in his case or if he thinks that questioning you further will prove fruitless or counterproductive, he may waive cross-examination or ask a few perfunctory questions. If, however, your testimony has been damaging to his client, the opposing attorney will want to argue that you are a liar or that you do not know what you are talking about. In either case, the usual approach is to try to get you to say things that the attorney can show are not completely true. He will then argue, "Since the witness lied or was wrong on this point, his entire testimony is unworthy of belief."

15. Here are a couple of "trick questions" that attorneys will sometimes use:
    a. "Have you talked to anybody about this case?" If you say "No," everybody will think that probably you are not telling the truth, because a good lawyer always talks to his witness before they testify. Simply say that you talked to whomever you did—the lawyer, the police, or anyone else.
    b. "Are you being paid to testify in this case?" The lawyer hopes that your answer will be "yes," suggesting that you are being paid to say what the lawyer who called you wants you to testify. Your answer should be something like: "No, I am not getting paid to testify. I turned the subpoena over to my employer, and I will receive my usual salary."
    c. "And nothing else happened after that?" Watch out. You might remember something else after a few more questions. Better answer this one with, "I don't remember anything else" or "That is all I can recall."

16. While testifying or cross-examination, don't look at the attorney who called you for help in answering the question. You're on your own.

17. Testifying for a substantial length of time is surprisingly tiring and can cause fatigue, crossness, nervousness, anger, careless answers, or a willingness to say anything in order to leave the witness stand. If you feel these symptoms, strive to overcome them, or ask the judge for a five-minute break or to allow you to have a glass of water. Also remember:
    a. Be natural. Be yourself. Don't try to be someone you're not. If you relax and tell the truth and remember you are talking to other people, you'll get along fine.
    b. After you have testified, do not tell other witnesses what was said during the testimony until after the case is over. Do not ask other witnesses about their testimony.

18. Now read these suggestions again. We think you'll find that some of them mean more the second time through.

■ ■ ■

Practical Courtroom Tips in a Domestic Case

[This pamphlet was adapted from a similar one which is the property of Mills and Weitzenkorn, P.C., of Denver, Colorado, and is used with their permission.]

1. **TELL THE TRUTH**—No one expects perfection, but if you tell the truth you will not be tripped up on cross-examination and the judge will believe you.

2. **DO NOT GUESS**—"I don't know" or "I don't remember" are acceptable answers, but guessing can get you into trouble on cross-examination.

   Remember, there's a real difference between "No" and "I don't remember." For example, if you answer on cross that you don't remember whether something happened, it means that it may or may not have happened. If the event could *not* have happened, then your answer should be "No."

   If you are asked, "Isn't it true that you kept $20,000 in a safe deposit box?" the answer is clearly "No, that is not true," as opposed to "I don't remember."

3. **BE SURE YOU HAVE HEARD AND UNDERSTAND THE QUESTION**—If you do not hear a question or do not understand it, do not try to answer based on what you think the question was. Instead, simply ask opposing counsel to repeat the question. Always wait for the lawyer to finish the question before beginning your answer. This may be difficult advice to follow. Remember, a question may actually contain several questions requiring several answers one at a time.

4. **TAKE YOUR TIME**—Use good judgment in answering questions. Consider every question and give it some thought, if necessary, but do not look like you are stalling for an answer.

5. **SPEAK LOUDLY ENOUGH FOR EVERYONE TO HEAR**—Do not chew gum. Keep your hands away from your mouth. Remember that you must verbalize your answers, not just nod your head. The court reporter must write down everything you have to say.

6. **LOOK AT THE JUDGE**—From time to time during your testimony, especially at important points, look the judge straight in the eye. Do not forget that the judge is the person who must be persuaded by what you have to say.

7. **DO NOT ARGUE WITH OPPOSING COUNSEL**—Keep your composure no matter what the other lawyer or your spouse does. Never lose your temper or let them provoke you. The judge may excuse a lawyer who misbehaves in the name of zealous advocacy, but if you act out, it will affect your credibility. The ruling of the judge will usually reflect a definite dislike for the spouse who is angry or flippant.

8. **BE COURTEOUS**—Say "yes, sir" or "ma'am" to opposing counsel, and if you must address the judge, use "Your Honor." Sometimes the other lawyer may interrupt you while you are answering. Let her finish the new question and then say, "Before I answer, I need to finish my answer to the last question."

9. **DO NOT MAKE JOKES OR WISECRACKS**—Remain a lady or gentleman at all times. Be honest, straightforward, and courteous. Watch the tone of your voice.

10. **IF YOU HEAR AN OBJECTION**—Stop answering immediately and say nothing until the judge rules on the objection. "Overruled" means you must answer, "sustained" means you must not. Do not worry about remembering legal terminology. Either the judge or the lawyers will tell you what to do. Never interfere with dialogue between the judge and lawyers about objections or other matters.

11. **DO NOT ANSWER A QUESTION WITH A QUESTION**—Opposing counsel is not on trial. Any combativeness toward that lawyer will irritate the judge.

12. **YOU MUST ANSWER EVERY QUESTION**—Do not bother to ask your lawyer or the judge if you must answer a particular question; unless an objection is made and sustained, you must answer.

13. **ON CROSS-EXAMINATION**—When you are being cross-examined, the other lawyer will be asking you questions that typically require a "yes" or "no" answer. Remember that the other lawyer is trying to get you to make statements that will hurt your case. Do not simply react to a question; it is important to *think* about your answers. Also, if the "yes" or "no" response that you give does hurt your case, the next words out of your mouth should be, "But can I explain?" The judge will allow you to explain your answer, which will lessen or completely remove the damage that would have been done by a simple one-word response.

14. **BE POSITIVE AND FIRM IN YOUR ANSWERS**—You know you are telling the truth and you are well-prepared, so do not be intimidated by the other lawyer. If you are worried about your answer, do not show it. Do not memorize what you are going to say. Memorized testimony is not believable.

15. **IT'S OK TO CRY**—Don't be surprised if during your testimony you become emotional and cry. It can be upsetting to talk about personal matters in court. The judge will understand, and, in fact, it may add to rather than detract from your credibility. If you need a tissue, a drink of water, or a break to compose yourself, just ask the judge for permission.

16. **REMEMBER THAT THE JUDGE IS WATCHING YOU**—Not only during your testimony, but also at counsel table. Do not overreact during the testimony of other witnesses. Do not lose your temper. It doesn't make points with the court, and it usually lessens the judge's respect for you.

17. **NOTES TO ME DURING TRIAL**—If you want to communicate with your lawyer while someone is testifying, write a note. Do not nudge or whisper to your attorney. It may be possible to listen, read, and write at the same time, but no one can listen to the witness, the lawyer, and the client all at the same time!

■ ■ ■

Part III

State Specific

Section 1

Adoption

Adoption and Illegitimate Children

1. Q. WHAT IS ADOPTION?
   A. Adoption is the creation by law of the relationship of parent and child between two individuals. Adoption terminates the relationship and all rights and responsibilities previously existing between a natural parent and child. The adoption process is closely regulated by the state.

2. Q. HOW ARE CHILDREN ADOPTED?
   A. Children may be placed for adoption in a variety of ways. These are as follows:

   a. An "agency placement" is the procedure for adoption used by county Departments of Social Services or licensed private adoption agencies.
   b. A "direct placement" or "independent adoption" is one made by the natural parents directly into an unrelated adoptive home without the assistance of an agency.
   c. A "relative adoption" is one in which a parent's relative (often a spouse) agrees to adopt the child of that parent.
   d. An "adoption facilitator" is an individual or nonprofit entity that assists natural parents in locating and evaluating prospective adoptive parents without charge.

Except for relative adoptions, all of these procedures require court approval and a preplacement assessment or home study, as will be explained later in this pamphlet. There is no one method that is better than another for a couple.

3. Q. MY WIFE AND I WANT TO ADOPT A CHILD. WHAT'S THE DIFFERENCE BETWEEN AGENCY PLACEMENT AND DIRECT (NON-AGENCY) PLACEMENT?
   A. It might seem at first much easier to adopt a child directly from the mother than to apply to a county Department of Social Services or a licensed private adoption agency. Many prospective parents are honestly concerned about fees, waiting lists, background checks, and home studies. As a practical matter, however, there may be many more problems (although these *can* be overcome) with direct placements than with agency adoptions. Direct placement, on the other hand, will require effort on the part of the prospective parents regarding the natural parents of the child (both in finding them and in obtaining valid legal consents to the adoption).

4. Q. WHERE CAN WE FIND OUT ABOUT ADOPTING A CHILD BY AGENCY PLACEMENT?
   A. There are several adoption agencies in North Carolina, including the local county Department of Social Services as well as private agencies. Check with your Department of Social Services or your lawyer for further information.

5. Q. CAN WE PLACE AN ADVERTISEMENT FOR A CHILD?
   A. No one may solicit children for adoptive placement except a licensed child placement agency, an adoption facilitator, or an individual with a completed preplacement assessment finding that the individual is suitable to be an adoptive parent (or that individual's immediate family). *Only a licensed*

agency, *Department of Social Services, or adoption facilitator may advertise in any periodical or newspaper, or by radio, television, or other public medium.* Violation of this provision is a crime in North Carolina.

6. Q. WHAT IS A PREPLACEMENT ASSESSMENT?

    A. A preplacement assessment, formerly known as a home study, is required in all adoptive placements, except where a biological parent places a child with a grandparent, sibling, first cousin, aunt, uncle, great-aunt, great-uncle, or great-grandparent of the child. It must be completed or updated within 12 months before the placement occurs. It may be prepared by any licensed child placement agency for a fee. The preplacement assessment must be based on at least one personal interview with each individual being assessed and must occur in the individual's residence. A copy of the completed preplacement assessment must be provided to the prospective adoptive parents and to the biological parent who placed the child for adoption.

7. Q. WHAT LEGAL STEPS ARE REQUIRED FOR ADOPTION?

    A. Here is a checklist of the steps that must be followed:

    a. The first step is to obtain a preplacement assessment.

    b. Consents will be obtained from the biological parents.

    c. The mother completes an affidavit indicating the name, last known address, and marital status of the parents.

    d. A petition will be filed by the prospective adoptive parents seeking the court's approval of the adoptive placement. The preplacement assessment, consents, and affidavit are filed with the petition. A certified copy of the background information about the child's health, social, educational, and genetic history provided by the placement agency or parents and a copy of any court order or pleading concerning custody or visitation with the child will also be filed with the petition. The petitioners must also file an affidavit accounting for any payment made in connection with the adoption. Finally, a document is filed with the petition identifying any individual whose consent may be required but has not been obtained at the time of filing the petition.

    e. Once the petition is filed, notice of the petition is served on any person whose consent was necessary but had not been obtained. Notice will also be served on the agency that placed the child for adoption and the agency that prepared the preplacement assessment.

    f. The court will order the preparation and filing of a report by the agency that placed the child or prepared the preplacement assessment. The report is to provide information to assist the court in determining whether the adoptive placement is in the best interest of the child and must be completed within 60 days of the receipt of the order by the agency.

8. Q. WHEN IS THE ADOPTION FINAL?

    A. No later than 90 days after the petition has been filed, the court will set a date for a hearing or disposition of the petition. The hearing or disposition will occur no later than six months after the petition is filed, unless the court extends the time. If the petition is not contested, a hearing will not be required. If a hearing is required because the petition is contested, the court will determine whether the adoption is in the best interest of the child.

9. **Q. WHEN MAY A PARENT'S CONSENT BE OBTAINED?**

   A. A father's consent may be obtained before the birth of the child. A mother's consent may not be obtained until after the birth of the child. There is no waiting period. A foreign order of adoption may be accepted in lieu of the consent of the biological parents or guardian.

10. **Q. ONCE A PARENT GIVES CONSENT, CAN HE/SHE CHANGE HIS/HER MIND?**

    A. Yes. The individual who gave the consent may revoke it by giving written notice to the person specified in the consent. The prospective adoptive parents must immediately, upon request, return the child to the person who gave consent.

    A consent to the adoption of an unborn child or a child who is three months old or less at the time the consent is given may be revoked within 21 days following the day on which it is executed, inclusive of weekends and holidays.

    A consent to the adoption of any child over age three months may be revoked within seven days following the day on which it is executed, inclusive of weekends and holidays.

    When the placement occurred before a preplacement assessment was completed and provided to the birth parent who placed the child for adoption, the revocation period is extended to five business days after that person receives the preplacement assessment, or the remainder of the revocation period, whichever is longer.

    If a second consent is obtained, it is irrevocable.

    The consent of a child over age 12 or of an adult adoptee may be revoked at any time before entry of the final order.

11. **Q. CAN WE HAVE A CONTRACT OR BINDING AGREEMENT FOR A PRIVATE ADOPTION?**

    A. No. A written agreement would not be enforceable because:

    a. North Carolina law does not recognize adoption contracts; and

    b. Such a contract would violate the birth mother's legal right to revoke consent within 30 days of signing the consent form.

    c. In addition, no such contract could ever anticipate the situation at birth—twins, triplets, healthy single infant, stillbirth, or child with birth defects. As a result, you cannot rely on an agreement or contract in private adoptions. Nothing can require the birth parents to give up the child at birth or abide by their consent to the adoption. Nothing can guarantee that the prospective adoptive parents will accept and keep the child offered for adoption.

12. **Q. IS INDEPENDENT PLACEMENT ADOPTION REALLY AN "OPEN ADOPTION," OR CAN THE NAMES OF THE PARTIES BE HIDDEN FROM EACH OTHER?**

    A. Confidentiality is not an issue in independent adoption, since by law the biological parents must be parties to the adoption and, therefore, must give informed consent. This means that the names of the adopting parents appear on the Consent to Adoption forms at the time the biological parents sign the forms. Also, since by law only the parents may place their child for adoption (unless the child has been released to a county Department of Social Services or a licensed private child-placing agency), the biological parents and adoptive parents obviously would have face-to-face contact with each other. The biological parents have every right to know the people with whom they plan to place their child, and should be encouraged to know enough about them to feel comfortable with their assuming a parental role through adoption. Quite candidly, there is nothing to stop either parent from telephoning the birth parents (before or after the adoption is final), writing to the child, or following the adoptive family at the local park or shopping mall.

13. **Q. WHAT IF THE BIOLOGICAL PARENTS WANT TO VISIT THE BABY?**
 A. Adoption arrangements which include plans for continuing contact between natural and adoptive parents or allow natural parents to have continuing contact with adopted children are called open adoptions. North Carolina does not favor open adoption arrangements. In North Carolina such arrangements are invalid. They cannot be a precondition to the adoptive placement. The consent of the biological parents must be unconditional. Such arrangements also will not invalidate an adoptive placement. Generally, the biological parents become legal strangers to the child once the adoption is final. They have no legal right to any further contact. However, they will know the names and addresses of the adoptive parents. There is no guarantee that they will not attempt to make unwanted contact. If so, they may be treated just like any other stranger. They are subject to civil and criminal laws that limit unwanted intrusions.

14. **Q. WHAT EXPENSES MAY WE PAY FOR IN CONNECTION WITH THE ADOPTION?**
 A. Effective July 1, 1996, adoptive parents may pay for the "reasonable and actual fees and expenses." These expenses include:

 a. Services of an agency in connection with an adoption;
 b. Medical, hospital, nursing, pharmaceutical, traveling, or other similar expenses incurred by a mother or her child incident to the pregnancy and birth or any illness of the adoptee;
 c. Counseling services for a parent or the adoptee;
 d. Ordinary living expenses of a mother during the pregnancy and for no more than six weeks after the birth;
 e. Expenses incurred in ascertaining the background information about an adoptee and the adoptee's biological family;
 f. Legal services, court costs, and traveling or other administrative expenses connected with an adoption; and
 g. Preparation of the preplacement assessment and the report to the court.

15. **Q. WHAT CANNOT BE PAID BY US?**
 A. Payments may *not* be made for:

 a. Placement of a child;
 b. Consent for adoption;

    c. Relinquishment of a child to an agency; or

    d. Assisting a parent or guardian in locating a prospective adoptive parent, or transferring custody of a child to an adoptive parent.

An affidavit of accounting identifying all expenditures made in connection with the adoption must be made at least 10 days before the entry of the final order.

    Violation of this section is a Class 1 misdemeanor subject to punishment in the court's discretion. Any subsequent violation is a Class H felony and may be punished by a fine of not more than ten thousand dollars ($10,000).

16. **Q.** WHAT ABOUT OUR LEGAL EXPENSES AND MEDICAL EXPENSES FOR THE BABY?

    A. Medical expenses incident to the birth of the child should be covered by your medical insurance policy. Check your policy for specific provisions. Generally, all legal expenses are the responsibility of the adopting parents. Legal expenses are reimbursable up to varying limits under some corporate benefits packages. Beginning in 1997, there is an individual income tax credit available for the payment of qualified adoption expenses up to $5,000 per child (and up to $6,000 for special needs children). Expenses include adoption fees, court costs, attorney fees, and other costs. The credit is available through the year 2001.

17. **Q.** ONCE MY CHILD IS ADOPTED, DO I HAVE ANY FURTHER LEGAL RIGHTS OR OBLIGATIONS TO THE CHILD?

    A. No. Once the child has been adopted, the natural parents cease to have any legal rights or obligations toward the child. If a natural parent owed a child support obligation, that obligation would stop once the child was adopted.

18. **Q.** I AM NOT MARRIED AND HAVE A CHILD OUT OF WEDLOCK. IF I DO NOT WANT TO PLACE THE CHILD FOR ADOPTION, CAN I OBTAIN SUPPORT FOR THE CHILD FROM HIS FATHER IF I KEEP THE CHILD?

    A. Yes. The law makes no distinction in support obligations between parents who are married when the child is born and parents of illegitimate children. Likewise, the law allows the courts to determine custody and visitation rights of parents of legitimate as well as illegitimate children, and there are no distinctions or preferences given to either mothers or fathers under the North Carolina General Statutes concerning who is entitled to custody of a child or what type of visitation should be allowed. Mothers are not *automatically* granted custody of illegitimate children, for example, and neither are fathers of illegitimate children barred from visitation rights with the children. It may be necessary, however, to obtain the services of a private attorney and file a complaint or motion for a hearing as to custody or visitation rights. Child support can be obtained with the assistance of the County Child Support Enforcement Agency.

19. **Q.** HOW CAN I PROVE TO THE COURT WHO IS THE FATHER OF MY ILLEGITIMATE CHILD?

    A. Anyone involved in a paternity/child support case can file a motion in court asking for a hearing and paternity tests (which involve the mother, child, and alleged father). The results are reported back to the court for further proceedings to determine paternity. The tests used most often to "prove" paternity are DNA tissue tests, which are very accurate and reliable. The person making the motion for paternity testing is usually required to pay for the testing, but the male can be ordered to pay back the cost of the tests if he is found to be the father of the child. DNA testing can be performed immediately after birth or before birth. Blood samples are no longer required. A cell sample may be taken from a swab of the mouth. Testing can be arranged by the Child Support Enforcement Agency.

■■■

Adoption Rights Letter

As part of the private adoption process, we require all interviewees to read and sign this Adoption Rights Letter to ensure that they understand and comply with North Carolina law.

Please print:

_____

(name of individual or couple)

_____

(address)

_____

(home phone)

_____

(work phone)

I/We acknowledge the following:

A. **PRIVATE ADOPTIONS ARE OPEN.** A valid private adoption in North Carolina requires the execution of forms which reveal the full names of the birth parents and the adoptive parents. There is no legitimate way to disguise identities, conceal names, or make this anything other than an open procedure in which each set of parents knows the identity of the other parents. Even though a new birth certificate is prepared after the final decree and the original birth certificate is sealed, it is much more likely that children will be able to identify or locate their birth parents (and vice versa) in a private adoption than in an agency adoption.

B. **NO PLACEMENTS.** This law firm is not a placement agency, and we do not set up adoptions or match parents and children. We do not maintain adoption lists, and we cannot act as a clearinghouse. It is against the law to place children for adoption without a license, and we want those who see us about adoptions to know this from the start. The lawyer's primary responsibility is to counsel and advise adoption clients, to prepare and file adoption papers, and to help with the Clerk of Superior Court and the Department of Social Services in completing the adoption.

C. **NO CONTRACTS.** No contract for adoption would, in our opinion, be enforceable in North Carolina to compel a couple to accept a child for adoption or to force a birth parent to place the child for adoption and not revoke his/her consent. We do not, therefore, prepare "adoption contracts."

D. **EXPENSES.** Adoptive parents may pay for the reasonable medical expenses which are actually incurred by the birth mother incident to the birth of the child. This includes the costs of prenatal care, delivery, and post-delivery in the hospital by the birth mother. You may also pay for costs of treatment for the child.

E. **NO PROMISES.** Private adoption is, in all honesty, a risky proposition. No one can guarantee the birth of a healthy infant. No one can certify that a child will not be born with AIDS, herpes, or drug/alcohol dependence. Getting a full medical history on birth parents may be difficult. No one can guarantee that an adoptive couple will remain married, have a happy marriage, will not divorce, or will not abuse or neglect the adopted child. A large element of risk is inherent in private adoptions.

F. **OUR PLEDGE.** We promise to work hard in each adoption case. Our fees are solely for counseling work, phone calls, office visits, document preparation, trips to court, and related matters. We cannot promise success with each proposed adoption. We will not promise to find a child (or a set of adoptive parents). We do not place children. We will be glad to answer any questions you may have about the information contained in this Information Letter.

G. **YOUR PLEDGE.** I/We have read this letter fully and understand the facts, policies, and information above. I/We have also read and received a copy of CLIENT INFORMATION LETTER #16, "ADOPTION." I/We have received a copy of this letter.

H. **RELEASE OF INFORMATION (OPTIONAL).** I/We hereby do/do not authorize the release of the information at #1 above in connection with private adoption.

(Signature)

(Signature)

(Date)

■■■

Adoption Road Map

While each adoption is unique, most adoptions of a given type follow the same general procedures. Each adoption process depends upon the nature of the placement: stepparent, relative, intrastate, interstate, or international.[1] The following is an outline of the process for a typical interstate adoptive placement in which a child is born in another state and the prospective adoptive parents live in East Carolina.[2] It is intended to help adoptive parents understand what will happen during the typical interstate adoption process and approximately when various events will occur. The circumstances of each adoptive placement are unique. This summary cannot address the issues presented by every case and is not intended to provide legal advice. You should consult an attorney about the law as it applies to the circumstances of your individual case.

    I. IDENTIFYING A CHILD
   II. PRIOR TO BIRTH
  III. AFTER BIRTH
  IV. AFTER PLACEMENT
   V. FINALIZATION

I. Identifying a Child

The first step in the adoption process is identifying a child that is available for adoption. The question asked most frequently by prospective adoptive parents is: How do we locate a child? Most prospective adoptive parents locate children available for adoption through friends and relatives, private adoption agencies, county departments of social services, or adoption facilitators. An adoption facilitator is an individual or nonprofit entity that assists biological parents in locating and evaluating prospective adoptive parents without charge.

The second most common question is: Can we place an advertisement for a child? In East Carolina, no one may solicit children for adoptive placement except a licensed child placement agency, an adoption facilitator, or an individual with a completed preplacement assessment finding that the individual is suitable to be an adoptive parent or that individual's immediate family. *Only a licensed agency, Department of Social Services, adoption facilitator or person with a completed pre-placement assessment[3] may advertise in any periodical or newspaper, or by radio, television, or other public medium. Violation of this provision is a crime in East Carolina.*

---

[1]The process is generally less complicated for relative, stepparent, and intrastate adoptions.
[2]Most states do not permit non-residents to finalize adoptions in the state where the child is born.
[3]Persons with a pre-placement assessment can advertise but must include a statement in the ad that 1) pre-placement assessment finds that they are a person suitable to be an adoptive parent; 2) identifies the name of the agency that completed the pre-placement assessment; and 3) the date of the pre-placement assessment.

II. Prior to Birth

A. THE PRE-PLACEMENT ASSESSMENT. Before an unrelated child is placed with prospective adoptive parents, a pre-placement assessment (PPA) should be prepared by a licensed child placement agency or county department of social services. A PPA may be prepared even though a specific child has not yet been identified for adoption. The purpose of the PPA is to evaluate the circumstances relevant to the individual's suitability to be an adoptive parent, including the quality of the environment in the home. Ideally, the PPA should be completed at or before the time a child is identified for adoption. If not, the preparation of the PPA can be expedited for an additional fee. If the PPA is not completed at the time the petition for adoption is filed, an explanation must be filed with the petition. A copy of the PPA must be provided to the parent placing the child for adoption.

B. BACKGROUND INFORMATION. The birth parent(s) will be asked to complete one or more forms to provide the adoptive parents with medical and social history and other relevant information about birth parents (hobbies, interests, talent and abilities). The birth parents, particularly the birth mother, will also be asked to allow the adoptive parents access to medical records for themselves and the child. At a minimum, prospective adoptive parents should have access to information regarding prenatal care.

III. After Birth

A. CONSENTS AND OTHER NECESSARY RELEASES. Once the child is born, the birth parents will be asked to formally give their consent to the adoptive placement. They, or at least the birth mother, will also be asked to sign a number of other documents to facilitate the legal and physical transfer of custody of the child to the adoptive parents. These documents are generally signed at the hospital. While there is no mandatory waiting period in East Carolina, these documents should not be executed until at least 24 hours after the birth of the child. We recommend waiting 24 hours to ensure that the birth mother has sufficiently recovered and is free from medications that might impair her capacity to give her consent. Other states do impose mandatory waiting periods. When applicable, they must be followed. Once the consents and authorizations are signed, physical custody of the child may be transferred to the prospective adoptive parents and they may remove the child from the hospital.

The same consents and releases will be sought from the birth father when his identity and whereabouts are known or can be determined with the exercise of due diligence. If his identity is not known or his whereabouts are known or can be determined with the exercise of due diligence, a different procedure is followed. The procedure will vary depending upon the individual circumstances of the case.

IV. After Placement

A. **INTERSTATE COMPACT COMPLIANCE.** Each of the United States has enacted a version of the Interstate Compact for the Placement of Children (ICPC). The administrators of the ICPC in each state supervise interstate adoptive placements to ensure that the legal requirements of both states are satisfied. In an interstate placement, the requirements of both the sending (where the child is born) and the receiving state (where the prospective adoptive parents live) must be satisfied before the child may be taken to the prospective adoptive parents home state.

B. **FILING THE ADOPTION PETITION.** Once the physical transfer of custody of the child has occurred, the prospective adoptive parents will sign a petition for adoption in which they seek the authorization of the court to adopt the child. The petition and accompanying documents will be filed in the county and state where the prospective adoptive parents reside.

C. **ADOPTIVE PLACEMENT PROGRESS REPORT.** Once the petition is filed, the court will order the preparation and filing of a report by the agency that prepared the pre-placement assessment. The report is to provide information to assist the court in determining whether the adoptive placement is in the best interest of the child. In preparing a report to the court, the agency must conduct two personal interviews with each petitioner in the petitioner's residence and at least one additional interview with each petitioner and the adoptee and observe the relationship between the adoptee and the petitioners. In East Carolina, the report must be completed within 60 days of the receipt of the order by the agency. If the agency identifies a specific concern about the suitability of the petitioner or the petitioner's home for the adoptee, the agency must file an interim report immediately, which identifies the concern. The agency must give the petitioner a copy of any such report.

V. Finalization

A. **ENTRY OF THE DECREE OF ADOPTION.** In East Carolina, no later than 90 days after the petition has been filed, the court will set a date for a hearing or disposition of the petition. The hearing or disposition will occur no later than six months after the petition is filed unless the court extends the time. The adoptee must have been in the physical custody of the petitioner(s) for at least 90 days. If the petition is not opposed, a hearing will not be required. If a hearing is required, the court will determine whether the adoption is in the best interest of the child based upon a preponderance of the evidence and must conclude that there has been substantial compliance with the statutory requirements. If the court denies a petition to adopt a minor, custody will revert to the birth parent(s).

If the petition is granted, as they usually are, the clerk of superior court issues the decree of adoption. Except in step-parent adoptions, a decree of adoption severs the relationship of parent and child between the individual adopted and that individual's biological or previous adoptive parents. A final decree of adoption effects a complete substitution of families for all legal purposes after the entry of the decree. It establishes the relationship of parent and child between each petitioner and the individual being adopted.

B. **ISSUANCE OF A NEW BIRTH CERTIFICATE.** The decree of adoption will direct the Division of Vital Statistics to issue a new birth certificate reflecting the adoptive parents' names and the child's new name. The Division of Vital Statistics issues a new birth certificate for the child and seals the old birth certificate. This usually takes thirty to sixty days after the final decree is issued. The adoptive parents may then apply for a social security number for the child.

C. **ADDITION CONSIDERATION.** As with any other life-changing event, the adoption of a child presents an occasion to reconsider previous plans. We recommend a thorough review of life insurance policies, investment and retirement account beneficiary designations. You should also prepare or revise last wills and testaments.

■■■

Adoption

Adoption is the creation by law of the relationship of parent and child between two individuals. Adoption terminates the relationship and all rights and responsibilities previously existing between a natural parent and child. The adoption process is closely regulated by the state.

The primary purpose of these regulations is to advance the welfare of minors by (i) protecting minors from unnecessary separation from their original parents, (ii) facilitating the adoption of children in need of adoptive placement by persons who can give them love, care, security, and support, (iii) protecting children from placement with adoptive parents unfit to have responsibility for their care and rearing, and (iv) assuring the finality of the adoption.

The secondary purposes are (i) to protect biological parents from ill-advised decisions to relinquish a child or consent to the child's adoption, (ii) to protect adoptive parents from assuming responsibility for a child about whose heredity or mental or physical condition they know nothing, (iii) to protect the privacy of the parties to the adoption, and (iv) to discourage unlawful trafficking in children and other unlawful placement activities.

As your lawyers, we have a duty to strictly comply with the statutory requirements for adoptive placements. Being sure that our clients are fully informed about and understand the adoption process is an essential part of our responsibility. The following is designed to address the most common questions clients have about adoptions.

1. **Q. How do we locate a child that is available for adoption?**
   A. Most prospective adoptive parents locate children available for adoption through

   a. Friends and relatives;
   b. Private adoption agencies;
   c. County departments of social services, or
   d. Adoption facilitators. An adoption facilitator is an individual or non-profit entity that assists biological parents in locating and evaluating prospective adoptive parents without charge.

2. **Q. Can we place an advertisement for a child?**
   A. No one may solicit children for adoptive placement **except**: a licensed child placement agency, an adoption facilitator, a county department for social services, or an individual with a completed pre-placement assessment finding that the individual is suitable to be an adoptive parent. Advertisements can be published only in a periodical or newspaper, on radio, television, cable television, or on the Internet. An individual with a completed pre-placement assessment finding that the individual is suitable to be an adoptive parent must include a statement that 1) the person has completed a pre-placement assessment finding that he or she is suitable to be an adoptive parent; 2) identifies the name of the agency that completed the assessment; and 3) identifies the date the assessment was completed. The advertisement may also state whether the person is willing to provide lawful expenses pursuant to North Carolina law. *Violation of this provision is a crime in North Carolina.*

3. Q. WHAT IS A PRE-PLACEMENT ASSESSMENT? IS IT REQUIRED? WHAT DOES THE PRE-PLACEMENT ASSESSMENT COVER?

A. A pre-placement assessment, formerly known as a home study, is required for all adoptive placements, except where a biological parent places a child with a grandparent, sibling, first cousin, aunt, uncle, great-aunt, great-uncle, or great-grandparent of the child. It must be completed or updated within 18 months before the placement occurs. It may be prepared by any licensed child placement agency for a fee. The pre-placement assessment must be based on at least one personal interview with each individual being assessed and must occur in the individual's residence. The pre-placement assessment will address the following issues:

a. Age and date of birth, nationality, race, or ethnicity, and any religious preference of the prospective parents;

b. Marital and family status and history, including the presence of any children born to or adopted by the individual and any other children in the household;

c. Physical and mental health, including any addiction to alcohol or drugs;

d. Educational and employment history and any special skills;

e. Property and income, and current financial information provided by the individual;

f. Reason for wanting to adopt;

g. Any previous request for an assessment or involvement in an adoptive placement and the outcome of the assessment or placement;

h. Whether the individual has ever been a respondent in a domestic violence proceeding or a proceeding concerning a minor who was allegedly abused, dependent, neglected, abandoned, or delinquent, and the outcome of the proceeding;

i. Whether the individual has ever been convicted of a crime other than a minor traffic violation;

j. Whether the individual has located a parent interested in placing a child with the individual for adoption, and a brief, non-identifying description of the parent and the child; and

k. Any other fact or circumstance that may be relevant to a determination of the individual's suitability to be an adoptive parent, including the quality of the environment in the home and the functioning of any children in the household.

The assessment must be completed within 90 days of receipt of a request. A copy of the completed pre-placement assessment must be provided to the prospective adoptive parents. The prospective adoptive parents are entitled to respond to any unfavorable assessment and to have their response reviewed by the agency. A copy of the pre-placement assessment must also be provided to the biological parent who placed the child for adoption. If a copy cannot be provided to one or both of the biological parents, an affidavit must be filed with the petition for adoption explaining why.

4. Q. WHAT LEGAL STEPS ARE REQUIRED?

A. *Obtain and file the necessary documents.* The first step is to obtain a pre-placement assessment. Consents will be obtained from the biological parents. The mother will complete an affidavit indicating the name, last known address, and marital status of the parents. A petition will filed by the prospective adoptive parents seeking the court's approval of the adoptive placement. The pre-placement assessment, consents, and affidavit will be filed with the petition. A certified copy of the background information about the child's health, social, educational, and genetic history provided by the placement agency or parents and a copy of any court order or pleading concerning custody or visitation with the child will also be filed with the petition. Finally, a document will be filed with the petition identifying any individual whose consent may be required but has not been obtained at the time of filing the petition.

Once the petition is filed, notice of the petition will be served on any person whose consent was necessary but had not been obtained. Notice will also be served on the agency that placed the child for adoption and the agency that prepared the pre-placement assessment. The court will order the preparation and filing of a report by the agency that placed the child or prepared the pre-placement assessment. The report is to provide information to assist the court in determining whether the adoptive placement is in the best interest of the child and must be completed within 60 days of the receipt of the order by the agency. The petitioners must also file an affidavit accounting for any payment made in connection with the adoption.

5. Q. WHEN IS THE ADOPTION FINAL?

A. No later than 90 days after the petition has been filed, the court will set a date for a hearing or disposition of the petition. The hearing or disposition will occur no later than six months after the petition is filed, unless the court extends the time. If the petition is not opposed, a hearing will not be required. If a hearing is required, the court will determine whether the adoption is in the best interest of the child.

6. Q. WHEN MAY A PARENT'S CONSENT BE OBTAINED?

A. A father's consent may be obtained before the birth of the child. A mother's consent may not be obtained until after the birth of the child. There is no waiting period. However, we recommend waiting at least 24 hours to ensure that the mother is free from the influence of medications that might affect her capacity to give a valid consent. An agency must provide consent within 30 days of receiving notice of the proceeding for adoption. A foreign order of adoption may be accepted in lieu of the consent of the biological parents or guardian.

7. Q. ONCE A PARENT GIVES CONSENT, CAN THEY CHANGE THEIR MIND?

A. Yes. The individual who gave the consent may revoke by giving written notice to the person specified in the consent within seven days following the day on which the consent was executed, inclusive of holidays and weekends. However, if the seventh day falls on a weekend or a North Carolina or federal holiday, then the revocation period continues until the next business day. If notice is given by mail, it is effective upon dispatch in the U.S. Mail.

The prospective adoptive parents must, immediately upon request, return the child to the person who gave consent.

Where placement occurred before a pre-placement assessment was completed and provided to the birth parent who placed the child for adoption, the revocation period is extended to five business days after that person receives the pre-placement assessment, or the remainder of the revocation period, whichever is longer.

If a second consent is obtained, it is irrevocable.

A parent or guardian whose consent was obtained by fraud or duress may move to have the decree of adoption set aside and have the consent declared void within six months of the time the fraud or duress is or ought reasonably to have been discovered. A parent or guardian whose consent was necessary but was not obtained may move to have the decree of adoption set aside within six months of the time the omission is or is thought reasonably to have been discovered.

The consent of a child over age 12 or of an adult adoptee may be revoked at any time before entry of the final order.

8. Q. ONCE THE REQUIRED CONSENTS ARE OBTAINED, HOW LONG IS IT BEFORE THE ADOPTION IS FINAL?

A. A petition must be filed within 30 days of the placement of a child for adoption. A dispositional hearing will be set within 90 days from the filing of the petition. A final order will be filed within 6 months of the filing of the petition.

9. Q. WHAT EXPENSES MAY WE PAY FOR IN CONNECTION WITH THE ADOPTION?

A. In the past, North Carolina had a very restrictive policy regarding payments in connection with adoptions. No payments of any kind were permitted. More recently, adoptive parents were permitted to pay for "the reasonable and actual medical expenses incurred by the biological mother incident to the birth of the child." Such payments had to be disclosed in the petition for adoption and the adoptive parents must represent that "there were no gifts or payments of, or promises to give or pay, any other fee, compensation, consideration, or thing of value . . ."

Under the revised Chapter 48, which became effective July 1, 1996, adoptive parents may pay for the "reasonable and actual fees and expenses" listed in G.S. § 48-10-103:

a. Services of an agency in connection with an adoption;

b. Medical, hospital, nursing, pharmaceutical, traveling, or other similar expenses incurred by a mother or her child incident to the pregnancy and birth or any illness of the adoptee;

c. Counseling services for a parent or the adoptee;

d. Ordinary living expenses of a mother during the pregnancy and for no more than six weeks after the birth;

e. Expenses incurred in ascertaining the background information required under G.S. § 48-3-205 about an adoptee and the adoptee's biological family;

f. Legal services, court costs, and traveling or other administrative expenses connected with an adoption; and

g. Preparation of the pre-placement assessment and the report to the court.

Note that payments may not be made contingent on the placement of the minor for adoption, relinquishment of the minor, consent to the adoption, or cooperation in the completion of the adoption. Except where there has been fraudulent action, if the adoption is not completed, a person who has made payments may not recover them. However, that person is not liable for any further payment unless the person has agreed in a signed writing with a provider of a service to make this payment regardless of the outcome of the proceeding for adoption. Also, agencies may charge or accept a reasonable fee or other compensation from prospective adoptive parents.

PAYMENTS MAY <u>NOT</u> BE MADE FOR:

a. placement of a child,
b. consent for adoption,
c. relinquishment of a child to an agency, or
d. assisting a parent or guardian in locating a prospective adoptive parent, or transferring custody of a child to an adoptive parent.

Violation of this section is a Class 1 misdemeanor subject to punishment in the court's discretion. Any subsequent violation is a Class H felony and may be punished by a fine of not more than ten thousand dollars ($10,000). An affidavit of accounting identifying all expenditures made in connection with the adoption must be made at least ten days before the entry of the final order.

10. **Q.** WHAT ABOUT OUR LEGAL EXPENSES AND MEDICAL EXPENSES FOR THE BABY?
    A. Medical expenses incident to the birth of the child should be covered by your medical insurance policy. Check your policy for specific provisions. Generally, all legal expenses are the responsibility of the adopting parents. Legal expenses are reimbursable up to varying limits under some corporate benefits packages. Beginning in 1997, there is an individual income tax credit available for the payment of qualified adoption expenses. Consult your tax adviser for specific information relating to what expenses and what amounts can be deducted.

11. **Q.** WHAT IF THE BIOLOGICAL PARENTS WANT TO VISIT THE BABY?
    A. Adoption arrangements which include plans for continuing contact between natural and adoptive parents or allow natural parents to have continuing contact with adopted children are called open adoptions. North Carolina does not favor open adoption arrangements. In North Carolina such arrangements are invalid. They cannot be a pre-condition to the adoptive placement. The consent of the biological parents must be unconditional. Such arrangements also will not invalidate an adoptive placement. Generally, the biological parents become legal strangers to the child once the adoption is final. They have no legal right to any further contact. However, they will know the names and addresses of the adoptive parents. There is no guarantee that they will not attempt to make unwanted contact. If so, they may be treated just like any other stranger. They are subject to civil and criminal laws which limit unwanted intrusions.

■■■

Section 2

Alimony and Child Support

Adultery

Preface

The purpose of this handout is to assist you in answering questions that you may have regarding adultery and the law in North Carolina. It is, of course, impossible to answer all of your questions in a short brochure such as this, so we want to encourage you to ask other questions of your lawyer at the appropriate time. Feel free to take this handout with you so that you may refer to these answers from time to time and have a better idea of how your case is being handled. If you have any comments or suggestions for improving this handout, please do not hesitate to let us know.

1. Q. **WILL PROOF OF ADULTERY HELP MY CASE?**
    A. This really depends on what kind of a case you have. Let's look at some definitions first. *Adultery* is sexual relations by a married person with a member of the opposite sex. *Illicit sexual behavior* is sexual relations of any kind with one not your spouse, including homosexual relations. Although the word "adultery" has been replaced in our domestic relations statutes with "illicit sexual behavior," adultery is still the most common form of this behavior, so it will continue to be used here in this handout. Adultery could be important in an alimony case, for example, but it has nothing to do, on the other hand, with the award of child support or the filing for an absolute divorce. Except in cases involving alimony where there is clear evidence of adultery, proof of adultery is seldom a "bomb" that will cripple the opposition and force them to make every concession you demand. The specific effect of adultery on various cases is covered in the questions and answers below.

2. Q. **WHAT IS PROOF OF ADULTERY?**
    A. Since adultery and extramarital affairs are carried on in secret, there is seldom any direct proof of adultery. You would be extremely unlikely, for example, to obtain 8" x 10" color glossy photos of your spouse and his/her lover "buck naked in bed" together without a serious chance of getting your head blown off by a double-barreled shotgun. At the other extreme, you will almost never be able to prove adultery through mere association or companionship, such as seeing your spouse in the company of a potential paramour. The most likely proof of adultery is indirect proof or circumstantial evidence.

3. Q. **WHAT ARE SOME OF THE LEGAL EFFECTS OF ADULTERY?**
    A. The chart on the next page shows the legal impact of adultery on various types of cases. The specific questions that follow provide a more detailed explanation.

4. Q. **WHAT IS CIRCUMSTANTIAL EVIDENCE OF ADULTERY?**
    A. Circumstantial evidence of adultery is defined as *inclination* plus *opportunity*. Inclination is the probability or likelihood that a person would commit adultery, given the chance to do so. Opportunity is the chance to do so. To use an example, a surveillance of Mr. Green shows that he spent three

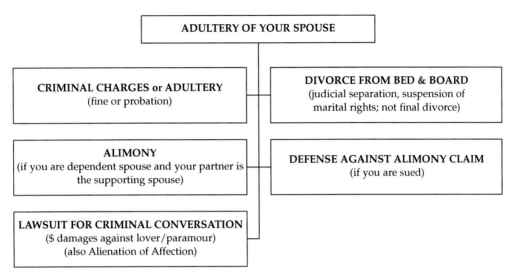

No relation (usually) to custody/visitation, unless potentially harmful impact on children
No relation (usually) to equitable distribution

nights in a row from 9:00 p.m. until 7:30 a.m. the next morning in the apartment of Ms. Brown. He is also observed hugging and kissing Ms. Brown. This set of facts would probably be sufficient circumstantial evidence to allow the jury to decide whether adultery had been committed, even though there was no **direct proof** of it. On the other hand, the mere presence of Mr. Green in the apartment of Ms. Brown from 9:00 p.m. until midnight on one particular night would **not** be sufficient. You must remember that the circumstantial evidence needed is such as to convince a reasonable juror (or, for example, an average person on the street, such as a neighbor or friend of yours) that adultery—sexual relations—occurred, not just that Mr. Green has been seeing Ms. Brown at some "indelicate" or unusual times under suspicious circumstances.

5. Q. MY SPOUSE HAS CONFESSED AND ADMITTED ADULTERY TO ME. ISN'T "WORD OF MOUTH" ENOUGH PROOF?
   A. Even though such an admission by a party is ordinarily a very strong kind of proof, classified as an admission against interest, the courts usually require some corroborating evidence to ensure that an adulterous affair has occurred. Some examples of independent corroborating evidence might be motel receipts, telephone bills, articles of clothing or jewelry of the paramour, unexplained and lengthy absences of the spouse, or any other evidence that would "link up" the bare assertion of adultery with the actual fact.

6. Q. CAN ADULTERY HELP ME WIN MY CUSTODY CASE?
   A. Probably not. Unless you can prove a *nexus* or significant connection between the adulterous conduct of your spouse and the welfare of your child, you stand little chance of prevailing in a custody suit merely by proving adultery on the part of your partner. A 1979 case in the North Carolina

Court of Appeals, *Almond v. Almond*, emphasized this point by holding that even continued and unconcealed cohabitation with a member of the opposite sex will not automatically disqualify a parent from getting or keeping custody of a minor child. If, on the other hand, you can show a **detrimental impact** on the child's welfare due to the adultery, you may be able to use that to improve your custody case. Such would be the case if, for example, your spouse's paramour had an alcohol or drug abuse problem, was physically abusive to your spouse or the child, or exposed an impressionable child (not an infant) to lewd or immoral conduct.

7. **Q.** SO ADULTERY HAS NOTHING TO DO WITH CUSTODY, RIGHT?
   A. Not so fast. There are at least two reasons why adultery is dangerous in custody cases:
   - First, while *the law* may say that adultery *per se* doesn't matter, *the judge* is the decision-maker in your case. The judge has a great deal of discretion in custody cases and in awarding or restricting visitation rights. Some judges might not be bothered or offended by adultery; others would be loath to grant custody or normal visitation rights to a parent carrying on an adulterous affair.
   - Second, while a divorce might end the marriage, it won't end the relationship with the other parent over the minor children. The parents will have to deal with each other on a frequent basis over a period of years, and post-divorce cooperation clearly is in every client's best interest. It is hard to imagine how having an affair before the divorce is complete can have a positive effect on the spouse's feelings for the adulterer, but the possibility that it will poison any spirit of cooperation is readily apparent. The need for future negotiation is inevitable, and negotiating with a friend is usually easier than negotiating with an enemy.

8. **Q.** CAN I FILE CRIMINAL CHARGES FOR ADULTERY?
   A. While adultery is still a crime in North Carolina under NC General Statutes 14-184, this type of "crime" is almost never prosecuted. If your spouse were found **guilty** based upon your evidence, the judge would most like impose a fine and probation, not a stiff prison term. Because your standard of proof is higher in a criminal case (**beyond a reasonable doubt**) than in a civil domestic case (**greater weight of the evidence**), you might not be able to prove your criminal case with the same kind of evidence that would easily persuade a domestic relations judge. Finally, as a practical matter, you would run the risk of looking very foolish to the magistrate and assorted court personnel as you try to swear out charges for something that is still a crime in North Carolina, is happening all too often in the community, and yet is almost *never* prosecuted by the District Attorney's Office.

9. **Q.** IS ADULTERY A GROUND FOR ALIMONY?
   A. No. Effective October 1, 1995, the grounds for alimony were removed. Nowadays, alimony is the amount given to a dependent spouse by the supporting spouse under court order. But adultery still plays a part, since the statute requires an award of alimony if adultery (now called "illicit sexual behavior") is proved on the part of the supporting spouse before the sepa-

ration. Adultery remains a ground for divorce from bed and board, which is judicially approved separation (not a true divorce).

10. **Q. DOES PROOF OF ADULTERY MEAN I AM ENTITLED TO ALIMONY?**

    A. No. No one is "entitled to alimony" until a court has ruled in his or her favor on all of the issues in such a case. There are at least three such issues. Alimony is only the first one of these, which is whether the opposing party (your spouse) has committed illicit sexual behavior before the separation. The second issue, which you must also prove, is that you are the *dependent spouse* and your partner is the *supporting spouse*. The third issue, if you have prevailed on the first two, is *how much alimony* should be awarded. For a further explanation of alimony, you should see our Client Information Letter on that topic. In general, however, good proof of adultery will often help win an alimony case by forcing a settlement on the opposing party. Proof of adultery is a very strong tool in prosecuting alimony cases.

11. **Q. CAN ADULTERY BE A DEFENSE IN ALIMONY CASES?**

    A. Yes. If you can prove that your spouse committed adultery before the separation, this amounts to an *absolute defense* against a claim for alimony. Regardless of the circumstances, financial or otherwise, the judge cannot enter an order of alimony for a spouse who is guilty of adultery. It is important, however, to be sure that the proof of adultery concerns a recent and unforgiven affair, not one that occurred 10 years ago or which has been discussed, forgiven, and put aside by the parties. This issue is also covered more fully in our Client Information Letter on alimony.

12. **Q. CAN I SUE MY SPOUSE'S LOVER?**

    A. Yes. Such suits are rare in other states, but North Carolina recognizes a cause of action, or legal claim, for "criminal conversation" (adultery) and allows you to file a suit demanding money damages. Such suits are often coupled with a claim for "alienation of affection," which is the intentional act of taking away or withdrawing your spouse's genuine love and affection for you in favor of some third-party paramour.

13. **Q. THAT SOUNDS GREAT. WHERE DO I LINE UP TO GET MY MONEY?**

    A. Not so fast—it is never quite that easy to file one of these suits and prevail to the extent that you actually receive the money which is called for in a favorable judgment for you. Although many lawyers would take a case such as this on a contingent-fee basis, meaning that they would be paid a percentage of the award if there was recovery, you will need at least the following in order to persuade a lawyer to take your case:

    - Clear liability, meaning good proof of adultery (or alienation of affection); and
    - A solvent defendant or wealthy paramour (also known as a "deep pocket") who has lots of money and assets so that you can collect on any judgment that is granted in your favor.
    - If you do not have both of these elements, you may still be able to get a lawyer to represent you in such a suit, but it is likely that the lawyer would need to be paid on an hourly basis as in most domestic relations cases—and this could easily cost between $5,000 and $20,000.

14. Q. WHY ARE THESE SUITS *REALLY* FILED?

    A. Most suits of this nature are, unfortunately, filed for nuisance purposes or as leverage in domestic settlements. While there have been some very large reported verdicts ($50,000–$250,000), the vast majority of these cases are settled for "nuisance value," that is, the cost of the plaintiff's attorney's fees plus a little "heartbalm money" for the plaintiff. In some of these cases, because of the privilege against self-incrimination, it is difficult to get any-one involved to testify, which further emphasizes the importance of inde-pendent corroboration and circumstantial evidence.

15. Q. WHAT ABOUT EQUITABLE DISTRIBUTION? IF MY SPOUSE BROKE UP THE MAR-RIAGE, DON'T I STAND A CHANCE OF GETTING A BETTER PROPERTY DIVISION AWARD FROM THE DIVORCE COURT?

    A. No. Marital misconduct is not a sufficient reason in the eyes of the law for granting a greater or lesser share of marital property to a spouse. In a line of decisions beginning in 1983, the North Carolina Court of Appeals has held that spousal misconduct, such as marital infidelity, cannot justify a judge's greater or lesser apportionment of marital assets. The only "fault" that will be considered by the divorce court in property division cases is *economic fault*. This generally means the spouse who damages, destroys, squanders, wastes, or dissipates marital property will share in less of the remaining marital assets. Although prolonged and extensive extramarital affairs can sometimes cause major financial losses to the marital estate (motel bills, expensive dinners, costly vacations with the paramour, etc.), seldom does adultery itself generate proof of substantial economic fault.

16. Q. SO I'M FREE TO CARRY ON WITH MY GIRLFRIEND WHILE MY PROPERTY SETTLE-MENT IS BEING NEGOTIATED, RIGHT?

    A. Wrong. Extramarital sexual relations before divorce can have an adverse affect on the other spouse, perhaps leading to unwanted complications. This risk is especially high if the other spouse did not know of the "other woman" or the "other man" before agreeing to negotiated settlement, but it can arise even if there was full knowledge beforehand. Infidelity typically engenders hurt, embarrassment, and anger, especially when the adultery is public knowledge. A relationship while the divorce is pending can create these feelings, and the risk is that the spouse will seek vindication or revenge. This motive may manifest itself in serious problems when your lawyer tries to bargain for a "fair" division of property or to avoid an exces-sive settlement demand from the injured spouse. Steer clear of adulterous conduct if you want your lawyer to be able to deal with opposing counsel based on facts and finances, rather than hurt feelings.

17. Q. WHAT CAN I DO IF I HAVE OTHER QUESTIONS?

    A. Please feel free to ask your lawyers for help and assistance. That is why we are here to serve you. Our clients' questions deserve straightforward answers in plain English, not "lawyer-ese," so that our clients can assist us in the preparation and resolution of the case, whether by trial or negotiated settlement.

■■■

Alimony

1. **Q.** IS ALIMONY ALLOWED IN NORTH CAROLINA?

   A. Yes. A new law in 1995 made substantial changes in the area of alimony. In North Carolina today, court-ordered spousal support is based primarily on **need**. This handout will cover court orders for the two kinds of spousal support that exist under state law—**post-separation support** and **alimony**. Provisions for spousal support may also be set out in a **separation agreement**. Separation agreements are covered in a separate handout.

2. **Q.** DOES THE COURT EVER AWARD TEMPORARY SPOUSAL SUPPORT AT THE START OF A LAWSUIT?

   A. Yes. This is called post-separation support [or PSS] and it must be ordered for a **dependent spouse** whenever the court finds that:

   - Her (or his) financial resources aren't enough to meet her reasonable monthly needs and personal living expenses; and
   - The **supporting spouse** has the ability to pay.

3. **Q.** WHAT CRITERIA MUST THE COURT CONSIDER IN DECIDING THESE TWO ISSUES?

   A. There are several, including the financial needs of the parties, their accustomed standard of living, the current employment income (and other earnings) of the parties, and their earning abilities. The judge must also consider their debts, their reasonable living expenses, and each party's legal support obligations—for each other, for a former spouse, for their minor children, and for other minor children of only one of the parties.

4. **Q.** CAN MY HUSBAND STOP ME FROM GETTING PSS BY PROVING THAT I'VE COMMITTED ADULTERY?

   A. Adultery by the dependent spouse isn't a bar to PSS. But if your husband brings up marital misconduct, then the judge is allowed to consider any marital misconduct by either party in deciding whether to allow PSS and how much to award.

5. **Q.** WHAT IS "MARITAL MISCONDUCT"?

   A. This is a new term that replaces the old "fault grounds" that used to be required for alimony in this state. Marital misconduct is pre-separation conduct that includes **abandonment** (both actual and "constructive"), cruel and barbarous treatment endangering a spouse's life, malicious turning out-of-doors, alcohol/drug abuse, "personal indignities" that render one's life burdensome and intolerable, reckless spending or waste of assets, willful failure to support, and **illicit sexual behavior**.

6. **Q.** WHAT IN THE WORLD IS "ILLICIT SEXUAL BEHAVIOR"? IT SOUNDS LIKE THE TITLE OF A BAD NOVEL!

   A. **Illicit sexual behavior** [or ISB, for short] is **any** sexual misconduct, including adultery as well as any form of intercourse with a person not your spouse, whether heterosexual or homosexual.

7. **Q. WHEN DOES THIS MARITAL MISCONDUCT HAVE TO OCCUR?**
   A. ISB must occur at or before the date of separation of the parties; post-separation misconduct is not allowed as evidence except to **corroborate**, or help prove, pre-separation marital misconduct.

8. **Q. IF MY WIFE IS GUILTY OF MARITAL MISCONDUCT, IS THAT WHERE THE CASE STOPS?**
   A. No. Whenever there is evidence of marital misconduct by the dependent spouse—the wife, in this case—the judge must also consider any marital misconduct by the supporting spouse. Thus the conduct (or, in this case, "misconduct") of both parties will be subject to scrutiny if the supporting spouse attempts to point out the flaws or faults of the dependent spouse.

9. **Q. WHEN DOES PSS END? DOES IT GO ON FOREVER?**
   A. PSS terminates at the earlier of:

   - the date set by the court for termination, if any;
   - the date of death of either party;
   - the occurrence of the remarriage or cohabitation (see discussion below) of the dependent spouse; or
   - the date on which alimony (see discussion below) is allowed or denied.

10. **Q. WHAT ABOUT ALIMONY—DOES THAT STILL EXIST?**
    A. Oh, yes—alimony is still "alive and well" in North Carolina. The approach to alimony, however, is somewhat different from that involved in post-separation support.

11. **Q. MUST "GROUNDS" BE SHOWN TO OBTAIN AN AWARD OF ALIMONY?**
    A. No. There is no longer any need to prove grounds for alimony. Under the current law, alimony is to be granted if:

    - the claimant (or party requesting alimony) is the **dependent spouse**;
    - the other party is the **supporting spouse**; and
    - an award of alimony is equitable under the circumstances after considering numerous factors set out in the statute.

12. **Q. WHAT ARE THESE "FACTORS" THAT THE COURT MUST CONSIDER?**
    A. There are 15 of them. They include such items as:

    - The marital misconduct (see explanation above) of either spouse;
    - The earnings, unearned income (dividends, interest, rent, etc.), earning capacities, and needs of the parties;
    - The length of the marriage, the standard of living of the parties during the marriage, and their respective contributions as homemaker;
    - The ages and the physical, mental, and emotional conditions of the spouses;
    - How each party has contributed to each other's education and increased earning power;
    - The impact of either parent being custodian of a minor child;
    - Each party's education and the time needed to educate or train a spouse to become self-sufficient;
    - The assets and debts of each party;
    - The tax impact of alimony (see discussion below); and
    - Any other economic factor that the court finds proper for consideration.

13. Q. **WHAT IF A PARTY IS FOUND TO HAVE COMMITTED ADULTERY—DOES THAT HAVE ANY IMPACT ON THE ALIMONY CASE?**
    A. Yes. The statute covers three possible scenarios regarding **illicit sexual behavior** [ISB], the new term that includes, but is broader than, adultery:

    - If the dependent spouse **only** is found to have committed ISB, then no alimony can be awarded and the case is over;
    - If only the **supporting spouse** has committed an act of ISB, then the court must award alimony to the dependent spouse; and
    - If both parties have committed ISB, then the court has the discretion to grant or deny alimony based on all the circumstances.

    As stated earlier in the question on marital misconduct in general, any act of **ISB** must occur at or before the date of separation of the parties; post-separation ISB may only be used as supporting evidence to prove ISB occurring at or before separation.

14. Q. **HOW CAN ALIMONY BE PAID?**
    A. The judge can order alimony to be paid on a periodic basis (i.e., in a monthly sum paid directly to the claimant by garnishment, or paid through the Clerk of Superior Court). It can also be paid in a lump sum, such as "the sum of $5,000 due on October 1 of this year" or even "the sum of $5,000, due in monthly installments of $500 each for 10 months." Alimony can be paid indefinitely or for a specific period of time, such as "for the next 24 months." The judge has these options for PSS also.

15. Q. **WHEN DOES ALIMONY END?**
    A. Alimony ends at the earlier of:

    - the date set by the court for termination, if any;
    - the date of death of either party; or
    - the occurrence of the remarriage or cohabitation (see discussion below) of the dependent spouse.

16. Q. **WHAT IS COHABITATION?**
    A. The law defines cohabitation as two adults living together continuously in a private heterosexual or homosexual relationship, and demonstrating all of the rights and duties of a marital relationship.

17. Q. **ARE THERE ANY OTHER WAYS TO STOP ALIMONY?**
    A. There are two legal acts that will bar the award of alimony (or PSS) in the first place. One is the granting of a **judgment of absolute divorce** with no claim pending for alimony. One of the effects of absolute divorce is to **bar a claim for alimony** if it has not been **asserted in a pleading before the divorce is granted**. The second bar is found when there has been a **waiver of alimony** in an agreement of the parties. A separation agreement can contain a waiver of alimony, and so can an antenuptial agreement. When a party gives up a right to alimony, she or he may not go back afterwards and retrieve the lost support right.

18. Q. **WHAT IS A "DEPENDENT SPOUSE"?**
    A. A dependent spouse is one who is actually and substantially dependent upon the other spouse for support or who is actually in need of support from the other spouse.

19. Q. WHAT IS A "SUPPORTING SPOUSE"?

    A. The supporting spouse is one who is actually capable of providing support for the alimony claimant. If there is no "surplus" left when the reasonable needs of the defendant are subtracted from his net monthly income, then it is arguable that he is not the "supporting spouse." Be careful with this sort of logic, however, since most alimony defendants will claim poverty and proclaim loudly their inability to provide spousal support. It is up to the judge to make a determination of the amount of the defendant's **reasonable monthly needs** so that the court can then find out how much money is "left over" to be used as alimony or PSS.

20. Q. ARE THERE ANY "ALIMONY GUIDELINES"? HOW IS THE AMOUNT OF ALIMONY DETERMINED?

    A. The amount of alimony is up to the judge. Although in some cases there may be an award of limited-term alimony, other judges might grant an open-ended award of alimony, reviewable by the court upon a motion alleging grounds for modification—namely, a substantial change of circumstances since the date of the original court order. Unlike the area of child support, there are no guidelines as to the amount of alimony. The award is completely in the discretion of the court, subject to the "factors" listed above for alimony.

    As a practical matter, the judge will usually attempt to find out what the **unmet needs** of the claimant are. This is the difference between her reasonable monthly needs and expenses and her net monthly income (if any). This amounts to the "deficit" which must be filled in order to support her properly.

    Next, the judge will attempt to find out what the "excess income" of the defendant is. If this exists, it becomes the "surplus" which is applied against the "deficit" in order to support the claimant properly. The judge will sometimes simply take the deficit of the plaintiff (or the surplus of the defendant) and convert it into the amount of alimony to be paid in a case, although this ignores the tax consequences of alimony set out below.

21. Q. MUST TAXES ALSO BE CONSIDERED IN DECIDING THE AMOUNT OF ALIMONY?

    A. Yes. Alimony is taxable to the payee and deductible by the payor. This is an important factor to remember when calculating alimony in negotiations. If Mrs. Smith needs, for example, $1,000 per month to meet the "financial deficit" she is experiencing, then she may need about $1,500 of taxable alimony in order to obtain $1,000 of post-tax alimony. By the same token, if Mr. Smith is able to pay $1,000 per month based on his income and reasonable monthly needs, this is $1,000 **after taxes**, and the real amount of alimony he should be able to afford might very well be about $1,500 with the **tax break** he gets by deducting this amount from his income. This hypothetical assumes the parties are in a 28 percent federal tax bracket and paying about 7 percent state taxes, which is the rate in North Carolina. In other words, a deductible sum of $1,500 per month will equal approximately $1,000 per month after taxes for one in these tax brackets, which is the correct way to figure alimony amounts.

22. **Q.** ARE THERE ANY OTHER TAX CONSIDERATIONS IN CLAIMING A DEDUCTION FOR ALIMONY?

    A. Under the IRS Code, there are several mandatory provisions that are required for alimony to be taxable to the payee and deductible by the payor. One such requirement is that the obligation must be in writing and, of course, a court order passes this test. In addition, it is required that payments end at the payee's death. These are also requirements of state law. Finally, tax-filing status is important also. Alimony is only deductible for the payor, and taxable to the payee, if the parties file separate returns. It cannot be deducted on a joint tax return.

23. **Q.** WHAT IS THE PROCEDURE IN A SPOUSAL SUPPORT CASE?

    A. There is no single "best" way to proceed, but a common approach would be to file a complaint for post-separation support and alimony and to schedule promptly a hearing on the claim for PSS. At a later time, the court would hear the claim for alimony, perhaps after the divorce of the parties or after their equitable distribution case had been decided. In an alimony case, either party can request a jury to determine the marital misconduct issues, but that is all the jury does—the judge makes the determinations of **dependent** and **supporting spouse**, assesses the factors, and decides the amount of alimony.

24. **Q.** IS ANY OTHER RELIEF AVAILABLE?

    A. Yes. As part of an alimony or PSS award, the court may also:

    - Award **attorney's fees** from the defendant to the claimant. Such fees are sometimes paid in a lump sum and sometimes in installments.
    - Grant **exclusive possession** of real or personal property (or title to personal property) to the claimant. This means, for example, that the court can grant to Mrs. Smith the use and possession of the Ford station wagon or, for that matter, the use and possession of the marital residence, to the exclusion of Mr. Smith. This amounts to an eviction order against the defendant, forcing him to leave the house.
    - Make provision for **medical expenses**. This typically includes medical insurance coverage and the responsibility for payment of uncovered health care expenses, either in part or fully.

25. **Q.** WHAT IF I HAVE ANY OTHER QUESTIONS?

    A. Please feel free to ask your lawyers for help and assistance. That is why we are here to serve you. Our clients' questions deserve straightforward answers in plain English, not "lawyer-ese," so that our clients can assist us in the preparation and resolution of the case, whether by trial or negotiated settlement.

■■■

Checklist for Child Support Options

Here is a checklist for options in child support. Please keep this copy and feel free to ask any questions you may have.

Monetary/Cash Amount

- ▸ Check state child support guidelines
- ▸ Check service regulations (in military cases)
- ▸ Allocate among children? [Always when representing the noncustodial parent!]

Health Care Insurance

- ▸ Private insurance
- ▸ TRICARE (in military cases)

Uncovered Health Care Expenses (UHCE)

- ▸ Portion paid by noncustodial parent:
  - • all
  - • half
  - • other fraction
  - • excess over stated amount
- ▸ Define UHCE or leave unspecified?
- ▸ Payment due when? To whom?

Life Insurance (in North Carolina, only by agreement)

- ▸ Amount of coverage
- ▸ On both parents or just noncustodial one?
- ▸ Change ownership of policy? Irrevocable beneficiary change?
- ▸ Choice of beneficiary:
  - • other parent
  - • child/children
  - • trust

Dependency Exemption

- ▸ Transfer to noncustodial parent or leave out?
- ▸ Give away or trade for increase in child support?
- ▸ Permanent or annual transfer?
- ▸ Complete transfer, or conditioned on faithful compliance with child support obligations?

College Expenses (in North Carolina, only by agreement)

- ▸ Length of obligation
- ▸ Items to be covered:
  - • room and board
  - • books
  - • tuition
  - • fees

- ▸ Conditioned on:
  - child's performance in school?
  - generally recognized degree?
  - accredited institution?
- ▸ Portion paid by noncustodial parent:
  - all   • half
  - other fraction   • specific amount

Reduction of Child Support for Visitation?

Termination of Child Support

- ▸ Always include death or emancipation (by marriage, military service, etc.) or child's moving away from custodial parent
- ▸ Other qualifying events:
  - age of majority
  - high school termination
  - college termination

■■■

Child Support

1. **Q.** How much child support should I receive if I'm separated from my spouse?

   A. There is no set amount that is "enough child support" in any given case. Child support varies according to the needs of the child or children, the incomes of the parents, the parents' reasonable needs, and the accustomed standard of living of the child(ren), among other things, and this is set out as the standards for determining child support under General Statute § 50-13.4(c).

2. **Q.** Who decides how much is enough? What if the other parent and I cannot agree on the amount of child support?

   A. If the two of you are able to reach agreement on a sum, that amount should be set out in a separation agreement. If the separation agreement sets out a specific sum, that figure will be binding. If the parties cannot agree, you may petition the court to set the amount of child support that will be required.

3. **Q.** What court decides child support?

   A. In North Carolina, the district court hears child support cases. A child support case is usually heard in the county where the child is living. If the father lives in another state and our state lacks any contacts with him, you may need to have the case heard there instead of here.

4. **Q.** Can the child support enforcement office help me?

   A. Yes. The county Child Support Enforcement Office can help you establish or enforce child support. This can also be done with a private attorney.

5. **Q.** How do I know how much child support I need?

   A. There is no "right amount" of child support. Many states have adopted child support guidelines. In North Carolina, these guidelines on child support are often used by the judge in setting child support and by the parties or attorneys in settling support cases.

6. **Q.** What if I need more child support?

   A. The Guidelines are flexible and allow for a child's special needs, extremely high or low income, and other factors the court finds to be important. Make a list of all monthly expenses for your household and apportion the expenses between yourself and the child or children. Be sure to set aside a certain portion of the rent, utilities, and food for each child. You should also consider whether to apportion such expenses as car payments, gasoline, and medical bills for each child. *You* must support the child or children, and *you* are the one who best knows the facts, needs, and expenses. The judge can go outside the Guidelines, but it is up to you to prove the need for a variance from the Guidelines.

7. **Q.** When my child is visiting my ex-husband, can he reduce the child support paid to me?

   A. No. Unless the court order or separation agreement specifically provides for a reduction, the child support payment should remain the same.

8. Q. **IF I CANNOT SEE MY CHILD FOR VISITATION, CAN I STOP PAYING CHILD SUPPORT?**
    A. Under North Carolina law, denial of visitation is not legal justification for withholding child support. Neither is lack of child support a legal excuse for refusing the other parent visitation rights. The parents do not have the right to try to link together these separate obligations. Even if a parent is not paying any child support, he may still visit his children. And even if a parent is not allowing visitation, the children are still entitled to child support.

9. Q. **WHEN DOES CHILD SUPPORT STOP?**
    A. Child support, without an agreement or court order, usually ends at the child's eighteenth birthday, although it will continue beyond then if the child is still in high school, so long as the child is not over 20 years old. A separation agreement or court order by consent may set a higher age, such as upon graduation from college or at age 21. Child support may end earlier than the above if the child is emancipated, such as by joining the military, moving away from home, or getting married.

10. Q. **CAN THE OTHER PARENT'S PAYCHECK BE GARNISHED FOR CHILD SUPPORT?**
    A. Yes. Under North Carolina law, garnishment of a paycheck for child support may be ordered for up to 40 percent of the net available pay. Garnishment is a court proceeding that requires a lawyer or the help of the Child Support Enforcement Office. Garnishment is allowed only if a *court order* for child support is violated; it does not apply if there is only a separation agreement. Wage assignment is also used to take child support directly from a parent's pay if there has been a prior child support order.

11. Q. **WHAT IF I NEED MORE CHILD SUPPORT IN THE FUTURE?**
    A. If the child support is set out in a court order, you may petition the court to increase child support if you can show that there has been a substantial change of circumstances since the date the order was signed. Such a change usually consists of increased living expenses, inflation, and an increase in the earnings of the other parent. Sometimes the parents can agree between themselves on a regular increase in child support. If they wish, they can enter into an agreement that adjusts child support annually on the basis of, say, the Consumer Price Index or the wage increases of the noncustodial parent. When the parents cannot agree, the court must resolve the matter, and the custodial parent must prove that present child support is inadequate.

12. Q. **CAN CHILD SUPPORT ALSO BE REDUCED?**
    A. Yes. The court has the power to modify child support upwards or downwards, so long as there has been a substantial change of circumstances since the entry of the original order. Thus, for example, a parent who just lost his job or has had a substantial pay cut could petition the court to reduce the child support payments that he is making.

13. Q. **CAN CHILD SUPPORT BE PAID THROUGH THE COURT?**
    A. Yes. If the court order says so, the child support may be made payable through the clerk of court. Payment to the clerk is the preferred method. This allows the parents to be sure that payments are properly recorded and avoids problems of payments made in cash directly to the custodial parent with no receipt given. If child support is paid through the clerk's office, the clerk will also help enforce the order through contempt proceedings if the

payor is in arrears. This is done at no cost to the custodial parent. When payment is made through the clerk, it must be in the form of cash, certified check, or money order so that the payment can be mailed out to the custodial parent right away, instead of waiting for a personal check to clear.

14. Q. ARE THERE ANY OTHER ASPECTS OF CHILD SUPPORT IN ADDITION TO THE MONEY PAID EVERY MONTH?

A. Yes. Such matters as medical expenses, tax exemptions, and college are also important parts of child support. You should try to reach an agreement on these with the other parent if possible. If you can't agree, then the court can decide the issues of medical expenses and tax exemptions; the expenses for a child's college education are beyond the court's powers.

15. Q. HOW DOES THE COURT DECIDE MEDICAL EXPENSES?

A. If one of the parents has medical insurance, that parent is usually required to keep it in place for the minor child or children. The remaining costs—*uncovered health care expenses*—are divided by the judge between the parents in a way that is fair. Often this means that the parents divide these expenses equally or in proportion to their incomes.

16. Q. WHEN CHILD SUPPORT IS DETERMINED BY THE COURT, WILL BOTH PARTIES' INCOMES BE CONSIDERED?

A. Yes. North Carolina law requires that the judge take into account both parties' incomes in setting child support.

17. Q. HOW DOES A JUDGE IN NORTH CAROLINA COMPUTE CHILD SUPPORT?

A. As of July 1, 1990, North Carolina has been using a child support guideline or formula called the *income shares model*. This approach takes the income of both parents and apportions the child support responsibility between them according to the ratio of their incomes to each other. The calculations are done on a set of preprinted child support worksheets. The incomes used are gross, pre-tax incomes. Thus, if the father earns *$3,000 per month* and the mother earns *$1,000*, the father's child support obligation will be three-fourths (and the mother's will be one-fourth) of the total needs of the child.

18. Q. HOW DOES THE COURT DETERMINE THE "TOTAL NEEDS" OF THE CHILD?

A. The total needs of the child will be presumed to be the Basic Child Support Obligation set out on the *child support schedules* available at the clerk's office. It is impossible to set out these figures here, but they cover the expected needs of one or more children whose parents earn up to $10,000 per month combined income. In general, the amount of the Basic Child Support Obligation is directly determined by the combined incomes of both parents. The higher the total income, the higher the obligation.

19. Q. WHAT SPECIAL ITEMS OR EXPENSES CAN BE CONSIDERED BY THE COURT IN SETTING CHILD SUPPORT UNDER THESE GUIDELINES?

A. In addition to the Basic Child Support Obligation, the judge should consider:

- payments or expenses for the support of other children;
- medical insurance premiums;
- day-care expenses necessary to enable a parent to get or keep a job;
- shared or split custody arrangements; and
- any other extraordinary costs or expenses related to the raising of a child.

20. **Q. WHAT IS SHARED CUSTODY?**
    A. The definition of shared custody (for child support purposes) is any arrangement where the "noncustodial parent" gets 123 or more overnight visits per year with the child. If this occurs, new rules apply for determining child support and a new worksheet must be completed for *shared custody*, as opposed to sole custody.

21. **Q. WHAT IS SPLIT CUSTODY?**
    A. Split custody is a custody arrangement in which each parent has physical custody of at least one child. In a split custody arrangement, an adjustment to child support is made because each parent will incur direct expenses for rearing one or more of the children. In this case also, a new child support worksheet must be used. These worksheets are also available at the courthouse.

22. **Q. WHAT IF I NEED MORE CHILD SUPPORT THAN THE GUIDELINES SHOW I SHOULD GET?**
    A. You can ask for a variance in child support so long as you provide written advance notice to the other side before the hearing. A variance could be needed because of unusually high needs of a child, extremely high or low income of a parent, or several other reasons. It is very important to document the reasons for a variance so that they can be shown clearly to the court in testimony or written evidence.

23. **Q. CAN THE COURT AWARD ATTORNEY'S FEES TO ME IN A CHILD SUPPORT CASE?**
    A. Under North Carolina law, if the person asking for attorney's fees is acting in good faith and is unable to afford the legal expenses of the lawsuit, she has hired a private attorney, and the other party is not paying adequate child support when the suit is filed, it is possible (but not mandatory) for the court to award reasonable attorney's fees as part of the custody order.

24. **Q. CAN A CHILD SUPPORT ORDER BE CHANGED?**
    A. No child support order is ever "permanent." However, once a parent is ordered to pay child support, the judge can change the order only if there is substantial change of circumstances relating to the needs of the child or the ability of the payor to make child support payments.

25. **Q. IF I'M ORDERED TO PAY CHILD SUPPORT, WILL I GET VISITATION RIGHTS?**
    A. Ordinarily, the noncustodial parent is entitled to reasonable visitation rights with a minor child except in extraordinary situations, such as when the noncustodial parent has a history of abusing the child. Visitation isn't related to child support, however, and you must file a motion for visitation if you want that awarded by the court.

26. **Q. CAN I REGISTER A COURT ORDER FROM ANOTHER STATE HERE IN NORTH CAROLINA SO THAT NORTH CAROLINA CAN TREAT IT AS ONE OF ITS OWN DECREES FOR PURPOSES OF CHILD SUPPORT ENFORCEMENT?**
    A. Yes. You may file and register the other state's decree with the Clerk of Superior Court in the county where you reside under the Uniform Reciprocal Enforcement of Support Act. You may also register a North Carolina decree in the state where the other parent lives for purposes of enforcing child support.

27. **Q. WON'T CHILD SUPPORT BE SETTLED WHEN I OBTAIN A DIVORCE?**
    A. Divorce decrees do not necessarily settle child support matters, and a support order can be entered before or after a final decree of divorce in North Carolina.

28. **Q. WHAT IF I HAVE OTHER QUESTIONS?**
    A. Please feel free to ask one of our attorneys. They are here to help you.

■■■

Child Support—How Much is Enough?

1. **Q. THE CHILDREN ARE LIVING WITH ME. HOW MUCH CHILD SUPPORT SHOULD I BE RECEIVING FROM THEIR FATHER?**

   A. There is no "right amount" for child support. If the two of you are able to reach agreement on a sum, that amount should be set out in a separation agreement. If you cannot agree, you may petition the court to determine the amount of child support that should be paid by the noncustodial parent to the parent with whom the child or children are living.

2. **Q. WHAT COURT DECIDES CHILD SUPPORT?**

   A. In North Carolina, the district court hears child support cases. A child support case is usually heard in the county where the child is living. If the father lives in another state and our state lacks any contacts with him, you may need to have the case heard there instead of here.

3. **Q. DO I HAVE TO HAVE A LAWYER PREPARE THE SEPARATION AGREEMENT OR PETITION THE COURT FOR ME?**

   A. A separation agreement should *always* be prepared by an attorney. This is a very important document, and both sides should be represented by attorneys to be sure the agreement is done properly and fairly. You should likewise have a lawyer when you go to court for child support. If you do not want an attorney or cannot afford one, the Child Support Enforcement Office can help you establish or enforce child support.

4. **Q. IF MY SPOUSE FAILS TO PAY CHILD SUPPORT, WHAT SHOULD I DO?**

   A. If your husband or wife is bound by court order or separation agreement to pay a certain amount of child support, you may ask the court to enforce the order (by contempt of court) or the agreement (by a lawsuit for breach of contract). A person found in contempt of court may be sentenced to jail for up to 30 days under North Carolina law for not obeying the prior child support order. Failure to obey a child support order can lead to other penalties as well, such as seizure of assets (a car or bank account, for example) or the assignment or garnishment of the other parent's wages.

5. **Q. HOW DO I KNOW HOW MUCH CHILD SUPPORT I NEED?**

   A. Many states have adopted child support guidelines. In North Carolina, these guidelines on child support are often used by the judge in setting child support and by the parties or attorneys in settling support cases.

6. **Q. WHAT IF I NEED MORE CHILD SUPPORT?**

   A. The Guidelines are flexible and allow for a child's special needs, extremely high or low income, and other factors the court finds to be important. Make a list of all monthly expenses for your household and apportion the expenses between yourself and the child or children. Be sure to set aside a certain portion of the rent, utilities, and food for each child. You should also consider whether to apportion such expenses as car payments, gasoline, and medical bills for each child. *You* must support the child or children and *you* are the one who best knows the facts, needs, and expenses. The judge can go outside the Guidelines, but it is up to you to prove the need for a variance from the Guidelines.

7. Q. WHEN MY CHILD IS VISITING MY EX-HUSBAND, CAN HE REDUCE THE CHILD SUP-PORT PAID TO ME?

A. No. Unless the court order or separation agreement specifically provides for a reduction, the child support payment should remain the same.

8. Q. IF I CANNOT SEE MY CHILD FOR VISITATION, CAN I STOP PAYING CHILD SUPPORT?

A. Under North Carolina law, denial of visitation is not legal justification for withholding child support. Neither is lack of child support a legal excuse for refusing the other parent visitation rights. The parents do not have the right to try to link together these separate obligations. Even if a parent is not paying any child support, he may still visit his children. And even if a parent is not allowing visitation, the children are still entitled to child support.

9. Q. WHEN DOES CHILD SUPPORT STOP?

A. Child support, without an agreement or court order, usually ends at the child's eighteenth birthday, although it will continue beyond then if the child is still in high school, so long as the child is not over 20 years old. A separation agreement or court order by consent may set a higher age, such as upon graduation from college or at age 21. Child support may end earlier than the above if the child is emancipated, such as by joining the military, moving away from home, or getting married.

10. Q. CAN THE OTHER PARENT'S PAYCHECK BE GARNISHED FOR CHILD SUPPORT?

A. Yes. Under North Carolina law, garnishment of a paycheck for child support may be ordered for up to 40 percent of the net available pay. Garnishment is a court proceeding that requires a lawyer or the help of the Child Support Enforcement Office. Garnishment is allowed only if a *court order* for child support is violated; it does not apply if there is only a separation agreement. Wage assignment is also used to take child support directly from a parent's pay if there has been a prior child support order.

11. Q. WHAT IF I NEED MORE CHILD SUPPORT IN THE FUTURE?

A. If the child support is set out in a court order, you may petition the court to increase child support if you can show that there has been a substantial change of circumstances since the date the order was signed. Such a change usually consists of increased living expenses, inflation, and an increase in the earnings of the other parent. Sometimes the parents can agree between themselves on a regular increase in child support. If they wish, they can enter into an agreement that adjusts child support annually on the basis of, say, the Consumer Price Index or the wage increases of the noncustodial parent. When the parents cannot agree, the court must resolve the matter and the custodial parent must prove that present child support is inadequate.

12. Q. CAN CHILD SUPPORT ALSO BE REDUCED?

A. Yes. The court has the power to modify child support upwards or downwards, so long as there has been a substantial change of circumstances since the entry of the original order. Thus, for example, a parent who just lost his job or has had a substantial pay cut could petition the court to reduce the child support payments that he is making.

13. **Q.** CAN CHILD SUPPORT BE PAID THROUGH THE COURT?
    A. Yes. If the court order says so, the child support may be made payable through the clerk of court. Payment to the clerk is the preferred method. This allows the parents to be sure that payments are properly recorded and avoids problems of payments made in cash directly to the custodial parent with no receipt given. If child support is paid through the clerk's office, the clerk will also help enforce the order through contempt proceedings if the payor is in arrears. This is done at no cost to the custodial parent. When payment is made through the clerk, it must be in the form of cash, certified check or money order so that the payment can be mailed out to the custodial parent right away, instead of waiting for a personal check to clear.

14. **Q.** ARE THERE ANY OTHER ASPECTS OF CHILD SUPPORT IN ADDITION TO THE MONEY PAID EVERY MONTH?
    A. Yes. Such matters as medical expenses, tax exemptions, and college are also important parts of child support. You should try to reach an agreement on these with the other parent if possible. If you can't agree, then the court can decide the issues of medical expenses and tax exemptions; the expenses for a child's college education are beyond the court's powers.

15. **Q.** HOW DOES THE COURT DECIDE MEDICAL EXPENSES?
    A. If one of the parents has medical insurance, that parent is usually required to keep it in place for the minor child or children. The remaining costs—*uncovered health care expenses*—are divided by the judge between the parents in a way that is fair. Often this means that the parents divide these expenses equally or in proportion to their incomes.

16. **Q.** WHEN CHILD SUPPORT IS DETERMINED BY THE COURT, WILL BOTH PARTIES' INCOMES BE CONSIDERED?
    A. Yes. North Carolina law requires that the judge takes into account both parties' incomes in setting child support.

17. **Q.** HOW DOES A JUDGE IN NORTH CAROLINA COMPUTE CHILD SUPPORT?
    A. As of July 1, 1990, North Carolina has been using a child support guideline or formula called the *income shares model*. This approach takes the income of both parents and apportions the child support responsibility between them according to the ratio of their incomes to each other. The calculations are done on set of preprinted child support worksheets. The income used are gross, pre-tax incomes. Thus if the father earns *$3,000 per month* and the mother earns *$1,000*, the father's child support obligation will be three-fourths (and the mother's will be one-fourth) of the total needs of the child.

18. **Q.** HOW DOES THE COURT DETERMINE THE "TOTAL NEEDS" OF THE CHILD?
    A. The total needs of the child will be presumed to be the Basic Child Support Obligation set out on the *child support schedules* available at the clerk's office. It is impossible to set out these figures here, but they cover the expected needs of one or more children whose parents earn up to $10,000

per month combined income. In general, the amount of the Basic Child Support Obligation is directly determined by the combined incomes of both parents. The higher the total income, the higher the obligation.

19. Q. WHAT SPECIAL ITEMS OR EXPENSES CAN BE CONSIDERED BY THE COURT IN SETTING CHILD SUPPORT UNDER THESE GUIDELINES?
    A. In addition to the Basic Child Support Obligation, the judge should consider:

    • payments or expenses for the support of other children;
    • medical insurance premiums;
    • day-care expenses necessary to enable a parent to get or keep a job;
    • shared or split custody arrangements; and
    • any other extraordinary costs or expenses related to the raising of a child.

20. Q. WHAT IS SHARED CUSTODY?
    A. The definition of shared custody (for child support purposes) is any arrangement where the noncustodial parent gets 123 or more overnight visits per year with the child. If this occurs, new rules apply for determining child support and a new worksheet must be completed for *shared custody*, as opposed to sole custody.

21. Q. WHAT IS SPLIT CUSTODY?
    A. Split custody is a custody arrangement involving each parent having physical custody of at least one child. In a split custody arrangement, an adjustment to child support is made because each parent will incur direct expenses for rearing one or more of the children. In this case, a new child support worksheet must be used. These worksheets are also available at the courthouse.

22. Q. WHAT IF I NEED MORE CHILD SUPPORT THAN THE GUIDELINES SHOW I SHOULD GET?
    A. You can ask for a variance in child support so long as you provide written advance notice to the other side before the hearing. A variance could be needed because of unusually high needs of a child, extremely high or low income of a parent, or several other reasons. It is very important to document the reasons for a variance so that they can be shown clearly to the court in testimony or written evidence.

23. Q. WHAT IF I HAVE OTHER QUESTIONS?
    A. Please feel free to ask our attorneys. They are here to help you.

■■■

Section 3

Fees and Flaws

Attorney Fees

1. Q. This divorce is my husband's fault! Won't he have to pay all my attorney's fees?

   A. The answer to this question is *yes* . . . and *no*. The payment of attorney's fees is governed by state statutes that set out specific instances in which attorney's fees can be awarded by a judge. *As a general rule*, each partner pays his or her own attorney's fees. Some exceptions are covered below. There is no law that requires the spouse "causing the separation" to pay the other party's attorney's fees.

2. Q. What if we're going to sign a separation agreement and not go to court at all?

   A. In this case, payment of the attorney's fees you incur in the drafting and negotiating of a separation agreement is a point to be negotiated as a part of your agreement. Even if your spouse initiated the separation, there is no law that requires him or her to pay the fees *you* may incur to obtain a separation agreement.

3. Q. Can a judge order my wife to pay my fees if I have to take her to court for custody of the children?

   A. The judge may order attorney's fees in custody cases if:

   • You are an interested party (such as a parent or relative);
   • You are acting in good faith; and
   • You do not have sufficient means with which to pay the costs and fees involved in bringing or defending the custody case.

   This decision is entirely up to the judge. The judge may decide not to award attorney's fees to you even if the above elements are met. And there is no guarantee that, when attorney's fees are granted, they will be adequate or equal to what you have spent.

4. Q. How about child support cases?

   A. Again, the law allows the judge to award you attorney's fees if you meet the above criteria *plus* the judge finds that the party ordered to pay support (the other parent) **refused** to provide adequate support at the time you filed your case. Thus, if you and your spouse separate, the children remain with you, and your spouse continues to provide an adequate amount of support, then you will *not* be entitled to an award of attorney's fees. What is "adequate support" will be up to the judge to decide; it may or may not be equal to the amount your spouse is actually required to pay.

5. Q. What if I have to go to court to get alimony?

   A. If you can prove to the judge that you are a dependent spouse, are entitled to alimony, and do not have the money to pay your attorney's fees, the judge may award you attorney's fees. Again, this is entirely up to the judge.

6. Q. Maybe I should ask about when I can't get attorney's fees!

   A. There are two actions in which an award of attorney's fees is NOT allowed. These are absolute divorce and property division. In these actions, no matter who is at fault or who wins, the law does not allow for the award of attorney's fees.

7. Q. IF THE JUDGE DOES GIVE ME ATTORNEY'S FEES, WILL MY SPOUSE HAVE TO PAY *ALL* OF MY ATTORNEY'S BILL?

A. Probably not. First, the judge can only order attorney's fees which relate to the issue he or she has heard. If the judge has only heard your action for custody and support, only the fees you have incurred for representation concerning custody and support can be awarded. Additionally, while the judge can order payment of "reasonable" attorney's fees, this may or may not be the entire bill. The amount is solely the judge's decision.

8. Q. ARE THERE ANY OTHER ACTIONS IN WHICH I MIGHT GET ATTORNEY'S FEES?

A. There are several other situations in which attorney's fees can be awarded. However, only three are likely to arise in your domestic case:

- FAILURE TO COMPLY WITH DISCOVERY. The parties to a lawsuit are allowed a period of time in which they can request the other party to produce documents or answer written or oral questions, so that each party can "discover" what information the other party has. If your spouse fails to comply with your discovery requests (fails to produce documents or produces altered documents, for example) and you are then forced to go to court to get an order requiring his or her compliance, you may ask for payment of your attorney's fees in connection with your spouse's failure to comply.

- "RULE 11" MOTIONS. Our law has many rules which govern how to file, serve, and try cases. One of these is Rule 11 of the N.C. Rules of Civil Procedure, which sets out the requirements for a valid pleading (your complaint or motion for alimony, custody, etc.). Rule 11 requires that each pleading be "well grounded in fact and in law" (that is, have a valid factual and legal basis), be filed after "reasonable inquiry" as to the truth of its allegations, and not be used solely for the purpose of delay, additional expense, or harassment. If a judge should find that the requirements of Rule 11 have been violated, he may award, among other things, the payment of a reasonable attorney fee.

- INJUNCTIVE RELIEF IN EQUITABLE DISTRIBUTION CASES. If you have to ask a judge to sign an injunction to prevent your spouse from damaging, removing, or destroying marital (or separate) property, the court can also award you attorney's fees up to the fair market value of the property involved.

9. Q. CAN I AT LEAST GET A TAX DEDUCTION FOR THE ATTORNEY'S FEES I WIND UP PAYING?

A. You may deduct those amounts which represent fees charged to you for tax advice or assistance in obtaining alimony. You will not receive much tax counseling from your domestic lawyer, but if alimony is an issue, the amount you pay for advice and litigation to obtain alimony is tax-deductible. If you are ordered to pay alimony, you may also deduct any attorney's fees you are required to pay for your spouse if they are clearly designated as part of the alimony you pay.

10. Q. WHAT IF I HAVE OTHER QUESTIONS?

A. Please ask our attorneys. They are here to help you.

■■■

Legal Malpractice

Preface

The purpose of this pamphlet is to assist you in answering questions that you may have regarding legal malpractice in the area of family law in North Carolina. These answers are, of course, very general in nature. For specific answers to your particular situation, be sure to consult with an attorney.

1. **Q.** HELP! MY LAWYER REALLY MESSED UP MY CASE BADLY. CAN I SUE HER?

   A. It depends on what the lawyer did and whether it constitutes "legal malpractice" or legal negligence. Legal negligence is, in plain words, being careless or sloppy in how you do things that are legal entrusted to you as a lawyer. It doesn't mean *intentional wrongdoing*, but it usually refers to lack of diligence, failure to follow up on things, or perhaps lack of legal knowledge or expertise in a particular field of law.

2. **Q.** WHAT IS LEGAL MALPRACTICE?

   A. The four essential legal elements are found in the "Four D's": (1) Duty, (2) Deviation, (3) Damages, and (4) Direct Relationship. The first of these is "Duty." There must be a duty on the part of the lawyer to do something or avoid something regarding you and your case. For example, your lawyer might have a duty to ask for documents from the other side to find out how much your husband had in his retirement account on your date of separation. Perhaps your lawyer might have a duty to prepare fully for a trial and be ready for the direct and cross-examination that will occur, as well as opening and closing argument, or your lawyer might have a duty to calculate correctly the amount of child support that you should receive. These are examples of duties in the area of family law.

3. **Q.** WHAT ABOUT "DEVIATION?"

   A. "Deviation" means that the lawyer deviated from, or breached, that duty. She did something to violate the duty that she owed to you, the client. For example, the lawyer had a duty to ask for the annual benefit statement from your husband to find out the value of his pension on the date of separation, and she didn't do this—that would be an example of deviation from the duty owed to a client.

4. **Q.** WHAT ARE "DAMAGES"?

   A. "Damages" means that you've suffered actual monetary damages because of the lawyer's actions (or failure to act). For example, you may have lost a claim to your husband's retirement benefits as a result of the lawyer's negligence, or perhaps the lawyer failed to assert a claim for equitable distribution in your court papers and you lost your right to ask the court to divide your marital property. However, it is important to note that you must show the likelihood that you would have recovered if not for the breach.

5. **Q.** OKAY, I THINK I UNDERSTAND THE FIRST THREE. WHAT'S "DIRECT RELATION-SHIP"?

   A. This just means that there must be a direct relationship between the act of the lawyer and the damage you suffered. For instance, if the reason that the attorney didn't have the annual benefit statement for the husband's pension is 1) because you were going to get it and failed to do so, or 2) because you told her to "skip it," that you weren't interested in his pension, then it wouldn't be the attorney's negligence that caused this loss, it would be your own conduct. The law states that the actions of the former lawyer must be approximate cause of the damages suffered by you. There cannot be any separate or intervening cause.

6. **Q.** IS THAT IT? IF I HAVE THOSE FOUR, DO I HAVE A GOOD CASE?

   A. Not so fast! In addition to the above four "legal elements" for malpractice, the attorney who handles your case will probably want to see *two* additional elements: "aggravation" and "a deep pocket."

7. **Q.** AGGRAVATION? THAT'S NO PROBLEM . . . I'M REALLY AGGRAVATED THAT SHE MESSED UP SO BADLY! THAT ONE'S COVERED.

   A. Not necessarily. Aggravation in this case means "aggravated facts," ones that would make a judge or jury outraged, incensed, mad, or angry when hearing about the case. In one case, it might be testimony that the client lost her house because of the lawyer's negligence, that the bank foreclosed on the house and she was tossed out on the street. In another case, it might be that the client had to cancel her wedding due to the actions of the lawyer. Whatever the fact, they need to be "aggravated" to give a reasonable chance of a good recovery in settlement or trial. In order to gauge whether there has been sufficient aggravation for the purposes of litigation, you should obtain the professional opinion of an attorney rather than rely on the opinions of friends and family.

8. **Q.** WHAT'S THIS ABOUT A "DEEP POCKET"?

   A. We want to be sure that your former lawyer has "deep pockets" for any damage award, or judgment, that is entered against her. If she's not covered by a legal malpractice insurance carrier, for example, then she might not be able to pay the judgment and we'd just be *out of luck*, even if we won the case itself.

9. **Q.** WHAT IF WE HAVE ALL OF THE ABOVE SIX PARTS OF THE CASE? DOES THAT MEAN WE CAN GO AHEAD AND FILE A LAWSUIT?

   A. No. We still have to make sure that the time limits haven't been exceeded. The law in general states that the suit for legal malpractice must be filed within three years of discovery of the error or omission, but in no event may it be filed over four years after the incident.

10. **Q.** IF THERE'S NO DEADLINE PROBLEM, WHAT'S NEXT?

    A. Then we try to settle the lawsuit. We meet with the other side as an attempt to agree on a resolution that will pay you back something for the losses you have suffered.

11. **Q.** IF WE CAN'T SETTLE THE CASE, THEN WHAT HAPPENS?
    A. We prepare the lawsuit and file it.

12. **Q.** AFTER WE FILE THE LAWSUIT, DO WE THEN GO TO TRIAL? HOW SOON WILL THE CASE BE TRIED?
    A. The next steps would include discovery (the exchange of documents and other information between the two sides in preparation for trial) and motions (to dismiss the case or to rule in our favor without a trial), and then a pretrial conference with the judge.

13. **Q.** WHAT HAPPENS IF WE GO TO TRIAL? HOW SOON WILL THE CASE BE TRIED?
    A. The trial usually involves a jury. The parties and their witnesses will testify (and be cross-examined) prior to the court's decision. It can take from one to two years to get a trial date in Wake County Superior Court for these cases.

14. **Q.** IS THERE ANY WAY THAT I CAN HELP MY ATTORNEYS WITH THE EVALUATION OF MY CASE?
    A. Yes. You can fill out the questionnaire below so that your attorneys will have a better idea of what your case involves and how they can help you. Use additional sheets of paper if necessary—we want to get "the full picture" of what happened in your case.

Please state the general nature of your case (i.e., custody, pension division, child support). _____

_____

_____

Next, state what specific things your former lawyer did (or didn't do) that are the basis of your complaint. _____

_____

_____

How have you been damaged as a result of these actions by your former lawyer? What monetary loss have you suffered? How did you calculate the money damages?

_____

_____

Are there any aggravating circumstances that we should know about? Please detail them here: _____

_____

And lastly, are there any other concerns you have, facts you need to pass on to us, or issues that you'd like to raise? If so, write them down here: _____

_____

_____

■■■

Notes

Section 4

Custody

Child Custody and Visitation

1. **Q. DO MOTHERS AUTOMATICALLY GET CUSTODY OF THEIR CHILDREN WHEN PARENTS SEPARATE?**

   A. The courts of most states, including North Carolina, do not establish an automatic preference for either mother or father, but they do look very closely at which parent will best promote the welfare and interests of the children of the couple. As a general rule, parents are joint guardians of their children, with equal rights to custody and control, in the absence of a court order.

2. **Q. WHAT KIND OF FACTORS DO THE COURTS CONSIDER IN GRANTING CUSTODY?**

   A. They usually look at who has primarily taken care of the child during the marriage (for example, washing, feeding, and clothing the child, or helping the child with homework), who has the best approach to discipline, who has cared for the child since the separation (if the couple has already separated), what work schedules either or both parents have, how each parent can provide for the physical, emotional, educational, religious and social needs of the child, and the temperament and character of each parent.

3. **Q. CAN THE COURT AWARD ATTORNEY'S FEES TO ME IN A CUSTODY CASE?**

   A. Under North Carolina law, if the person asking for attorney's fees is acting in good faith and is unable to afford the legal expenses of the lawsuit, it is possible (but not mandatory) for the court to award reasonable attorney's fees as part of the custody order.

4. **Q. DO I HAVE TO FILE FOR CUSTODY IN NORTH CAROLINA?**

   A. Not necessarily. While usually a custody suit is filed where the child is presently residing, a person can file an action involving custody of a minor child in the "home state" of the child (i.e., where the child has lived for the last six months) or in any state where the child and one parent have substantial and significant contacts and connections (such as former neighbors, teachers, doctors, relatives, and so on). If this would be in another state, you may file there.

5. **Q. HOW CAN THE ISSUE OF CUSTODY BE RAISED?**

   A. This is done by filing a complaint with the court. The complaint for custody must be served on the other parent. After that, a hearing may be scheduled on custody and visitation rights.

6. **Q. CAN A CUSTODY ORDER BE CHANGED?**

   A. No custody order is ever "permanent." However, once a parent is awarded custody in a court order, the judge can change the custody order only if there is a substantial change in circumstances since the time of entry of that prior order. It must be proven that the change has a direct impact on the child's welfare. The change may be either beneficial or adverse. The change in circumstance must be such as to require a change of custody, not some lesser change (such as a change in visitation schedule).

7. **Q.** WILL MY SEPARATION AGREEMENT PROTECT ME FROM THE OTHER PARENT SNATCHING MY CHILD?

   A. No. A separation agreement is only a contract between you and the other parent. It is not a court order unless it is incorporated into a decree or order of a court. A court order is enforceable by contempt of court. Court orders of one state can be filed and registered in another state and thus be treated as if they were issued by the second state for purposes of enforcement. None of this applies to separation agreements.

8. **Q.** CAN I REGISTER A COURT ORDER FROM ANOTHER STATE HERE IN NORTH CAROLINA SO THAT NORTH CAROLINA CAN TREAT IT AS ONE OF ITS OWN DECREES FOR PURPOSES OF ENFORCEMENT?

   A. Yes. You may file and register the other state's decree with the Clerk of Superior Court at the county courthouse. You may want to register the decree in the county where you reside or in the county where the other parent lives.

9. **Q.** IF ANOTHER PARENT DOES NOT LIKE THE PRESENT CUSTODY ORDER, CAN HE OR SHE FILE FOR CUSTODY IN ANOTHER STATE?

   A. Under the Uniform Child Custody Jurisdiction and Enforcement Act, the court in a custody case must always inquire into whether the child or children have been the subject of custody litigation in any other state. When a judge finds that another court has made an award of custody, the judge should refuse to rule on the case and refer the parent to the court that originally entered the custody order. Only if that original court no longer has jurisdiction and has released or transferred jurisdiction to the new state court may that court assume jurisdiction to hear the custody case (unless there is an immediate and clear emergency affecting the child's welfare).

10. **Q.** WON'T CUSTODY BE SETTLED WHEN I OBTAIN A DIVORCE?

   A. Divorce decrees do not necessarily settle custody matters. A custody order can be entered before or after a final decree of divorce in North Carolina.

11. **Q.** MY DAUGHTER IS TWELVE. CAN'T SHE TELL THE JUDGE WHERE SHE WANTS TO LIVE?

   A. In North Carolina, the child's preference between parents is an important factor to be considered when deciding the issue of custody. However, the child's preference is not conclusive or binding on the issue of custody. There is no set age for when a child can testify.

12. **Q.** CAN ALL CHILDREN TESTIFY IN COURT AS TO THEIR PREFERENCE?

   A. The courts do not allow every child to testify as to his preference. Whether a child is old enough is a matter to be decided by the trial judge. This means that the judge must decide that the child is capable of testifying truthfully.

13. **Q.** HOW CAN A JUDGE DETERMINE WHETHER A CHILD IS ABLE TO TESTIFY?

   A. The trial judge must determine that the child is "of sufficient age, discretion and maturity" so that he can formulate and express a rational opinion as to custody. If you have other questions in this area, please ask for Client Information Letter Number 50, "Testimony of Your Child."

14. Q. CAN A NON-PARENT OBTAIN CUSTODY OF A CHILD INSTEAD OF A PARENT?

A. There is a parental preference rule which states that a birth parent (mother or father), who is of good character and who is a proper person to have custody of the child, is usually entitled to custody against all other persons. If, however, the parents have abandoned, abused, or neglected the child, then a third party can intervene to request custody.

15. Q. IF MY SPOUSE IS GRANTED CUSTODY, WILL I GET VISITATION RIGHTS?

A. Ordinarily, the noncustodial parent is entitled to reasonable visitation rights with a minor child except in extraordinary situations, such as when the noncustodial parent has a history of abusing or neglecting the child. Visitation can be flexible and unstructured, assuming the parties can get along and agree on the times and terms of visitation, or it can be highly structured and rigid, with certain days and times set out with great specificity. Ask for our Client Information Letter Number 32 on specific visitation rights to see the options available in this area.

16. Q. WHAT IF I HAVE OTHER QUESTIONS?

A. Please feel free to ask our attorneys. They are here to help you.

■■■

Custody Checklists

Custody Checklist #1

Findings of Fact for Custody Order

See: Green v. Green, 54 N.C. App. 571, 284 S.E.2d 171 (1981) and Montgomery v. Montgomery, 32 N.C. App. 154, 231 S.E.2d 26 (1977)

1. Residence of parties
2. Information regarding custody jurisdiction
3. Factual background—marriage, separation, names and ages of child(ren)
4. Procedural background
5. Employment and income of each party
6. Reputation and character of each party
7. Physical ability of each party to care for child
8. Mental ability of each party to care for child
9. Emotional ability of each party to care for child
10. Facts regarding fitness of each party to care for child—habits, church, attitudes, drinking
11. Living situation of each party
12. Any special needs of child—medical, transportation, education, psychiatric, day care, etc.
13. Any special needs of either party
14. Relationship between Plaintiff and child (i.e., Plaintiff shows love and affection toward child and child reciprocates; or partiality; or unresponsiveness)
15. Relationship between Defendant and child
16. Living situation of child during marriage and after separation
17. Custodial history—who took major responsibility for child care during marriage and after separation
18. Child care when custodian is absent
19. Living situation of child—well-adjusted or not; healthy; well cared for; happy in current situation or not
20. Relationship between parties—cooperation, conflict, indifferent or otherwise
21. Relationship between each party and child
22. Fit and proper—either or both parents
23. Best interest of child

Custody Checklist #2

Transfer of Custody from Prior Court Order

See: Rothman v. Rothman, 6 N.C. App. 401, 170 S.E.2d 140 (1969) and Barnes v. Barnes, 55 N.C. App. 551, 286 S.E.2d 586 (1982)

1. Change of circumstances since last court order
2. Must *affect welfare* of child
3. Effect must be *adverse* or *harmful*
4. Must be *substantial* so as to require motion to get custody

Custody Checklist #3
Testimony of Client and Witnesses

1. EDUCATION
   - Grades
   - Awards
   - Homework
   - Absences
   - Teacher Conferences
   - Tests . . . Aptitude and Achievement
   - Extracurricular activities
2. DISCIPLINE
   - Each parent's approach
   - Spanking
   - Rewards
   - Reprimands
   - Allowances
   - Withdrawal of privileges
   - Logic, predictability, and structure
3. CHORES FOR CHILD
   - Clothes/Laundry
   - Bedroom
   - Housecleaning
   - Cooking
   - How assigned?
   - Performance
4. CLOTHING
   - How child is clothed by each parent
   - Style of clothing
   - Maintenance and cleaning of clothing
5. FINANCES
   - Child's reasonable monthly needs
   - Use of money for child support
   - Incomes of parents and other sources of money
   - Child support actually paid
6. CHILD'S SURROUNDINGS
   - Playmates and friends
   - Neighbors
   - Schools, playgrounds, parks, etc.
7. CHILD CARE ARRANGEMENTS
   (by father, mother, third parties, such as sitters, grandparents, etc.)
   - Feeding
   - Clothing
   - Washing and bathing
   - Health care
   - Chores
8. RELIGION
   - Church attendance
   - Youth groups
   - In-home instruction

9. LEISURE TIME
(vacations, weekends, holidays, after school)
- Camp
- Music
- Scouts
- Dance
- Athletics

10. LIVING ARRANGEMENTS FOR CHILD AT EACH RESIDENCE
- Bedrooms
- Play areas

11. VISITATION ARRANGEMENTS
(regular or irregular, conflicts or cooperation, etc.)

12. RELATIONSHIP WITH OTHER SIBLINGS
(brothers/sisters, stepchildren, etc.)

13. MEDICAL/DENTAL CARE

14. DAILY SCHEDULE FOR CHILD AND PARENT

15. PARENTAL TRAINING AND ABILITIES

16. SPECIAL PROBLEMS OR CONSIDERATIONS OF CHILD OR EITHER PARENT

Custody Checklist #4

Concerns of the Judge

WHICH PARENT:
- is more likely to encourage visitation?
- is more respectful toward the other parent?
- will maintain greater continuity of contact with friends, relatives, neighborhood, and school?
- relates better with children and provides more productive support, stimulation, and guidance?
- is the more effective disciplinarian?
- is more likely to be mature and responsible in children's upbringing?
- is less likely to discuss with the children the failure of the marriage?
- is more able to provide an emotionally secure role model?
- is more resourceful in getting help?
- is more flexible and adaptable?
- has more time to devote to the children?
- has shown greater interest in the children and their activities?
- uses more "quality time" with the children?

Custody Checklist #5

Who Does What?

WHO HAS THE RESPONSIBILITY?
- M - Mother
- F - Father
- C - Child
- O - Other—If shared, circle all involved

FAMILY TASKS	RESPONSIBILITY?			
ROUTINE FOOD SHOPPING	M	F	C	O
PREPARATION OF EVERYDAY MEALS	M	F	C	O
PREPARATION OF SPECIAL MEALS	M	F	C	O
SPECIAL HOUSEHOLD PURCHASES (such as furniture, appliances, etc.)	M	F	C	O
ROUTINE PURCHASES	M	F	C	O
ROUTINE HOUSECLEANING	M	F	C	O
• sweeping/vacuuming	M	F	C	O
• mopping/waxing	M	F	C	O
• dusting	M	F	C	O
• picking up clutter	M	F	C	O
• bathrooms	M	F	C	O
• changing bed linens	M	F	C	O
• taking out garbage	M	F	C	O
MAJOR HOUSECLEANING	M	F	C	O
• windows	M	F	C	O
• curtains	M	F	C	O
• kitchen appliances/cabinets	M	F	C	O
• walls	M	F	C	O
WASHING CLOTHES	M	F	C	O
IRONING/MENDING	M	F	C	O
HOUSEHOLD MAINTENANCE	M	F	C	O
YARD WORK	M	F	C	O
CHILD CARE	M	F	C	O
• Preparation for school	M	F	C	O
• Helping with homework	M	F	C	O
• Care of children in emergency/illness	M	F	C	O
• Care of children on school holidays	M	F	C	O
• Preparation of children for bed	M	F	C	O
• Disciplining children	M	F	C	O
TRANSPORTING CHILDREN	M	F	C	O
• Purchasing clothes for children	M	F	C	O
• Birthday planning for children	M	F	C	O
• Doctor/dentist visits for children	M	F	C	O
• Obtaining child care (baby sitters, etc.)	M	F	C	O
HOLIDAY PLANNING	M	F	C	O
FINANCES (budgeting, bill paying, etc.)	M	F	C	O

■■■

Custody Mediation

Preface

Custody mediation is a growing trend around the country and offers parents a way to focus on the welfare of their children and resolve problems over child custody and visitation without the bad feelings and sometimes *bad results* which may accompany a custody suit. Conflict is natural when parties separate, especially considering the emotional upheaval of divorce. Mediation can assist parents in resolving conflicts over the children in a constructive and healthy way.

* * * * *

1. Q. WHAT IS CUSTODY MEDIATION?
   A. Custody mediation is a cooperative problem-solving process in which parents sit down with a mediator to discuss their goals and disagreements for the purpose of trying to reach an agreement regarding the custody and care of their child or children.

2. Q. WHAT DOES THE MEDIATOR DO?
   A. A mediator is a neutral and objective professional who is trained in problem solving. His or her role is to help the parties resolve their conflicts regarding their child in a cooperative manner. The mediator will:
   - Encourage parents to discuss their desires and plans for their child and come to a common understanding of each parent's goals.
   - Help parents focus on the child and his or her future care rather than on the past events which have caused anger or bad feelings between the parties.
   - Assists parents in exploring possible solutions to problems and reaching an agreement on issues that affect the health, education, and well-being of the child.

3. Q. WHAT DOES THE MEDIATOR *NOT* DO?
   A. The mediator does not take sides. He or she is neutral and objective. The mediator does not give legal advice. The mediator does not make decisions for the parties; rather, he or she assists the parties in reaching their own agreement.

4. Q. DO I HAVE TO GO THROUGH CUSTODY MEDIATION?
   A. Where there is a mediation program established (such as in Wake County) and the pleadings or motions in a case involve issues of custody, visitation, or a motion for contempt relating to custody issues, mediation is required. However, in cases where there is undue hardship to a party, a party resides more than 50 miles from the court, or there are concerns such as those outlined in #6 below, a party may ask the court to waive mandatory mediation.

5. Q. WHAT ARE THE BENEFITS OF MEDIATION?
   A. Mediation helps the parties place the primary focus on what is best for the child and not on what happened in the marriage and who is to blame. It reinforces the idea that while divorce may end a marriage, it does not end

a family. Mediation assists the parties in reaching an agreement about how to continue to be parents in a reorganized family. Since mediation allows the parents to be directly involved in the decision-making process, it often leads to more lasting results. It can help parties communicate with each other more effectively to solve problems and reduce conflict, which is damaging to the children. Resolution of issues through the mediation process can reduce the stress and anxiety of divorce for both parents and children. It can also allow the parties to resolve custody and visitation issues at a much lower cost than through a custody trial.

6. Q. WHEN IS MEDIATION *NOT* ADVISABLE?
   A. Mediation may be inappropriate where there are safety concerns for one of the participants. Where there is a history of domestic violence (hitting, throwing things, emotional and verbal abuse), substance abuse, or when one party has severe psychological, psychiatric, or emotional problems, mediation may not be advisable. If any of those conditions exist in your case, tell your attorney so that a motion to exempt from the mediation process is made.

7. Q. CAN MY ATTORNEY COME WITH ME?
   A. In many court-ordered custody mediation programs (such as in Wake County), attorneys cannot attend the mediation sessions. However, it is a good idea to meet with your attorney prior to mediation so that you have a thorough understanding of your legal rights and options, and afterwards *to review any agreement reached through mediation.* In other circumstances, such as private mediation, attorneys can be present at the mediation sessions if everyone agrees.

8. Q. HOW MUCH DOES MEDIATION COST?
   A. There is no cost for mediation through the court-ordered mediation program for parents involved in a custody or visitation lawsuit in Wake County. This service is provided free of charge through the court system. Private mediators (i.e., those not in the mandatory mediation process) provide this service at an hourly rate, and the cost is generally shared by the parties. Even where there is a charge for mediation services, this process can actually reduce the overall cost to the parties by helping them reach a satisfactory resolution without lengthy and expensive litigation.

9. Q. CAN WHAT I SAY IN THE MEDIATION SESSION BE USED AGAINST ME IN COURT?
   A. Mediation proceedings are private and confidential. Communications from the parties to the mediator or between the parties in the presence of the mediator during a mediation session are absolutely privileged and inadmissible in court.

10. Q. HOW DOES MEDIATION WORK IN WAKE COUNTY?
    A. Approximately 45 days after a new custody or visitation lawsuit is filed or 25 days after an action to modify an existing custody or visitation order is filed, the Custody Mediation Office will contact the parties or their attorneys by letter to let them know when they must appear for the orientation session. Orientation sessions are held at 12:00 noon every other Wednesday

and last about one hour. At the end of the session, the parties will make an appointment with the mediator and mediation will usually take place within the following two weeks.

11. **Q. WHAT HAPPENS IF WE REACH AN AGREEMENT THROUGH MEDIATION?**

A. The first step in the custody mediation process is filing a claim for custody with the court. Then, upon notice of the pending custody action, the custody mediation office will schedule custody mediation orientation, which you and the other party will attend and be instructed as to how custody mediation works. While at orientation, the parties typically set a date for the actual mediation, which can be one or more meetings. If an agreement is reached, *do not* sign a parenting agreement then and there; have a lawyer review the terms before signing (see Q12 below). If no agreement is reached, then the parties must attend a parenting class. Once the parenting class is complete, the parties can elect to return to mediation. Otherwise, the next step is to schedule the custody hearing to be heard by or in front of your assigned judge.

12. **Q. DO I HAVE TO REACH AN AGREEMENT IN MEDIATION?**

A. No. Although reaching an agreement through custody mediation offers many benefits (see #5 above), you are not required to reach an agreement. You should discuss with your attorney, prior to the mediation session, areas where you might be able to compromise. In mediation, you are not required to agree to anything with which you are not comfortable. However, if you the cannot reach any agreement, both parents will need to begin the time-consuming and expensive process of preparing for a trial in which a judge will decide what is best for their children.

■■■

Notes

_____

_____

_____

_____

_____

_____

_____

_____

_____

_____

_____

_____

Custody and Child Support:

The Interstate Connection

Custody

1. **Q.** Help! My ex-wife took our children from Texas, where I have an order giving me custody, and drove to North Carolina. Do I need an order from a Texas judge? A private attorney in North Carolina? Can a sheriff's deputy help me? Where do I go from here?

    A. Slow down—that's a lot of questions. We'll try to answer them all, but first you need to know about the Uniform Child Custody Jurisdiction and Enforcement Act. A summary is provided in this "TAKE-1" handout.

2. **Q.** What is the statute you just mentioned?

    A. The Uniform Child Custody Jurisdiction and Enforcement Act (UCCJEA) is a law that's found in all 50 states plus the District of Columbia. It is just about the same everywhere, and it provides a lot of protection in cases of child removal or kidnapping. For example, it allows you to register your "foreign custody order" (that's the one from Texas) in North Carolina.

3. **Q.** Register my Texas order? What good will that do?

    A. Registering your foreign custody order allows the court in North Carolina to enforce it just as if it had been entered here by a judge in this state.

4. **Q.** Sounds pretty good. How do I do it? Do I have to file a complaint or a motion to get my papers from Texas registered there?

    A. "Registration" under the UCCJEA means filing with the court:

    1. A letter or other document requesting registration;
    2. Two copies (including one that is a *certified copy*) of the foreign court order, plus an affidavit that, to the best of your knowledge and belief, your Texas order has not been modified; and
    3. Except as otherwise provided in G.S. 50A-209, your name and address (or that information for the person who is seeking registration) and the same information for any parent or person acting as a parent who has been awarded custody or visitation in the child-custody order which you want registered.

The specifics are found on page 1 of one of the court forms, AOC-CV-660 (Petition for Registration of Foreign Child Custody Order). Here are the forms from the Administrative Office of the Courts (AOC) which are available for the foreign custody order registration process:

AOC-CV-660	Instructions For Registration Of Foreign Child Custody Order (Side 1)/Instructions For Expedited Enforcement Of Foreign Child Custody Order (Side Two) (New 12/06)	PDF Ready
AOC-CV-660	Petition For Registration Of Foreign Child Custody Order (New 12/06)	PDF Ready (Fillable)

AOC-CV-661	Notice Of Registration Of Foreign Child Custody Order (New 12/06)	PDF Ready (Fillable)
AOC-CV-663	Motion To Contest Validity Of A Registered Foreign Child Custody Order And Notice Of Hearing (New 12/06)	PDF Ready (Fillable)
AOC-CV-664	Order Confirming Registration Or Denying Confirmation Or Registration Of Foreign Child Custody Order (New 12/06)	PDF Ready (Fillable)
AOC-CV-665	Petition For Expedited Enforcement Of Foreign Child Custody Order (New 12/06)	PDF Ready (Fillable)
AOC-CV-666	Order For Hearing On Motion For Expedited Enforcement Of Foreign Child Custody Order (New 12/06)	PDF Ready (Fillable)
AOC-CV-667	Warrant Directing Law Enforcement To Take Immediate Physical Custody Of Child(ren) Subject To Foreign Child Custody Order (New 12/06)	PDF Ready (Fillable)
AOC-CV-668	Order Allowing Or Denying Expedited Enforcement Of Foreign Child Custody Order (New 12/06)	PDF Ready (Fillable)

They are available from the website of the AOC at this address: http://www.nccourts.org/Forms/FormSearchResults.asp

5. Q. WHAT DOES THAT MEAN—THE PART ABOUT G.S. 50A-209?

A. G.S. 50A-209 says you don't have to provide this information if you state in your affidavit that the health, safety, or liberty of the child/children would be endangered by disclosure. In that situation, the information must be sealed and may not be disclosed to the other party or the public unless the court, after a hearing, orders it in the interest of justice.

6. Q. WHAT HAPPENS NEXT?

A. One copy of the registration petition and one copy of the registration notice must be served upon the defendant (that's your ex-wife) and any other person listed in paragraph 3 of the Petition for Registration of Foreign Child Custody Order. Instructions regarding service are found in the "Notice to Plaintiff" section of the Notice of Registration, AOC-CV-661. Then the court proceeds to determine whether to confirm the order or not. There must be a hearing to determine whether the order is confirmed. The notice states that a registered order is enforceable as of the date of the registration just as if it had been entered by a judge here. The notice also states that a hearing to contest the validity of the registered order must be requested within 20 days after service of notice; if the other side doesn't contest the registration, this will result in confirmation of the custody order.

7. Q. WHAT CAN MY EX-WIFE DO WHEN NOTIFIED ABOUT THE REGISTRATION?

A. The other side can do nothing, which usually means that the foreign order will be confirmed by the judge here, or else the other side, your ex-wife, can contest the registration, which means challenging the validity of the Texas custody order. If the other side files a motion to contest the validity of the foreign order, you will receive a copy of the motion and a notice of hearing informing you of the date and time the court will hear the matter. If no one files a motion to contest the validity of the foreign child custody order, the clerk of court will mail you a copy of the Order Confirming Registration. If there is a question about the existence of a custody order or the authority of the court to exercise custody jurisdiction, that question, by law, must be given priority on the court's calendar and handled expeditiously.

8. **Q.** SO A FOREIGN CUSTODY ORDER MUST BE REGISTERED IN EVERY CASE BEFORE NORTH CAROLINA WILL ENFORCE IT?

A. No. A foreign child custody order IS NOT required to be registered before it can be enforced in North Carolina. If you are seeking immediate enforcement of a foreign child custody order, see Instructions for Petition for Expedited Enforcement of a Foreign Child Custody Order, Form AOC-CV-665. If you want law enforcement officers to immediately pick up the children, you must check the box before paragraph 10. A warrant directing law enforcement to pick up the children immediately can be issued only by a district court judge, and the warrant is available only if the judge determines that the children are in danger of immediate serious physical harm, or there is an immediate danger of their being removed from the state. You must testify to the judge, or produce another witness to testify, that there is a need for law enforcement to get the children immediately. You will also need to complete portions of Form AOC-CV-667, which is the warrant form. If the warrant is not issued, the judge will consider your request for custody of the children at the hearing that will be set when you file the Petition for Expedited Enforcement of Foreign Child Custody Order.

9. **Q.** WHEN WILL THE JUDGE HEAR MY CASE?

A. After you file the Petition for Expedited Enforcement of a Foreign Child Custody Order, the court must issue an order stating the hearing date. A judge must consider your request for enforcement of the child custody order on the next judicial day after the Petition for Expedited Enforcement is served upon the other side. If your hearing date arrives and the other side hasn't been served, the judge will probably continue the case so that service can be had on the other party, your ex-wife, or upon any other person who has, or claims to have, custody of the children.

10. **Q.** SO THERE'S NOTHING THAT MY EX CAN DO TO CONTEST THE PETITION?

A. There are several defenses available to her. The instructions on the expedited enforcement order state that custody will be granted to you at the conclusion of the hearing unless she appears at the hearing and is able to prove one of these:

1. The foreign custody order has been stayed, vacated, or modified, or was entered by a court that didn't have jurisdiction to do so; or
2. The foreign order has not been confirmed, and the other party was entitled to receive notice before it was entered.

If a defense is proven to the court, then the order will not be confirmed, and the registration will be vacated.

11. **Q.** ONCE I HAVE GOTTEN CONFIRMATION OF MY TEXAS CUSTODY ORDER HERE IN NORTH CAROLINA, CAN I FORGET ABOUT HEARINGS ON CUSTODY OR VISITATION BACK THERE?

    A. Not at all. Texas still has original jurisdiction. Unless at some future point in time the case gets fully transferred to North Carolina for misconduct by one of the parents or because NC is a more convenient forum, Texas remains the court with the primary responsibility regarding child custody in your case.

Child Support

12. **Q.** I NEED SOME HELP WITH CHILD SUPPORT. I HAVE A COURT ORDER AGAINST MY EX-HUSBAND FOR CHILD SUPPORT. IT WAS ENTERED IN IOWA. CAN I REGISTER IT HERE FOR ENFORCEMENT?

    A. UIFSA (the Uniform Interstate Family Support Act) is the law in all states. It provides that a child support order (or an income-withholding order in a support case) issued by another state may be registered in North Carolina for the purpose of enforcing the order against the payor.

13. **Q.** WHAT'S INVOLVED IN REGISTERING A FOREIGN CHILD SUPPORT ORDER?

    A. To register your Iowa order, which is known as a "foreign child support order," you need to file:

    1. a letter of transmittal requesting registration of the order for enforcement;
    2. two copies, including one certified copy, of the order for which registration is sought, and copies of all orders modifying the order;
    3. certification of the amount of any arrearage under the order;
    4. the name of the obligor (that's your ex-husband), his address (if known), his Social Security number, the name and address of his employer, the source of any other income of his, and a description and location of any available property which he owns in this state; and
    5. your own name and address, as well as the agency or person to whom support payments are to be sent.

14. **Q.** CAN I ALSO FILE A MOTION FOR ENFORCEMENT OF MY IOWA ORDER?

    A. A motion seeking enforcement of a registered order may be filed at the time the order is registered for enforcement or after a registered support order is confirmed. The petition must state the grounds for the remedy that is being sought.

15. **Q.** IT SOUNDS LIKE THERE ARE TWO THINGS GOING ON HERE—REGISTRATION AND CONFIRMATION. WHAT'S THAT ABOUT?

    A. Registration occurs when you submit your order to the court with the above documents and information. Then the notice of registration, AOC-CV-505, is sent to the other side. It warns him about the registration process, what it involves, and the results of ignoring the notice.

16. **Q. WHAT DOES THE NOTICE SAY?**

    A. The Notice of Registration states that:

    *If you want to contest the validity or enforcement of the registered Foreign Support Order, you **must** file a written request for hearing asking the Court to vacate registration of the order, asserting any defense regarding alleged noncompliance with the order, or contesting the amount of arrears allegedly owed under the order or the remedies that are being sought to enforce the order. Your request for hearing must be filed with the Clerk of Superior Court within twenty (20) days after the date of mailing or personal service of this notice. **Failure to contest the validity or enforcement of the registered Foreign Support Order in a timely manner will result in confirmation of the order and the alleged arrears, and precludes further contest of the order with respect to any matter that could have been asserted.***

    At the hearing, the payor (your ex-husband) may ask the judge to vacate the registration. He may contest the amount of back support that you are requesting. He may contest the enforcement remedy being sought (such as seizure of property or garnishment). And he may assert a defense against his alleged noncompliance with the order. He cannot, however, challenge the fundamental provisions of the registered order; that is only available in the original court where the order was entered. Nor may he ask the court to modify the registered order unless he meets certain requirements of the law. There are only a limited number of defenses available to him for challenging registration. If he does not succeed in challenging registration, then the order is confirmed.

17. **Q. WILL THE JUDGE TREAT A REGISTERED ORDER FROM IOWA JUST LIKE A NORTH CAROLINA ORDER FOR ENFORCEMENT?**

    A. No. The order must be confirmed, not just registered. Then, upon confirmation, the judge can grant you any remedies that a child support order entered in North Carolina would allow.

18. **Q. DOES THAT MEAN THAT THE JUDGE CAN ORDER PAYMENTS THROUGH THE COURT?**

    A. Payments no longer go "through the court." The agency that collects child support and sends it to the parent with custody is called "Centralized Collections." This agency will also keep records of payments received in case there is a dispute about child support payments. The judge will often use this agency as the collection mechanism for child support.

19. **Q. WHAT ABOUT DIRECT PAYMENTS FROM MY EX-HUSBAND? IF THAT'S ORDERED, I'M AFRAID THAT HE WON'T MAKE THEM ON TIME IN THE FULL AMOUNT.**

    A. Good point. In North Carolina, the rule is that payments must be made by garnishment from his employer unless the two of you agree otherwise, or unless the court is convinced that an alternative means is available to guarantee payment of child support to you. When payments are made directly to you by the other side, there's always the risk that they won't be made in the full amount, they will be late, or the check will "bounce" when you try to deposit it at the bank. Some non-custodial parents also think that they can make deductions from child support for things that they provide for the children, or to punish the custodial parent for something she has done. Garnishment and using Centralized Collections are the best ways to ensure proper accountability for the payment of child support.

20. **Q.** CAN I SPEED UP THE CHILD SUPPORT HEARING PROCESS AT ALL? I'M AFRAID THAT IT'LL TAKE THREE OR FOUR MONTHS TO GET A HEARING DATE!

   A. The law in North Carolina (N.C. Gen. Stat. 50-32) states that child support is supposed to be on a fast track when there is a motion or complaint pending for establishment of support. This is known as "Expedited Process." The statute says that:

   Except where paternity is at issue, in all child support cases the district court judge shall dispose of the case from filing to disposition within 60 days, except that this period may be extended for a maximum of 30 days by order of the court if:

   (1) Either party or his attorney cannot be present for the hearing; or

   (2) The parties have consented to an extension.

21. **Q.** SO ONCE I HAVE GOTTEN CONFIRMATION OF MY CHILD SUPPORT ORDER HERE IN NORTH CAROLINA, I CAN FORGET ABOUT HEARINGS ON CHILD SUPPORT BACK IN IOWA?

   A. Not at all. Iowa still has original jurisdiction. Unless at some future time the case gets fully transferred to North Carolina for specific reasons set out in the statute, Iowa is the court with the primary responsibility regarding child support in your case.

■■■

Joint Custody

Preface

The purpose of this handout is to assist you in answering questions that you may have regarding joint custody. It is, of course, impossible to answer all of your questions in a short brochure such as this, so we want to encourage you to ask other questions of your lawyer at the appropriate time.

"Joint Custody" is a term that comes up very often while parties are negotiating and discussing child custody and visitation. It is also a term which is frequently misunderstood. This Client Information Letter attempts to explain the meanings, effects, benefits, and disadvantages of joint custody.

1. Q. **What is "Joint Custody"?**
   A. Joint custody is not defined by the North Carolina General Statutes. The statutes provide only that a court can order joint custody. However, most lawyers agree that joint custody can be defined in two ways:

   Joint legal custody. This term means that the parents will share in making all major decisions that affect the child. These decisions might include whether or not the child will go to private or public school, undergo elective surgery, or move with one parent to another state. It does not mean that the parents will jointly make day-to-day decisions. Neither does it mean that the child will spend the same amount of time with each parent.

   Joint physical custody. Sometimes referred to as "shared custody," means that each parent will have an equal or nearly equal amount of time with the child. This can be accomplished in many ways. For example, the child can alternate weeks with each parent or spend three and a half days of each week with each one. However, the child must have a permanent address for purposes of school and medical records, so one parent's home should be designated as the "primary residence."

2. Q. **What are the effects of Joint Legal Custody?**
   A. Just as the definitions of joint custody differ, so do the effects of a joint custody arrangement. Joint legal custody will require both parents to discuss the child's needs more frequently than with a sole custody arrangement.

   Joint legal custody means that both parents will need to cooperate with each other and reach agreements where the child is concerned. This may not be easy to do. If you and your spouse have been able in the past to set aside your other differences and discuss and agree on matters concerning the child, joint legal custody may be an acceptable solution. However, if your disagreements include issues concerning the child, the arguments and disagreements will continue well beyond your divorce and will frustrate any attempt at true joint legal custody.

3. Q. **What are the benefits of Joint Physical Custody?**
   A. Joint physical custody was seen at one time as a wonderful answer to the problem of a child's growing up without the opportunity to spend equal time with both parents. Ideally, a shared custody arrangement means that

both parents maintain a "real home" for the child, including a room, toys, and clothes. This helps reinforce the idea that families are forever. In sole custody arrangements, the non-custodial parent's every-other-weekend visits may not allow a real parent-child relationship to form or continue. Both parent and child are trying to do everything in one weekend. A joint physical custody arrangement can allow both parents to spend real parental time with the child and thus develop a better relationship.

4. Q. **WHAT ARE THE DISADVANTAGES OF JOINT PHYSICAL CUSTODY?**

   A. Recently, it has become apparent that joint physical custody is not the ideal solution it was once thought to be. Too often the child may be shuttled back and forth between parents and have no real feeling of a "home." Consistency is often difficult to achieve in such an arrangement. The rules may be different at each parent's home—bedtime is 8:30 p.m. at Mom's but 10:00 p.m. at Dad's. Schoolwork sometimes suffers. For example, homework assigned while the child is staying at one home, but due to be turned in when he is at the other, can be inadvertently overlooked. Friends are different at each home and harder to keep up with, the babysitter may be different each time, and so on. Children who have difficulty adapting to change may find joint physical custody too chaotic. Generally, the parents must work very hard at such an arrangement. Joint physical custody seldom reduces hostility between the parties and may even increase it. It requires two parents who maintain a commitment over time to put the needs of the child first and are able to create a conflict-free zone for their child. Parents who choose joint physical custody must be willing to have open and frequent communication with each other. Joint physical custody requires two parents committed to be co-parents.

5. Q. **WHEN IS JOINT PHYSICAL CUSTODY NOT ADVISABLE?**

   A. Joint physical custody is not advisable where there is a history of domestic violence, drug or alcohol abuse, child abuse or neglect by a parent, or where a parent suffers from a debilitating mental illness. Since joint physical custody requires joint decision making and a tremendous amount of cooperation between the parents, joint physical custody is not appropriate where there is a history indicating that the parents are unable to agree on child rearing. In addition, joint physical custody is not a good choice where the child involved becomes overanxious or confused when asked to cope with numerous things or has a temperament which makes it difficult for him or her to adapt easily to change.

6. Q. **WHAT EFFECT DOES A SHARED CUSTODY ARRANGEMENT HAVE ON CHILD SUPPORT?**

   A. For purposes of determining child support, shared custody is defined as a parent's visiting with the child for 123 or more overnights a year. "Shared custody" will result in a different amount of child support than in a sole custody situation. The increased overnights will be figured into the calculations and the parent will receive a "credit" for that time. This is based on the theory that the parent must provide substantial support for the child during the extended visits and therefore the other parent is saved that expense. Joint legal custody, however, has no effect on child support.

7. Q. CAN I BE GRANTED JOINT CUSTODY BY THE COURT?

   A. If the decision concerning joint custody cannot be reached by you and the other parent, you will have to ask the court to award joint custody. You should first decide whether you want joint legal or physical custody.

- If you want joint physical custody, you must have a workable schedule to propose.
- You must also be able to show that you have the time, the room, and the ability to care for the child, and that such an arrangement will be the least disruptive to the child.
- Beyond that, for both joint legal and physical custody, you should be able to show the judge that you have always been substantially involved with the child's upbringing and have previously helped care for and make decisions concerning the child.
- You should be able to demonstrate that you and the other parent have usually been cooperative and communicative as to the child and that you have the ability to continue this relationship during your separation and divorce.
- Finally, all of your evidence should indicate to the judge that a joint custody arrangement would be in the best interest of the child.

8. Q. MY SPOUSE WANTS JOINT CUSTODY. HOW CAN I KEEP THIS FROM HAPPENING?

   A. Again, if this decision is left to a judge, you must show the judge the opposite of the above. Based on changing perceptions about joint custody, courts seem to be less inclined now to start with the assumption that joint custody is better than primary/secondary custody arrangements. It might be difficult for your spouse to convince a court that joint custody is appropriate when you can show that your spouse has rarely agreed with you on issues concerning the child, has had very little to do with caring for and raising your child, or if during your separation the child has been made a part of your disagreements and arguments. The court will need to know that you and your spouse are not good candidates for joint custody and that joint custody is not in the child's best interest.

9. Q. WHAT ARE THE ADVANTAGES AND DISADVANTAGES OF JOINT CUSTODY?

   A. As mentioned earlier, joint custody, either legal or physical, gives both parents a greater opportunity to interact with the child and be a continuing part of the child's life. Sometimes this means that child support payments are made more regularly, and each parent will have a better idea of where and for what the support is used. Many times a child can continue to maintain a relationship with both parents that may not otherwise be possible.

   However, under joint custody the parents also have greater contact with each other than they would with a sole custody arrangement. For two bitter and uncooperative people, this probably means that the arguments, disagreements, and anger will continue. This in turn will create tension that is communicated to the child, and all the benefits of joint custody could well be negated by the parents' behavior.

10. Q. HOW DO I KNOW IF JOINT CUSTODY WILL BE RIGHT FOR ME—AND OUR CHILD?

   A. A joint custody arrangement can be a good solution or a bad solution. Whether or not such an arrangement is right for you, your spouse, and your child depends entirely on the relationship that all of you have, and this relationship should be carefully considered when you make your decisions concerning custody. You should consider your child's age, temperament, and coping style; the current quality and nature of the parent-child relationships; and the practicality of such an arrangement. A successful joint custody arrangement requires a great deal of maturity and cooperation, and a commitment to making the child's needs a priority. A very important measure of whether or not joint custody is right for you is whether you and the other parent can be good "co-parents." Co-parenting requires mutual commitments:

- Both parents will continue to be fully involved in making major decisions about their children's health, education, welfare, and religion.
- Parents will not place the children between them and their conflicts. Parents must be businesslike partners. As business partners, the parents are not in love and may (and often do) have areas of disagreement. When there are disagreements regarding the children, the parents are cordial and work out their differences in a fair and equitable manner.
- Both parents view themselves as having a family. Neither parent refers to the other as a "visitor." Each has a family home and each is entitled to make decisions and have a lifestyle which the children will be a part of when in that parent's home. Neither parent may interfere with the other's lifestyle or home life; each parent must support the other's relationship with the children.
- Children are not allowed to "play" one parent off of the other. Decisions are made by the parents, then handed down to the children. The parents must guide the children, not the other way around.
- Parents must communicate with each other. This means *regular* discussions of children's activities, needs, progress, and conditions. There must be a sharing of significant events in the lives of the children.
- Parents must concede that they are *jointly* responsible for the rearing of the children and will work together to equitably share children's expenses, living arrangements, and care. Both must invest time in teachers' conferences, doctors' appointments, religious activities, etc.
- Parents must agree that, even though they have differences, they will value and respect each other as a co-parent, and this means that the children need to be involved with both parents.
- Court must be seen only as the *final option*. All other means of settling problems must be tried first.

If some or all of the requirements of co-parenting are lacking from your relationship with the other parent, joint custody could be a very poor solution.

Joint custody, both legal and physical, can have an excellent effect on both the child and the parents—if the parents are able to work together on issues concerning the child. However, it can have disastrous results for the child if the parents cannot or will not co-parent. The relationship you have with your spouse concerning your child will be the largest factor affecting the outcome of any joint custody arrangement you might choose.

■■■

Section 5

Last Will and Probate

All About Probate

1. Q. WHAT IS PROBATE?

A. Probate is the procedure of settling the estate of a deceased person. The estate of one who has died consists of the property of that person upon death.

2. Q. WHO IS RESPONSIBLE FOR PROBATE IN MY ESTATE?

A. If you have made a will, you have probably named a person, called the *Executor*, in that document. If you have no will, the court will appoint someone, usually the next-of-kin, to be the *Administrator* of your estate for this purpose.

3. Q. WHAT ARE THE DUTIES OF MY EXECUTOR?

A. The duties of the Executor are the same as those of the Administrator.

1. Safeguard the estate's property;
2. Inventory the property;
3. Submit accounts and inventories to the court as required;
4. Pay the debts and expenses of the deceased (including funeral and burial expenses, costs of last illness, and outstanding medical bills);
5. Pay any federal or state death taxes; and
6. Distribute the estate to those named in the will or, if no will exists, to the next of kin.

4. Q. WHO PAYS FOR ALL THIS?

A. Your estate does. In general, your estate is responsible for all your debts, bills, and expenses. These must be paid before any remaining assets in your estate can be given to your next of kin or your heirs under the will. Your Executor has no duty to pay these costs out of his or her own pocket and is not normally personally liable for your debts. Your Executor has the duty to release enough of your assets to allow the payment of expenses such as taxes, credit card balances, and hospital bills.

5. Q. IF I AM APPOINTED AS SOMEONE'S EXECUTOR, DO I GET PAID?

A. An Executor (or an Administrator) can request the court to provide two types of compensation:

1. Direct reimbursement for out-of-pocket expenses, such as postage stamps, bank charges, and mileage; and
2. Payment for services rendered as an Executor or Administrator (unless the will directs otherwise). The amount of this latter payment will vary, of course, depending on the amount of work done, the time spent on the estate, the complexity of the work, and the size of the estate.

6. Q. DOES MY EXECUTOR HAVE TO PAY A FEE OR POST A BOND TO SETTLE MY ESTATE?

A. There are various expenses necessary to settle an estate. Fees must be paid to the court upon filing and closing the estate. A bond is sometimes required, especially if there are minor children or an out-of-state Executor/Administrator involved. These costs are, of course, paid by the estate.

7. Q. ARE MY CREDITORS NOTIFIED OF MY DEATH?

A. Your Executor/Administrator must place a legal notice in the newspaper for your creditors after the court has appointed him or her to handle your estate. The notice must:

1. Give the name of the deceased and the name and address of the Executor or Administrator;
2. Be published once a week for three weeks in a row in the locality where the deceased had his or her home; and
3. State that all claims of creditors must be made within six months of publication of the notice.

Once this is done, the publisher prepares an Affidavit of Publication and this is put in the court file. Any claims not presented to the Executor or Administrator within these six months need not be paid.

Those claims which are valid and which are presented within the six-month period, including debts and expenses known to the Executor or Administrator, must be paid out of the available funds in the estate.

8. Q. WHAT ARE THE INVENTORIES AND ACCOUNT I MUST FILE AS AN EXECUTOR OR ADMINISTRATOR OF SOMEONE'S ESTATE?

A. Using North Carolina as an example, when you initially apply to the Clerk's Office for appointment, you will need to fill out an initial inventory. This is so you can give a preliminary account or a rough estimate of the assets in the estate. Within the first three months after you are appointed, you must file the Ninety-Day Inventory, which is the first formal accounting of the assets in the estate of the deceased—real estate, cars and trucks, furniture, pension benefits, bank accounts, jewelry, and so on. If you have completely settled the estate within 12 months of qualifying as Executor or Administrator, you will then file the Final Inventory, listing the following:

a. Amount of total assets as shown on the Ninety-Day Inventory you have already filed;
b. Additional assets received by the estate since the filing of the Ninety-Day Inventory (with description and fair market value);
c. Expenses, debts, taxes, and bills paid by the estate; and
d. Distribution of the estate to the heirs (how and to whom).

If you haven't completed settlement of the estate, you must file an Annual Inventory showing items a, b, c, and d above. A simple estate can usually be closed in a period of 7–12 months.

9. Q. CAN I GET INTO THE SAFE DEPOSIT BOX OF THE DECEASED?

A. Yes. The law provides that you can have access to the safe deposit box of the person whose estate you are settling, so long as you are accompanied by someone from the Office of the Clerk of Superior Court on your first visit. At that time, the official (usually a deputy or assistant clerk) will supervise the opening of the box, inventory the contents, and turn the contents which belong in the estate over to you for safekeeping. The inventory is returned to the Clerk's Office for filing.

10. Q. How do I handle the money of the deceased?

A. You should immediately set up an "estate account" at a local bank as soon as you have been appointed Executor or Administrator. You can arrange this at any local bank, and there is a small charge for printing the checks showing your name, your title (Executor/Administrator), the name of the deceased, and other information. Having a separate account is a good step toward preventing the mixing or "commingling" of your own personal funds and those that belong to the estate.

With the estate account set up, you can deposit or transfer the funds of the deceased into this separate account. Some items, such as paychecks, insurance premium refunds, or employee death benefits, may be deposited directly into the estate account. In the case of other assets, such as bank accounts, certificates of deposit, stocks and bonds, you will need to obtain a tax waiver from the North Carolina Department of Revenue (if the item is worth more than $10,000) to be able to transfer the asset into the estate account. The tax waiver application form is available from the Clerk's Office, from any local office of the Department, or from the statewide office in Raleigh.

11. Q. Are the life insurance proceeds part of the estate?

A For tax purposes, life insurance proceeds are counted as part of the taxable estate if the policy was owned by the deceased. You must account for the proceeds of such a policy on the tax return (state and, if necessary, federal) of the estate. On the other hand, only life insurance proceeds payable to the estate are listed on the inventory filed with the Clerk. Those policies and proceeds made payable to individual beneficiaries pass by contract, outside of the estate, directly to the named beneficiary.

12. Q. Once I have paid all the fees and expenses and accounted for all the property, how do I close the estate?

A. First you would prepare the applicable state Inheritance and Estate Tax Return (if required) and, if a large estate is involved, a Federal Estate Tax Return for the estate as well. A state tax return must usually be prepared. The North Carolina Department of Revenue will furnish you with a form, upon payment of any taxes due, which certifies that the estate is cleared for closing. The next step is to distribute the estate among the heirs-at-law (if there is no will) or the designated beneficiaries (if a will has been admitted to probate). You should obtain a receipt from all heirs or beneficiaries stating that they have received their entire share of the estate of the deceased (signed, dated, and witnessed). After you have distributed or divided the property, submit those receipts along with the Final Inventory to the Clerk's Office. You will also need canceled checks or "paid receipts" for all expenses, fees, and bills that have been paid. Once that Office is satisfied that you have accounted for all assets and expenses, the estate will be closed.

■■■

Health Care

Power of Attorney & Living Wills

Health Care Powers of Attorney

On July 3, 1991, the North Carolina General Assembly adopted House Bill 821, which allows an individual to designate a Health Care Attorney-in-Fact (Health Care Agent). The new act is codified at G.S. 32A-15 *et seq.* In addition, the bill also amends the Natural Death Act, G.S. 90-321, and provides a new living will form. The law took effect October 1, 1991.

Pursuant to G.S. 32A-17, any person having understanding and capacity to make and communicate health care decisions, who is 18 years of age or older, may make a **Health Care Power of Attorney**. Any competent person not engaged in providing health care to the principal [the one making the power of attorney] and who is over the age of 18 may act as the designated health care agent. The Health Care Power of Attorney must be in writing and signed by two *qualified* witnesses who are not related to the principal and who are not providing medical care to the individual.

The Health Care Attorney-in-Fact may be granted full power and authority to make health care decisions for the principal, subject to the limitations set forth by the principal in the document. The decisions would include such matters as the choice of intravenous feeding or hydration, the use of drugs to alleviate pain, and the decision whether or not to resuscitate the patient/principal.

Some of the more pertinent provisions of the Act are as follows:

- The Power of Attorney does not become effective until the physician or physicians designated in the Power of Attorney determine in writing that the principal lacks sufficient understanding or capacity to make or communicate his or her own health care decisions.

- Once the Power of Attorney becomes effective, it remains so even if the principal is incapacitated.

- Determination of the individual's understanding or capacity to make or communicate health care decisions can be made by the principal's attending physician if the physician or physicians designated in the document are unavailable or unwilling to make such a determination.

- A Health Care Power of Attorney is revoked by death of the principal and may be revoked by the principal at any time so long as he or she is capable of making and communicating health care decisions.

The execution of a Health Care Power of Attorney does not revoke, restrict, or otherwise affect any non-health care powers granted in a **general power of attorney**. However, health care powers granted pursuant to a Health Care Power of Attorney are superior to any similar powers granted by the principal to an Attorney-in-Fact under a general power of attorney. A Health Care Power of Attorney may be combined with or incorporated into a general power of attorney.

In addition, the Health Care Power of Attorney can contain provisions relating to appointment, resignation, removal, and substitution of the health care agent. The Power of Attorney is revoked upon the appointment by the court of a guardian of the person or a general guardian; however, the statute provides that the Health Care Power of Attorney may designate who is to be appointed guardian of the person of the principal and the court **must appoint accordingly**, except for good cause shown.

The Health Care Power of Attorney is not a substitute for a Living Will; in fact, it may be combined with or incorporated into a Declaration of a Desire for Natural Death, or "Living Will."

Living Will Revisions

G.S. 90-321 authorizes the execution of a Declaration of a Desire for Natural Death. Until recently modified, the statute provided that if a person's condition were found to be **terminal and incurable**, then the Declarant could authorize a physician to withhold or discontinue extraordinary means. "Extraordinary means" is defined as any medical procedure or intervention which, in the judgment of the attending physician, would serve only to postpone artificially the moment of death by sustaining or restoring or supplanting of vital function.

G.S. 90-321 was recently amended to broaden the circumstances under which a living will can be used. As modified, G.S. 90-321 provides that if a Declarant is found by the attending physician to be in **a terminal and incurable condition** or is diagnosed as in **a persistent vegetative state**, the physician can withhold or discontinue extraordinary means and/or artificial nutrition or hydration as specified by the Declarant. The old declaration form did not contain any alternatives; the new declaration form requires that the Declarant make decisions regarding the matters discussed above.

Please ask us if you would like our office to prepare either of these documents for you.

■■■

Your Last Will and Testament

Do you need a will? If you do, what should it contain, and how do you go about preparing it? Our office drew up this Information Letter to help you answer these questions. It is intended to be used with the help of your attorney.

Deciding what to say in your will is an important decision. Following through with your decision by making a will is just as important. Our office can offer you assistance in preparing your will. After reading this pamphlet, and when you are ready to have your will prepared, complete one of our Will Questionnaire forms. Set up an appointment if you want to discuss the will or go over questions about your estate. Otherwise, you may send us the completed Questionnaire. We'll prepare a draft of your will from the instructions you give us and it will be reviewed by an attorney. When it is ready, we will call you to come in and sign it in front of two witnesses and a notary.

Your decision to make a will is one of the most important things you can do on behalf of your family. Please consider carefully all the information below concerning this document.

1. Q. **WHAT IS A WILL?**
   A. A will is a document which directs how and to whom the property in your estate shall be distributed after your death. In addition, your will should name a person you want to settle your estate after your death. If you die without a will, relatives would inherit according to the laws of North Carolina, and this could result in someone you do not like (or don't even know) getting all or part of your property.

2. Q. **SHOULD YOU HAVE A WILL?**
   A. Some people believe that they do not need a will because they have few assets of any value. Others believe that even without a will their property will go to their spouses. If you die without a will (or *intestate*), the state will distribute your property among your relatives, but it may be in a manner you never intended. For example, you spouse may be entitled to claim only a partial share of your property, with your minor children inheriting the rest of your property in equal shares. This shared ownership could cause serious problems for your spouse in managing the property or trying to sell it. A will offers you the opportunity to make these matters easier for the surviving members of your family, and it gives you flexibility in leaving different items of property to different people. State law does not do either of these things.

   There are other important reasons for having a will that are often overlooked. If you and your spouse die at the same time in an automobile accident, then state law would name your nearest relative to receive your property, even if you did not want him or her as your heir. A carefully drawn will can prevent much uncertainty, even in the event of a common disaster for you and your spouse.

   If you die without a will, state law prescribes how your property will be divided among the relatives who survive you. Their degree of kinship to you may be an important factor in such a situation. Making a will gives *you* the choice of how your property will be divided.

Dying without a will means the court will name a person to administer your estate, pay your debts, pay your taxes, and distribute your property. This appointee is called the *ADMINISTRATOR* of your estate. On the other hand, if you have a will you may name a relative, close friend, or even an institution (such as a bank or lawyer) to take care of these matters. This person is called your *EXECUTOR*.

3. Q. WHAT ARE THE LEGAL REQUIREMENTS FOR A VALID WILL?

A. A will must meet specific and formal requirements of state law. These vary from state to state. If they are not met, your will may be declared invalid. If that happens, your property will be distributed as though you had died without a will.

WITNESSED WILL: Your will should be typed, signed, and witnessed to be effective. It is to your advantage to have the will signed, witnessed, and executed at our office. We use a self-proving clause attesting that the maker of the will and the witnesses signed in the presence of each other and before a notary public. This procedure is accepted by the courts of North Carolina and would usually avoid the necessity of trying to track down the witnesses to testify that they witnessed the signing.

HANDWRITTEN WILL: North Carolina recognizes a will written completely in the handwriting of the maker. These are called *HOLOGRAPHIC* wills. NOTHING except your handwritten words can appear anywhere on the document. No witnesses to the signing are required. Upon the death of the maker of the will, the court will require witnesses to testify that the handwriting and signature are that of the person who died, and that the will was found in a place where the deceased kept important papers and documents. If a holographic will is contested by a potential heir and it is declared invalid by the court, it is usually because of poor draftsmanship, because the will was not entirely in his or her handwriting, or because it was found in the wrong place at the time of death. If a will is declared invalid by the court, the effect is as though you had died without a will.

ORAL WILL: Oral wills (sometimes called *NUNCUPATIVE* wills) are generally valid in North Carolina if made upon one's deathbed before two disinterested witnesses. Such a will must be made at the time of one's last illness or when death is approaching. If the maker of the will recovers, then the will becomes invalid.

PROMISES: In order to be legally effective, any attempt to promise a gift of your property at death must meet the formal requirements of a will. A simple oral promise that a particular person will get something at your death is meaningless and of no legal effect. If you intend for property to be transferred in a particular way after your death, make sure you include it in your will.

4. Q. HOW DO YOU REVOKE OR CHANGE A WILL?

A. Your will can be revoked or changed at any time before your death. The best way to revoke a will is to destroy the original and execute a new will. Trying to change your will by scratching out parts of it or writing in changes will probably cancel the entire will. A written amendment to a will is called a *CODICIL*.

Why would you want to revoke your will? Events such as death of an intended beneficiary, divorce, new property holdings, additional births, and new tax laws are some likely reasons.

5. Q. What should go into your Will?

A. Naming your beneficiaries: The most obvious decision required in making a will is who is to get your property when you die. You should have a good idea of how you want your property divided when you come to our office. You should also consider providing for contingency beneficiaries in the event your primary beneficiaries are not alive at the time of your death.

If there are items of your property which you would like to leave to a particular person, you can do this by making what are called specific bequests. Each item must be described in detail and the person so named will receive it at your death if it is still available.

Assets can also be divided among groups of people. You can provide for distribution should some of the members of the group die before you do. Different legal items in your will have different effects, and you should understand their basic meanings.

Suppose your family is composed of you, your brother, Sam, and your sister, Sue. Sue has two children, Dave and Dan. A diagram of your family might look like this:

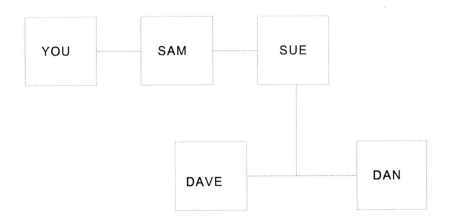

If you want Sam and Sue to share your property equally when you die, you can say so in your will. But what if Sue dies before you do? You can direct that her share be divided equally between her children by using the term *per stirpes*. The effect of that term is that Dave and Dan would share the one-half interest that their mother (Sue) would have received had she survived—the net effect being that Dave and Dan would each receive one-third of the estate with Sam receiving half of the estate. This same form of distribution can be used in leaving your property to your own children or any group of heirs.

There are other alternatives. For example, if you leave your estate to Sam and Sue and their children per capita and if Sue dies before you, then Sam, Dave, and Dan will each get one-third of your estate. Your will should appoint an alternate Executor should your first choice be unwilling or unable to accept the task. Your attorney will draw up a will using proper legal terminology to produce any division you wish, but you must know (and describe to us) what you want.

B. CHOOSING AN EXECUTOR: The choice of an Executor is an important one. The Executor should be trustworthy, willing, and capable of handling finances and property. It is the responsibility of the Executor to take your will to court for probate. Probate is the process by which the court decides whether a will is valid and thereafter supervises the distribution of property according to the will. The Executor will have to qualify before the court in your county of residence and is entitled to receive compensation for services performed for the estate.

Once officially appointed by the court, your Executor will be responsible for:

1. Collecting and safeguarding your property;
2. Filing property inventories in court;
3. Having your property appraised (if necessary);
4. Giving legal notice to creditors;
5. Paying all debts of the estate;
6. Preparing and filing state and federal tax returns (if necessary) and paying any taxes that may be due;
7. Filing an accounting of the handling of the estate assets with the court; and
8. Distributing your estate to your named beneficiaries.

You should appoint an alternate Executor should your first choice be unwilling or unable to accept the task. You should appoint an in-state Executor or else expect that the court may require a bond to be posted, with the costs coming from your estate.

C. CHOOSING A GUARDIAN: There are two types of guardians: (1) guardian of the person, and (2) guardian of the property. The same person can serve as both. The guardian of the person is responsible for raising your children in the event of the death of you and your spouse. The person or couple you select will stand in your place as parents, legally responsible for the welfare of your children. The guardian of the property is charged with the responsibility of preserving the property of the children and utilizing its funds for maintenance, care, and education of the children. As each child turns 18, that child's share of the estate must be distributed to him or her. You can defer the distribution beyond 18 with a trust.

If one parent of the child survives, no guardian is needed. If the parents of minor children have been divorced and one parent has been granted custody, the death of the custodial parent generally means that the other parent will become the child's guardian without court intervention. This means that if you are divorced with custody of children from a previous marriage, your nomination of a different guardian of the person will probably not be effective in North Carolina, but it might be advisable to nominate a guardian anyway to provide for the care of your children in case the other parent dies before you. Divorced parents frequently wish to name a guardian of the estate other than the ex-spouse, and the court will usually honor such an appointment.

In naming a person as guardian for young children, consideration should be given to naming a contemporary of yours rather than an older person (such as your parents). Such a contemporary would be better able to cope with raising them. Please remember that the designation in your will of a guardian is merely a nomination, as the court can appoint someone else if your nominee cannot or will not serve. If this is contested, the court will choose the best-qualified person.

6. Q. OTHER WAYS PROPERTY IS PASSED AT DEATH
A will is not the only means of disposing of property at death. For example, the proceeds of life insurance policies pass pursuant to the life insurance *contract* to the named beneficiary, not pursuant to your will. Property held in joint tenancy with right of survivorship (such as a jointly owned house or bank account) automatically passes to the survivor *by operation of law*. Trusts are sometimes used to distribute property in conjunction with wills.

A. BY CONTRACT: When you purchase life insurance, normally you name a beneficiary. This is the person who will receive the proceeds of your policy on your death. A will cannot change the beneficiary you name in your life insurance policy because an insurance policy is a contract between you and the insurance company in which the company promises to pay to the person named in the policy the face amount on your death. Only if you name your estate as beneficiary in the policy will the proceeds be distributed to your estate and pass through your will. Retirement benefits (such as 401k plans or IRA's) pass the same way.

B. BY OPERATION OF LAW: Almost all kinds of property may be held in joint tenancy "with right of survivorship." On the death of one of the joint owners, the other owner takes title to the deceased's share automatically. It does not pass by will. Examples of property that is often owned in this manner include bank accounts, motor vehicles, and homes. Taking the title in this manner does not necessarily mean that inheritance, estate, or income taxes are avoided; however, it does prevent the property from having to go through the probate process. Whether that is a benefit of any significance depends upon the nature and size of your estate. Accounts held in this fashion are often labeled "JTWROS," which stands for **"Joint Tenancy With Right of Survivorship."** The law requires this kind of ownership to be created clearly and explicitly. If there is any vagueness, the property will pass to your heirs, not to the co-tenant, at your death. When it is real estate that is held jointly between spouses, it is called "Tenancy by the entirety."

C. TRUST: A trust is an instrument through which you give legal title to property to a trustee appointed by you to be used as you instruct for the benefit of a third party, called the *beneficiary*. The trustee can be a friend, relative, banking institution, or any other person with the duties to administer the trust in accordance with your wishes, which are set forth in the provisions of the trust document. Trusts can be simple or extremely complex, can serve many functions, and are often used in conjunction with a will. They are frequently set up to ensure that minor children will have money available for their education, to provide for the continuing support of spouses or elderly parents, or to protect assets from being squandered unwisely. There are many other purposes for using trusts, and your attorney can discuss with you the possible uses of trusts in your estate plan.

7. LARGE ESTATES

Be sure to let your lawyer know your total assets and whether your estate might grow significantly in the future, either by appreciation of assets or by future inheritances or gift. With such information, the lawyer can review several estate-tax-saving devices of which you should be aware.

8. CONCLUSION

Wills are valuable and useful documents because they enable you to control the distribution of your property after your death. It is important for each spouse to have a will so that the wishes of each can be carried out. Please feel free to ask any questions as we go through the process of preparing and executing your Last Will and Testament.

■ ■ ■

Living Wills

1. Q. WHAT IS A LIVING WILL?

   A. A Living Will is a declaration of the desire to die a natural death, without extraordinary or artificial life support systems or devices. Its formal name is "Declaration of a Desire to Die a Natural Death."

2. Q. WHAT ARE THE PURPOSES OF A LIVING WILL?

   A. A Living Will can serve many purposes. First, it allows you to retain control over what happens at the end of your life if you are incompetent to make such decisions. A second purpose is removing the burden of decision-making from your loved ones and also the accompanying guilt that is often experienced by your family. Third, it allows you to reflect on and consider, before you become terminally ill, your ability to endure pain or lingering illness.

3. Q. IS A LIVING WILL A LEGAL DOCUMENT?

   A. Yes. North Carolina recognizes an individual's right to a natural death. The statute, NCGS Section 90-320, states that if an individual has *declared* his desire that his life not be prolonged by *extraordinary means*, and if it is determined by the attending doctor that his condition is terminal, irreversible, and incurable, and this is confirmed by another doctor, then the extraordinary medical means may be withheld. This also applies to patients who are found to be in a persistent vegetative state. "Persistent vegetative state" means that a patient's medical condition, in the judgment of the attending physician, involves complete loss of self-awareness and cognition and the patient will die in a short period of time without the use of extraordinary means or artificial nutrition and hydration.

4. Q. WHAT ARE "EXTRAORDINARY MEANS"?

   A. EXTRAORDINARY MEANS are defined as any medical procedure or intervention which, in the judgment of the attending doctor, would serve only to artificially postpone the time of death. These may include mechanical ventilation and artificial nutrition and hydration.

5. Q. WHAT ARE THE FORMALITIES OF A LIVING WILL?

   A. A Living Will should be prepared by an attorney. Living Wills must be witnessed and notarized. The witnesses cannot be related to the person making the Living Will or be potential heirs. Neither the attending doctor nor any of the employees of the doctor or hospital may be witnesses.

6. Q. HOW CAN A LIVING WILL BE REVOKED?

   A. A Living Will can be revoked by destroying the original and all copies of the document itself. It can also be revoked if you communicate your intent to do so to the attending doctor.

7. Q. WHERE SHOULD THIS DOCUMENT BE STORED?

   A. A Living Will is an *action document*. Make sure copies are kept with your doctor's records and also given to family members. Do not keep it in a safety deposit box or locked safe because people may not think to search in these places or may not have access to them.

8. **Q.** CAN I GIVE SPECIFIC MEDICAL DIRECTIVES AS TO MEDICAL CARE I WANT TO BE PROVIDED OR AVOIDED? CAN I ALSO APPOINT AN AGENT TO MAKE MY HEALTH CARE DECISIONS?

A. If you anticipate being unable to participate in making important decisions regarding your medical care, you may want to appoint an agent to make these choices on your behalf. You may do this by executing a Health Care Power of Attorney. This document is executed prior to your incapacity. By this document you may appoint a health care agent who is empowered to give, withhold, or withdraw consent to medical treatment when you lack the understanding or capacity to make or communicate such decisions. It will become effective *only* upon your incapacity, and will give your health care agent authority to request that life-sustaining procedures be withheld, even in the absence of a Living Will. Your attending physician must determine in writing that you lack the understanding or capacity to make or communicate decisions relating to your health care before your agent will obtain this authority under the Health Care Power of Attorney. Please ask for our Family Law Information Letter on "Health Care Power of Attorney and Living Wills" for further information on this topic.

■ ■ ■

Powers of Attorney Questionnaire

(**NOTE**: Please ask for our Client Information Letter #7, "Powers of Attorney," for more information on this subject.)

1. **What type of Power(s) of Attorney are you requesting?** [Check all that apply]
   ___ Special Power of Attorney
   [*Note: Insert location of form after the name of each type of POA, to make it easier for staff to locate and draft the document*](e:\forms\pow-att\special.poa)

   ___ General (Statutory) Power of Attorney
   (e:\forms\pow-att\poweraty.gen)

   ___ Health Care Power of Attorney
   (e:\forms\pow-att\health.car)

   ___ Adoption Power of Attorney
   (e:\forms\pow-att\adoption.poa)

   ___ Bill of Sale Power of Attorney
   (e:\forms\pow-att\billsale.poa)

   ___ Special Power of Attorney (Guardianship)
   (e:\forms\pow-att\guardian.poa)

2. **We need the following information to complete your Power(s) of Attorney. Please fill in all of the blanks as completely as possible.**

   Your *full* name:
   [A] _____
   Your city AND county of residence:
   [B] City _____ County of _____
   State of _____
   Full name of person you want to act as your agent:
   [C] _____
   Address of the person named above (not P.O. Box):
   [D] _____
   _____

   This person's relationship to you: _____
   Home phone: **[E]** _____; Work phone: **[F]** _____
   If this person is unable or unwilling to serve, who do you want to name as your alternate agent? Full name of person you want to act as your alternate agent:
   [G] _____
   Your relationship to the above-named person: _____
   Address of the person named above (not P.O. Box):
   [H] _____
   _____

Home phone: **[I]** _____; Work phone: **[J]** _____

Should the above-named person be unable or unwilling to serve, who do you want to name as your *second* alternate agent?

Full name of person you want to act as your *second* alternate agent:
[K] _____

This person's relationship to you: _____

Address of the person named above (not P.O. Box):
[L] _____

_____

Home phone: **[M]** _____; Work phone: **[N]** _____

Do you want the power of attorney to be effective immediately or to take effect only if you are incapable of handling your own affairs?

[Choose One]   ____ Effective now   ____ Effective later

For Health Care Power of Attorney Only:

Full name of the physician(s) you desire to make decisions concerning your health care during your incapacity:
[O] _____

Limitations: What limitations do you want to place on your physician(s) at the time you become incapacitated? (i.e., no intravenous feeding, no respirator, etc.)
[P] _____

_____

* *

For Adoption Power of Attorney Only:

Full name of child (on birth certificate):
[Q] _____

Date of birth:
[R] _____

Full adoptive name you will give the child:
[S] _____

* *

Do you also want a Living Will? _____

(This is a declaration of the desire to die a natural death, without extraordinary life support systems, if you are in a terminal, incurable, and irreversible state or in a persistent vegetative condition, such as in a coma.)

■■■

Powers of Attorney

1. Q. WHAT IS A POWER OF ATTORNEY?

A. A power of attorney is a document that allows someone else to act as your legal agent. Thus, a power of attorney can be used to allow a friend to sell your car, to let your spouse ship your household goods, or to authorize a relative to take your child to the hospital. It can create valid and legal debts in your name or it can authorize a person to pay off your debts.

2. Q. ARE THERE DIFFERENT KINDS OF POWERS OF ATTORNEY?

A. Yes. The two types of powers of attorney are *general* and *special*. A general power of attorney allows that person you name (or your *agent*) to do any and all things that you could legally do, from registering a car to selling a house. A special (or limited) power of attorney lists a particular act that the agent is authorized to do and limits the agent to that act. The agent can be authorized to do several changes in a single special power of attorney.

3. Q. WHEN DOES A POWER OF ATTORNEY EXPIRE?

A. A power of attorney may expire either on your death or upon your mental or physical incompetence. A power of attorney which survives your incompetence is called a *durable power of attorney*. This type of document will last beyond your physical or mental incompetence. Also, you may insert a clause in the document which states that the power of attorney is automatically terminated on a certain date or is terminated when you file a written revocation with the Register of Deeds.

4. Q. WHAT ARE SOME OF THE THINGS A SPECIAL POWER OF ATTORNEY CAN DO?

A. You can use a special power of attorney to allow someone to do almost all legal actions that you can do yourself. Thus, for example, you could prepare a special power of attorney that lets your designated agent:

a. Buy or sell real estate;
b. Purchase a car or sell your furniture;
c. Sign your paycheck or withdraw money from your bank account;
d. Admit your child to the hospital for necessary medical care;
e. Ship or store your luggage and household goods;
f. Sign your name to a lease or an agreement to connect utilities, such as electricity, gas, oil, or telephone service; and
g. Cash or deposit a tax refund check or transfer stocks and bonds.

These are just a few of the many things that can be done with a specific power of attorney. All you have to do is prepare the special power of attorney with a specific description of the particular act or deed to be done (and listing the agent that you authorize to do it).

5. Q. WHY DOESN'T EVERYONE HAVE A POWER OF ATTORNEY?

A. A power of attorney can be very useful if you have one in effect when you need it. But a power of attorney can be abused as well as used; there can be disadvantages to having one as well as advantages. A husband who just separated from his wife might use the power of attorney she gave him to clean out her individual bank account. A well-meaning older person might give a power of attorney to a younger relative, only to discover that the relative squandered and spent the assets of the older person. A power of attorney always has the potential for being a very helpful or very dangerous document for those reasons. The important thing to remember is that you are going to be legally responsible for the acts of your agent. Therefore, you must exercise great care in selecting the person to be your agent.

6. Q. ARE THERE ANY SPECIAL REQUIREMENTS FOR POWERS OF ATTORNEY?
   A. A power of attorney must always be signed in front of a notary public. If you wish, it can be recorded at the county Register of Deeds office in North Carolina where it is to be used. If the power of attorney is to survive your mental or physical incompetence or will be used to transfer real estate, then you must record this power of attorney with the Register of Deeds in the county listed in the power of attorney.

7. Q. DOES EVERY BUSINESS OR BANK HAVE TO ACCEPT MY POWER OF ATTORNEY?
   A. No. In North Carolina, banks and businesses are free to accept or reject a power of attorney. Some businesses or banks require that the power of attorney be recorded, while others do not. Some banks will accept only a special power of attorney. You should check with the business or bank before obtaining or using a power of attorney to be sure that it will be accepted.

8. Q. DOES A POWER OF ATTORNEY EXPIRE UPON MY DEATH OR MENTAL INCAPACITY?
   A. A power of attorney expires on the death of the grantor (the person signing it) or of the agent named in it. Many people choose to have an additional clause in a power of attorney that makes provision for mental incapacity. In such a case, the power of attorney would usually state that it would survive any mental incompetence of the grantor. In North Carolina, such a power of attorney must be recorded at the county Register of Deeds if the grantor later becomes mentally incapacitated. You should remember, however, that a valid power of attorney must be signed while the grantor is sane and mentally competent.

9. Q. WHAT IF I HAVE OTHER QUESTIONS OR SPECIFIC PROBLEMS I WANT HELP IN SOLVING?
   A. See your attorney as soon as possible. Seeing a lawyer early may not only solve a problem you have, it may also resolve or avoid a problem in the future, on this or other unrelated subjects. Seeing your lawyer early is practicing "preventive law."

■■■

Will Questionnaire
(Please print clearly)

1. **YOUR FULL NAME**

   _____

   (First)   (Middle)   (Last)

2. **LEGAL RESIDENCE**

   _____

   (Street Address)

   _____

   (City)   (County)   (State)

3. **FULL NAME OF SPOUSE**

   _____

   (First)   (Middle)   (Last)

4. **NAME AND RESIDENCES OF ALL YOUR CHILDREN** (Natural, adopted, illegitimate, etc.) Use reverse side if necessary. If minor, insert age.

   A. _____ (____)

   (Name)   Age

   _____

   City/State

   B. _____ (____)

   (Name)   Age

   _____

   City/State

   C. _____ (____)

   (Name)   Age

   _____

   City/State

   D. _____ (____)

   (Name)   Age

   _____

   City/State

5. **ESTIMATED SIZE OF YOUR ESTATE:** Include 100 percent of all insurance, real property less mortgage, and all *other* assets. (Circle estimate)

   Approx. or under: $200,000 $300,000 $400,000

   Approx. $500,000 or over

6. **WHOM DO YOU WANT TO RECEIVE YOUR REAL PROPERTY AT YOUR DEATH?***

   Full Name: _____

   Relationship: _____

   Address: _____

   City/State: _____

---

*In North Carolina and most states, you cannot disinherit your spouse. You will need a divorce decree or a signed separation agreement to leave your spouse out of your will, and leaving him or her $1 will not solve the problem.

7. **WHOM DO YOU WANT TO RECEIVE YOUR PERSONAL PROPERTY AT YOUR DEATH?**

   Full Name: _____

   Relationship: _____

   Address: _____

   City/State: _____

8. **IF THE ABOVE PERSON(S) DIE BEFORE YOU, WHOM DO YOU WANT AS YOUR ALTERNATE BENEFICIARY?**

   Full Name: _____

   Relationship: _____

   Address: _____

   City/State: _____

   Full Name: _____

   Relationship: _____

   Address: _____

   City/State: _____

9. **IF EITHER OF THE ABOVE PERSON(S) DIES BEFORE YOU, WHOM DO YOU WANT TO RECEIVE HIS OR HER SHARE?** [*CHECK ONLY ONE*]

   ☐ The surviving beneficiary under #8 above?

   ☐ The children of that deceased person?

   ☐ The *heirs* of that deceased person, including his or her spouse?

10. **IF YOU LEAVE A MINOR CHILD BEHIND AT YOUR DEATH, WHOM DO YOU WANT TO BE THE CUSTODIAN (OR *GUARDIAN OF THE PERSON*) OR CHILD(REN)?****

    Full Name: _____

    Relationship: _____

    Address: _____

    City/State: _____

11. **WHOM DO YOU WANT TO NAME AS ALTERNATE CUSTODIAN?**

    Full Name: _____

    Relationship: _____

    Address: _____

    City/State: _____

**The other parent of a child is *usually* named by the court as the successor custodian. If you name someone else, the court may, in a contested case, disregard your wishes and appoint the other surviving parent as custodian.

12. **IF YOU LEAVE A MINOR CHILD BEHIND AT YOUR DEATH, WHOM DO YOU WANT TO BE THE FINANCIAL TRUSTEE (OR *GUARDIAN OF THE ESTATE*) OF THE CHILD(REN)?**

Full Name: _____

Relationship: _____

Address: _____

City/State: _____

13. **WHOM DO YOU WANT TO NAME AS ALTERNATE FINANCIAL TRUSTEE?**

Full Name: _____

Relationship: _____

Address: _____

City/State: _____

14. **WHOM DO YOU WANT TO NAME AS YOUR EXECUTOR (THE ONE WHO PROBATES YOUR ESTATE, PAYS YOUR TAXES, AND DISTRIBUTES YOUR PROPERTY)?**

Full Name: _____

Relationship: _____

Address: _____

City/State: _____

15. **IF THE ABOVE-NAMED EXECUTOR DIES BEFORE YOU, WHOM DO YOU WANT TO NAME AS YOUR ALTERNATE EXECUTOR?**

Full Name: _____

Relationship: _____

Address: _____

City/State: _____

16. **OTHER INFORMATION TO BE CONSIDERED IN THE DRAFTING OF MY WILL:**

(**Note:** Do not use a will to dispose of life insurance proceeds or retirement assets. To do this, you will need to change beneficiaries through the appropriate company using the proper form.)

_____

_____

■■■

Section 6

Marriage and Divorce

Starting the Divorce Process:

An Overview

Studies have shown that the experience of separation and divorce are so traumatic as to rank second only to the death of a close loved one in terms of emotional turmoil, pain, and stress. Not only are separation and divorce accompanied by feelings of guilt, rejection, embarrassment, and anger, but the process also causes fear and uncertainty among those who experience it. Reserves of inner strength are often as necessary as external financial reserves in order to get through the process intact.

The first step to conquering fear of the unknown is to learn as much as possible about the process. A good lawyer can often explain the procedures clearly, assist in escalating goals, and propose a positive strategy to achieve those realistic results. Set out below are questions and answers about the process of divorce and separation that will help take the mystery out of it. A good attorney can clarify and refine the specific points, since no article can truly explain the law of 50 states clearly and thoroughly.

   1. Q. WHAT ISSUES CAN BE RESOLVED IN A DICORCE?
       A. The breakup of a marriage often involves five issues: property division, alimony, child support, custody/visitation, and divorce. And each of these can be resolved by consent (a negotiated settlement) or contested in court. Let's take a close look at how the process works.

   At the outset it should be noted that not all states handle divorce the same. There are two different legal structures for divorce and dissolution that exist in the United States. In some states, such as New York and Wisconsin, the divorce is a "package deal." All issues must be resolved by the parties (through agreement) or by the court (through trial) before the divorce is granted. "My wife/husband won't give me a divorce" is sometimes the cry heard in these jurisdictions, because the only alternative to a long, messy, and expensive trial is a settlement driven or guided by the other party. In these states, *divorce* is the end result of the process; when you get your divorce, everything else is already in place. The other issues in the case are raised mandatorily by law or court rule, and all issues regarding the marriage are before the court for decision whenever one party files for a divorce.

   In other states, such as Delaware and North Carolina, the divorce case is not necessarily joined with the other issues and may be heard shortly after the filed lawsuit has been served on the other side. Custody may be contested (or settled) in a different lawsuit or joined in the divorce suit. The same applies to child support, alimony (also called maintenance or spousal support), and property division (or equitable distribution). In these states, divorce is not necessarily the *end* of the case; it may just as easily be the *beginning* of the case, to be followed by court decisions (or agreements) as to any issues in the marriage that are brought up by the parties in the lawsuit. Each of these issues can be heard on different timetables—before or after the divorce—by the court.

2. Q. WHERE DO I START?

A. Getting the right lawyer is often the first step for a husband or wife. There are many ways to select an attorney if you do not have one in mind already. In some cases, you may have been represented previously by an attorney who could help you in your present situation. Then again, there may be a friend or relative who has been represented by a good lawyer in a case similar to yours. It might be a good idea in either of these cases to see if that lawyer might be able to handle this matter for you. Many bar associations maintain a lawyer referral service. You can also choose a lawyer based on advertising or any number of other ways. The important thing is that you choose a lawyer who is able to handle your case and able to work with you. Any way of selecting a lawyer is satisfactory if it achieves these goals, for it is very important for the client to have confidence in his or her attorney.

What you say to your lawyer is "privileged information." Generally speaking, what you tell your attorney must be held in confidence unless you give permission otherwise. In addition, your civilian attorney has the duty to:

- Let you make the major decisions in your case, such as pleading guilty in a criminal case or accepting a compromise or settlement in a civil case; and
- Remain open and honest with you in all aspects of your case, including the chances of success, the good and bad sides of your position, the time needed, and the fee required.

3. Q. HOW MUCH WILL ALL OF THIS COST ME?

A. Lawyers set fees in a number of ways. The major types of fees are flat rates, contingency fees, and hourly billing. Lawyers may use a flat fee in handling certain domestic cases where the work involved is usually straightforward, predictable, and routine. Thus many lawyers use a flat rate or set fee in uncontested divorces, adoptions, and name changes. A flat fee is paid in advance (ordinarily) and does not vary depending on the amount of time or work involved. No refund is due if the work takes less time than expected, and no additional charge is made if the case is longer or more complex than usual.

An hourly rate is most common when the client's work will be substantial, but it is difficult to estimate how much time it will take. Thus, for example, a lawyer might charge on an hourly rate for a contested custody or alimony case. It is fairly common for the lawyer to require a retainer to be paid before starting on the case. This amounts to a deposit or down payment to make sure that the client is serious about the case and is financially prepared to cover the costs that may be incurred. The size of the retainer and whether any part of it is refundable will vary from case to case and lawyer to lawyer.

In certain family law cases, the court may order one party to pay some or all of the other's legal expenses. The court can make such an award in cases involving alimony, child support, custody, and paternity, by way of example. It is important to remember, however, that the award of attorney's fees in such cases is not mandatory or automatic. It depends on a variety of factors, such as good faith, need, lack of adequate support, and so on. The courts see these awards of attorney's fees as a way to pay back or reimburse people for attorney's fees already paid or presently due. It is very difficult to retain an attorney from the outset based on the promise or hope of court-awarded attorney's fees at a later date. This is especially true because many times a person will not obey the court's order to pay the other party's attorney, and so further court work may be necessary.

4. Q. HOW CAN I MAKE SURE THAT MY LAWYER IS DOING THE JOB I WANT HIM/HER TO DO?

A. Here are some tips on the important matters that involve your lawyer and some areas where complaints are common.

- Be sure to insist that your lawyer explain specifically (1) what will be done in your case and (2) how much it will cost. If you wish, you can ask the lawyer to put this in writing. This includes the contract that binds you and the attorney—make sure you get a written contract, and then read it!
- Ask for an estimate of the total charges and ask what services are included in this estimate. Ask what your attorney expects to be the steps you go through and how much time (or expense) they might involve—if you hire an experienced lawyer, he or she should be able to at least "outline" the process for you with a fair degree of accuracy. [Note: At the same time, please be aware that it is hard to tell what might happen or how long something might take in a legal dispute. It's impossible to predict with any degree of accuracy what will happen, for example, in a divorce and separation case. While many of these are resolved as standard "uncontested divorces" with no alimony, property, or child-related issues involved, there are a great many cases that are completely unpredictable in this field of law, so don't expect a specific dollar amount to be quoted to you as "the entire fee" in anything but a standard uncontested divorce. In fact, be wary of attorneys who promise to handle your entire case for a fixed sum, since it is impossible at the outset to tell what will occur in all except the most routine of uncontested divorce cases—one in which both parties want to get divorced, there are no issues of alimony, property division, custody, or child support, and there is no problem serving the other party with the divorce papers.]
- Clients should receive frequent case updates and regular communications from their attorneys; the rules of most state bars require this. Be sure to ask about this if you want to ensure that your lawyer knows you want to be kept current regarding your case.
- You should also get copies of the "pleadings"—motions, complaints, counterclaims, petitions—that have been filed in your case, as well as any order or judgment that the judge signs.
- The lawyer should release your file to you upon request and with reasonable notice.
- Do not tolerate unreturned phone calls; nothing makes a client angrier (and justifiably so) than a lawyer who won't answer a phone call or a letter from a client requesting information.
- Consider hiring a lawyer who specializes in your particular kind of case. Many states allow lawyers to become specialists and list themselves as such if they meet certain qualifications. A specialist is usually more likely

to know the "ins and outs" of your case than an attorney who is a "general practitioner." Many states have lawyers who are *certified* as specialists in family law by the state bar.

When you first meet with your lawyer, make sure you go over the important facts of your case and outline for him or her the goals you have. While we all have hopes, desires, and dreams, it is vital to keep those goals realistic and achievable; don't expect your case to go anywhere if your goals are to embarrass the other side, bring her to her knees, or "break her" financially. Your lawyer has a duty to be open and honest with you, explaining the "pros and cons" of your case, the strengths and weaknesses. Make sure your lawyer is not going to get into a personality conflict with the other attorney; your money will be wasted on an unproductive "spitting contest." Consider your finances to decide "how much case you can afford."

5. Q. **WHAT IS INVOLVED IN "GOING TO COURT"?**
   A. If you must go into litigation, you need to know something about the process—you can't play ball if you do not know the rules! Litigation always starts with the filing of a complaint or petition, which states what the facts of the case are and what relief is requested, along with a summons, which states that the other side has been sued and has a certain period to respond. The other side usually files an answer or response within the 20–30 days following the service of these papers on him or her. Sometimes additional documents must be filed by the spouses, according to state or local rules. Examples might be financial affidavits or declarations, which state the incomes and expenses of each party, or property inventories, which show what each party claims to be marital or separate property, as well as the value placed on each item. Sometimes the courts also require parties to file a copy of tax returns or pay stubs with these declarations or affidavits.

   Contested domestic cases can take a long time to resolve. While the entire case is still pending, the next stage in some cases is sometimes one involving temporary, interim, or emergency hearings. A party may need the court to make an emergency ruling on issues of custody or visitation, especially where there is a "tug of war" going on between the parents or something occurs that is a serious danger to the children. The court often considers the need for interim spousal support or child support at a temporary hearing in the weeks or months after the case is filed; if the court didn't do this in some cases, the other party might be brought to her knees quickly without financial help. Some courts use the time after filing to conduct a hearing on *interim allocation*, which means a temporary division or distribution of marital assets pending the final hearing. This can also be useful in providing each party with sufficient means to pay the lawyers, psychologists, or accountants that may be necessary to assist in resolving the case or preparing for trial.

6. Q. **I THINK MY HUSBAND IS HIDING INFORMATION. HOW CAN I FIND THIS OUT?**
   A. You might find the answer in the "discovery" stage of litigation. Discovery is a word that means "finding out information that the other side has." Many court rules state that the process of discovery goes on in the first 90–120 days after the lawsuit is filed, or even longer in complex cases. This is probably the most important part of trial preparation—finding out what the case is all about, from the other side's perspective.

There's always "informal discovery," which usually means obtaining things yourself from the other side without formal notices or requests. This can be done surreptitiously, as when Mrs. Smith makes a copy of her husband's bank statements and then returns them to their file before leaving the home. It can also be done openly by the attorney's simply asking the other side for a copy of certain papers, receipts, titles, or deeds; if the adversaries are friendly and the marital dispute is under control, which often depends on the personalities of the attorneys and the level of animosity of the parties, it is possible to save hundreds or even thousands of dollars by simply agreeing on a "discovery plan" to allow each party, within reason, to obtain relevant documents from the other side by requesting them in a letter. While there are no penalties or sanctions for failure to produce or reply, as exist with formal discovery, the savings in time and money can be substantial if the parties and their lawyers are willing to cooperate.

Formal or traditional discovery, on the other hand, has structures, deadlines, definitions, and rules that must be obeyed.

Here are some examples:

- *Interrogatories* are written questions that must be answered by the other side under oath within a certain number of days (usually around 30) from when they are served by mail on opposing counsel.
- *Document requests* require the other side to produce documents at a specified place and time for inspection and copying.
- You can use a *request for entry upon land* to get into the office or home of the other party to inspect, inventory, and photograph (or videotape) what's there.
- A *deposition* is oral testimony given under oath in front of a court reporter. There is no judge present, and it's usually done in a lawyer's office. It results in a typed transcript of the testimony, and it can be very useful in exploring what facts or data the other side has, what accusations will be made, and how the other side is thinking about the case. It costs more, of course, than the use of interrogatories, but it usually produces better responses from the other side—answers that are more complete and more spontaneous, as well as the ability for your lawyer to ask "follow-up questions."

7. Q. **WHAT WILL HAPPEN IF WE END UP IN COURT?**

A. *Going to trial* doesn't just happen. It's the end-point of a long process that includes getting the client ready (rehearsal for the hearing, overview of questions that *will be asked* and *may be asked*, and reviewing documents that will be introduced as evidence), getting the client's witnesses ready, preparing exhibits for introduction, and setting the case on the calendar for weeks, or even months, in the future. Lawyers frequently prepare *written briefs* for the trial, which summarize and explain points of law that may be involved in the case.

On the day of trial, the judge will usually "call the calendar," which means announce the names of the cases that are on the court calendar for that day. *Yes*, there are other people getting a divorce, and *yes*, they also have *their* cases set on *your day*! It is the job of the judge to figure out which ones can be tried that day and which ones must be continued. If a continuance is not ordered for your case, then it will be tried. The trial usually consists of several sections:

- The plaintiff's (or petitioner's) case involves his or her testimony, immediately followed by cross-examination by the other side's lawyer. Here is where the plaintiff's exhibits and documents are often introduced. Then the witnesses for the plaintiff testify (and are cross-examined by the other side also), and they likewise may offer documents into evidence.
- The defendant (or respondent) has the same opportunity—to give testimony and present evidence, and to offer witnesses. The same opportunity for cross-examination by plaintiff's attorney exists.
- Most domestic cases are heard in front of a judge alone, although there are occasionally cases that, by state law, are allowed to be tried before a jury.
- After the presentation of both sides, each side is given the opportunity for rebuttal, which is testimony that denies or contradicts what the other side has presented.
- The lawyers will have the opportunity for final argument or "closing statement," which allows them to summarize their evidence and argue for the results they seek.
- Then comes the decision by the court. This is sometimes is right after closing statement, and sometimes occurs days or weeks after the trial has concluded (if the judge takes the case "under advisement").
- Once the decision has been made, it is noted in the court records and announced (formally in court or sometimes informally by phone conference). If the parties weren't at the decision conference, they will be notified by their respective attorneys.
- Entry of the order, judgment, or decree is the next stage. Sometimes this is done by the court, but, more often than not, it is the job of the attorneys to write up a decision for the judge to sign. This often means that they have to meet with each other or with the judge when they are preparing *findings of fact* for the judge on contested issues. This process alone can take days, weeks, or even months in a complex or hotly contested case.

8. **Q.** **Isn't there any alternative to a long trial?**
   A. Why would anyone go through this, you might ask—aren't there any alternatives? The answer is *yes*. There are three alternatives: mediation, arbitration, and negotiation. These options are usually less expensive than going to trial and, if handled correctly, less time-consuming.

   Arbitration is process by which a neutral third party renders a binding decision on the issue or issues presented—alimony, pension division, child support, etc. The arbitrator acts in much the same fashion as a judge in a civil trial, but he or she is usually paid by the parties (in equal or unequal shares), and the proceedings are usually faster and less formal than a trial. The arbitrator's job is not to choose sides but rather to listen to the facts of the case and then render a decision.

   Mediation is an informal dispute resolution where a neutral third party, a trained mediator, helps you and your spouse reach an agreement satisfactory to both of you. The mediator's role is to *help* the parties resolve their conflicts. Choosing sides or giving legal advice is not a mediator's duty. The mediator does not make any decisions for you, but rather encourages both parties to work together to make their own decisions. Mediation has become an increasingly popular option to trial, not to mention a cheaper option (in some cases it is free). Every state has its own requirements for mediation. In some counties it can be required by the court, and in others it is optional. And the parties, independently of the courts, can hire a mediator for a settlement conference, with the cost to be shared by both.

A negotiated settlement, involving the parties and their lawyers, is a third option to trial. This can be a productive way to settle some or all of the issues on the table. If all of the issues cannot be settled, a meeting like this is a good way to decide a majority of the issues and reserve the issues in controversy for trial. Taking some of the issues off the table will likely make trial shorter and the process less expensive and stressful. It is also a good way to bargain through the items on the table and see if there is room for negotiation.

Mediation and negotiation are give-and-take situations. Nothing can be demanded from the other side, and usually a good deal of compromise is necessary. It is important to examine exactly what you want to happen in your case and to be aware of your "bottom line." Fair negotiations and an open mind between the parties are essential to the success of these alternate resolutions. Bringing your anger over past events into the ring will ensure the failure of any settlement possibilities.

When will these alternatives to trial work? When both parties are willing to work together to form an amicable agreement in the best interest of all concerned, these alternatives will be a success. When are these three options to trial not a good idea? When a case involves physical abuse, substance abuse, or severe depression and anger, trying one of these settlement options may be a waste of time and money for both parties.

■■■

Dating During Divorce

Preface

The purpose of this pamphlet is to assist you in answering questions you may have regarding dating during divorce and the law in North Carolina.

1. **Q.** AFTER I SEPARATE FROM MY SPOUSE, AM I FREE TO DATE OTHER PEOPLE?

   A. Yes and no. You are free to associate with whomever you choose. However, until a final decree of divorce is entered, you are still married. Sexual relations with anyone other than your spouse is still a crime in North Carolina. Adultery is a misdemeanor, but since the district attorney usually has more pressing matters to handle, criminal prosecution is not your primary concern. Your chief concerns should be how a new relationship will affect:

   i. custody or visitation with your children;

   ii. your children and your relationship with them;

   iii. whether you pay or receive spousal support;

   iv. the amount of spousal and/or child support that you receive or pay; and

   v. your ability to effectively negotiate a property settlement with your spouse.

2. **Q.** BUT ADULTERY HAS NOTHING TO DO WITH CUSTODY, RIGHT?

   A. Not so fast. There are several reasons why adultery is dangerous in custody cases:

   - First, while *the law* may say that adultery per se doesn't matter, *the judge* is the decision-maker in your case. The judge has a great deal of discretion in custody cases and in awarding or restricting visitation rights. Some judges might not be bothered or offended by adultery; others would be loath to grant custody or normal visitation rights to a parent carrying on an adulterous affair.

   - Second, while a divorce might end the marriage, it won't end the relationship with the other parent over the minor children. The parents will have to deal with each other on a frequent basis over a period of years, and post-divorce cooperation clearly is in every client's best interest. It is hard to imagine how having an affair before the divorce is complete can have a positive effect on the spouse's feelings for the adulterer, but the possibility that it will poison any spirit of cooperation is readily apparent. The need for future negotiation is inevitable, and negotiation with a friend is usually easier than negotiating with an enemy.

   - Third, child support is important in every child custody or visitation case. Generally, the North Carolina Child Support Guidelines will determine the amount of child support paid or received in a given case. The Guideline amount is presumed to be sufficient to meet the reasonable needs of the child(ren). Under the Guidelines, the amount of child support is determined by the incomes of the parents. But the court may deviate or vary from the Guideline amount under appropriate circumstances. For example, if one parent is living with another person and sharing expenses, the needs of the child(ren) for fixed expenses like housing, electricity, natural gas, water, and other utilities are reduced because of the presence of another person in the residence.

- Finally, most new relationships that begin before a divorce is final are unlikely to succeed. When children have been made part of that relationship, they experience another loss. Children who suffer repeated losses can become reluctant to develop closer relationships. Not only is this damaging to the children, but many judges are very concerned about the impact of introducing children to a significant other while a divorce is pending.

3. Q. WHAT DOES DATING HAVE TO DO WITH WHETHER I PAY OR RECEIVE SPOUSAL SUPPORT?

A. Maybe a lot. This subject is covered more fully in our Family Law Information Letters #14 and #34, but in general, you should know that the law regarding spousal support changed effective October 1, 1995. For cases filed *prior to October 1, 1995*, the spouse seeking support had to prove that the other spouse was guilty of some marital fault. Among other things, this fault included adultery, indignities, and constructive abandonment. Dating or other social activities with a person to whom you are not married may be relevant to establishing one or more of the fault grounds necessary for an award of spousal support by the court. This is true even after you have separated from your spouse. For cases filed *on or after October 1, 1995*, marital misconduct is not essential for a claim for post-separation support or alimony. Marital misconduct occurring after the date of separation is only relevant to prove that similar behavior also existed before the date of separation. Marital misconduct includes "illicit sexual behavior" and indignities. A dependent spouse who has committed an act of illicit sexual behavior before the date of separation cannot be awarded alimony. A supporting spouse who has committed an act of illicit sexual behavior before the date of separation must pay alimony. When both spouses have committed acts of illicit sexual behavior, the court will weigh the relative fault of the parties to determine whether support should be awarded. "Illicit sexual behavior" includes sexual intercourse and other sexual acts engaged in with someone other than your spouse. Your relationship with a person of the opposite sex may be considered an indignity or constructive abandonment of your spouse, even if you have not engaged in sexual acts.

4. Q. WHAT DOES DATING HAVE TO DO WITH HOW MUCH I PAY OR RECEIVE IN SPOUSAL SUPPORT?

A. Dating will have little or no impact on how much spousal support you pay or receive, unless you share a residence or "cohabitate" with someone. Cohabitation means: "the act of two adults dwelling together continuously and habitually in a private heterosexual relationship . . . or a private homosexual relationship. Cohabitation is evidenced by the voluntary mutual assumption of those marital rights, duties, and obligations which are usually manifested by married people, and which include, but are not necessarily dependent on, sexual relations."

If you share a residence with someone, this living arrangement affects the amount of your monthly expenses and your need for support from your spouse or your ability to contribute to the support of your spouse. This is true whether you are romantically involved with this person or not. If you are romantically involved with a person with whom you share a residence, a court may determine that you are cohabiting with that person. Cohabitation by a spouse receiving support can be a basis for the reduction or termination of spousal support.

5. **Q.** BUT IF I DON'T HAVE CHILDREN AND ALIMONY IS NOT AN ISSUE, I CAN CARRY ON MY EXTRAMARITAL RELATIONSHIP WHILE MY PROPERTY SETTLEMENT IS BEING NEGOTIATED, RIGHT?

   A. Wrong. Extramarital sexual relations before divorce can have an adverse affect on the other spouse, perhaps leading to unwanted complications in your settlement negotiations. This risk is especially high if the other spouse did not know of the "other woman" or the "other man" before agreeing to a negotiated settlement, but it can arise even if there was full knowledge beforehand. Infidelity typically causes hurt, embarrassment and anger, especially when the adultery is public knowledge. A relationship while the divorce is pending can create these feelings, and the risk is that the spouse will seek revenge or vindication. This motive may manifest itself in serious problems when your lawyer tries to bargain for a "fair" division of property or to avoid an excessive settlement demand from the injured spouse. Steer clear of adulterous conduct if you want your lawyer to be able to deal with opposing counsel based on facts and finances, rather than hurt feelings.

6. **Q.** I'VE HEARD ABOUT "HEART-BALM" LAWSUITS AGAINST "THE OTHER WOMAN" OR "THE OTHER MAN." CAN DATING AFTER SEPARATION GIVE CAUSE TO THAT KIND OF LAWSUIT?

   A. Heart-balm lawsuits against "the other man or woman" mean that your spouse files an alienation of affection claim and a claim for criminal conversation. Early in 2002, the Court of Appeals ruled that a claim of alienation of affection pertains to a dating relationship *during* the marriage. However, a criminal conversation claim can be maintained and successfully litigated when sexual acts occur before or after the date of separation. Heart-balm lawsuits are complicated and often very expensive if taken to trial. Therefore, if you engage in sexual conduct with the person you are dating, you could be exposing them to a criminal conversation lawsuit.

■■■

Dealing with Debt and Divorce

Many marital property division cases are made up largely of debt, not assets. As a result, when a client comes to our firm concerned about how property is to be divided post-separation, we often need to focus the client's attention on the issue of *marital debt*. A "marital debt" is a very special kind of debt. It must be incurred during the marriage and before the date of separation. And it must either be for the joint benefit of the parties or for the purchase of marital property. The name on the debt—husband, wife, or both, is irrelevant. Either or both may be legally obligated for the debt. *Geer v. Geer*, 353 S.E.2d 427 (N.C. App., 1987). The burden of proof is on the party seeking to classify the debt as marital. *Caudill v. Caudill*, 509 S.E.2d 246 (N.C. App., 1998). In most cases, debt incurred during the course of the marriage is deemed "marital."

In many households the amount of marital debt exceeds the worth of the marital assets. If the existing debts are from joint accounts and further financial liability is possible, there are a number of steps that you need to address.

1. **GET A COPY OF YOUR CREDIT REPORT.** Unless the marriage has been for less than five years, it is unlikely that you are going to remember every in-store credit application that either you or your spouse filled out during the marriage. Reviewing the credit report will allow you to examine all possible sources of financial liability.

2. **REVIEW YOUR CREDIT REPORT.** You will need to take action regarding those accounts held in joint names. As a courtesy, the opposing party or the opposing attorney should be notified that you are about to close all joint accounts. Be aware that if you do not take this step, you risk flaring tempers and escalating the cost of litigation in the case. If you are aware that your spouse often uses the joint account, this is especially so.

3. **CLOSE THE ACCOUNT AS SOON AS POSSIBLE.** You may not be able to close some accounts, either because there is an outstanding balance that you cannot pay or if you do not qualify for a credit card in your sole name to which you can transfer the balance of the account. Nonetheless, you need to give each creditor formal notice that you wish to close or limit liability for the account. In practical terms, you should call each creditor holding a joint account. Each creditor should be told that you will not be responsible for any further financial liability on that account and that you request that no additional charges be made on the account.

4. **FOLLOW UP IN WRITING.** After you call each creditor you need to write a letter, retaining a copy for your own records, confirming that the account has been closed and that you will not be responsible for any further financial liability on that account. This is the best protection for you in the event that the opposing party reopens the account the following day and makes additional charges, which is always a possibility. Keep in mind that this action does not provide you absolute protection. In the event that the opposing party were to re-open a joint account and incur financial liability and then not pay on that debt, it remains a distinct possibility that the creditor would come after you for repayment. However, if you take these simple steps, it is less likely that a creditor could successfully sue for collection on that debt.

Please note that in some cases you will discover the existence of accounts that you did not open or for which you cannot recall signing a credit application. Indeed, we have had cases where the opposing party forged our client's signature. In that event, the creditor needs to be contacted immediately, and you should obtain copies of the original credit application. Most large creditors have a fraud department which investigates this type of occurrence. If the opposing party is thought to have forged credit applications, it is unlikely that you will be held responsible for that debt. Further, you should consider filing criminal charges against the opposing party for fraud.

If there is a large amount of debt in the marital estate, the possibility of bankruptcy should be discussed. If you believe that there may be a chance that the opposing party will assume joint debts in a property settlement and then declare bankruptcy soon thereafter, you may have a problem. Although the Bankruptcy Reform Act of 2001 makes marital debt non-dischargeable under Chapter 7, you may still be subject to the annoyance of creditor calls during dinner and the receipt of "nasty-grams" in the mail demanding payment on the joint debt. If this happens, you may be left with the feeling that your property settlement wasn't worth the paper it was written on.

In order to prevent this from happening to you, you should give notice to each and every joint creditor, alerting them to the fact that this debt has been assumed by the opposing party. This notice can be made by forwarding a copy of either a memorandum of the property settlement, which identifies the joint debts assumed by the opposing party, or a copy of the court order, which orders the opposing party to pay on the specific debts. At the same time you forward these documents, you should request from the creditor a formal notice stating that you no longer have a financial responsibility on the joint debt.

■■■

Divorce, Alimony, and Property Division

1. **Q.** CAN I DO THIS BY MYSELF, OR WILL I HAVE TO HAVE AN ATTORNEY OBTAIN A DIVORCE IN NORTH CAROLINA FOR ME?
   A. You should definitely get an attorney to file for divorce and get a judgment of divorce in North Carolina. While the state laws do not specifically require that you have an attorney, it is sometimes very difficult to get the judge to grant you a divorce if you are not represented by a civilian lawyer when you go to court.

2. **Q.** WHO PAYS FOR MY LAWYER?
   A. As a general rule, you must retain and pay for your own attorney in a divorce case. There is no law that requires a judge to order your spouse to pay your lawyer's fees in a divorce action in North Carolina.

3. **Q.** WHAT IF MY SPOUSE WON'T GIVE MA A DIVORCE?
   A. The judge is the person who grants a divorce, not your spouse. Once you have filed the divorce complaint at the courthouse, your attorney will serve a copy of the summons and complaint on your spouse, by sheriff or by certified mail. If no answer is filed within 30 days after service, you will probably be granted a divorce by default. If your spouse contests the divorce action by filing an answer denying one or more of the statements in your complaint, a hearing will be set during which the two of you can testify and the judge can decide what the truth is.

4. **Q.** IS MY DIVORCE FINAL WHEN THE JUDGE SIGNS THE JUDGMENT?
   A. Yes. You are then legally divorced. There is no waiting period after entry of judgment.

5. **Q.** CAN I RESUME THE USE OF MY MAIDEN NAME AT THE TIME OF DIVORCE?
   A. Yes. You may ask for the right to resume your maiden name in the divorce papers your lawyer files for you. This is routinely granted by the judge. Even if you do not ask for your maiden name back at the time of the divorce, you can file for resumption of your maiden name after the divorce is granted.

6. **Q.** CAN I USE "MENTAL CRUELTY" OR ADULTERY AS A GROUND FOR DIVORCE HERE?
   A. No. In North Carolina the only ground for divorce that is ever used is separation for over one year. The other ground, three years' incurable insanity, is almost never used. Most divorces granted on separation grounds are uncontested. This is essentially a "no-fault" divorce with no proof necessary as to who left whom or what reason was involved.

7. **Q.** IF MY HOME IS ANOTHER STATE BUT I AM STATIONED IN NORTH CAROLINA, CAN I FILE FOR DIVORCE IN THIS STATE?
   A. North Carolina law states that you may file for divorce here if you are a true legal resident of North Carolina and have been living here for at least six

months prior to the date of filing. If your spouse is a legal resident of North Carolina and resides here, you may also file here for divorce. You may want to find out whether you can file for divorce in your home state (other than North Carolina), and for this you should see a legal assistance attorney. He or she can discuss with you the laws of your home state as to procedures for divorce, hiring an attorney, grounds, cost of filing, and other issues.

8. Q. DO I HAVE TO HAVE A "LEGAL SEPARATION" TO GET A DIVORCE HERE, OR DO I HAVE TO "FILE FOR SEPARATION" IN NORTH CAROLINA?

A. All you need to do to obtain a divorce in North Carolina is live separate and apart from your spouse for *more than* one year with the intention that the separation be permanent. You do not need to show the judge a copy of a separation agreement, since such a document doesn't necessarily prove that you have indeed separated from your spouse. There is no such thing as "filing for separation" in North Carolina, although there are certain cases in which a judge can grant a "divorce from bed and board," or judge-approved separation, which allows you to live separate and apart from your partner.

9. Q. CAN THE JUDGE IN NORTH CAROLINA ORDER A PROPERTY DIVISION AT THE TIME OF DIVORCE?

A. After the divorce has been granted, the judge can divide the marital property of the couple if the court has been requested by either or both of them to do so. The court would not have the power to divide the marital property if neither party asked the court to do so before the divorce judgment was entered or if the parties had already executed a separation agreement that fairly divided their property.

10. Q. IS THERE SOME PROPERTY THAT THE JUDGE CANNOT DIVIDE?

A. The judge in North Carolina cannot divide *separate property,* and there are several kinds of separate property. Property acquired by either party before the marriage cannot be divided. Neither can property acquired by either party by gift or by inheritance, even if it is later traded or exchanged for another item. Business and professional licenses are also separate property.

11. Q. HOW WILL THE JUDGE DIVIDE OUR PROPERTY?

A. There is a strong presumption in North Carolina law that the fairest split would be an even division of all the marital property, regardless of who has title to the property, who paid for it, and so on. Under certain circumstances, however, the judge might decide that a 50-50 split is not fair to one or both of the parties. The statutes have a list of factors that the judge may then use to determine an unequal division of property between the couple. The judge will consider such matters as monetary and homemaker contributions to the marriage by each party; tax consequences of an unequal division; efforts of a spouse to preserve and increase the value of marital property; actions by a spouse to squander, waste, or dissipate assets; the health of each party; and the financial situation of each spouse.

12. **Q. CAN I GET THE JUDGE TO ORDER MY SPOUSE TO PAY MY ATTORNEY'S FEES IN A PROPERTY DIVISION CASE?**

A. The courts in North Carolina can't award attorney's fees in most property division cases. You will have to retain and pay for your own attorney to represent you, and you may also have to pay for an accountant or an appraiser if expert witness testimony is necessary in your case. You can, however, ask the court to allow you an "advance" or interim allocation of marital property pending a final hearing, and this could be used by you to pay the above fees.

13. **Q. WILL I HAVE TO PAY ALIMONY TO MY WIFE?**

A. It depends. The courts in North Carolina allow for the payment of two kinds of spousal support—alimony and post-separation support. Post-separation support will be ordered if (1) your wife is the **dependent spouse**; (2) you are the **supporting spouse**; and (3) her financial resources aren't enough to meet her reasonable monthly needs and personal living expenses. Alimony will be ordered if (1) your wife is the **dependent spouse**; (2) you are the **supporting spouse**; and (3) an award of alimony is equitable under the circumstances after considering numerous **factors** set out in the statute. These factors include such matters as marital fault before the separation, the incomes and needs of the parties, the length of the marriage, the physical, mental, and emotional conditions of the parties, the property and debts of the parties, the tax impact of alimony, and any other relevant economic factor.

14. **Q. WHAT IF MY WIFE COMMITTED ADULTERY—DOES THAT HAVE ANY IMPACT ON THE ALIMONY CASE?**

A. Yes. The statute covers three possible scenarios regarding **illicit sexual behavior** [ISB], the new term that includes, but is broader than, adultery:

- If the dependent spouse **only** is found to have committed ISB, then no alimony can be awarded and the case is over;
- If only the **supporting spouse** has committed an act of ISB, then the court must award alimony to the dependent spouse; and
- If both parties have committed ISB, then the court has the discretion to grant or deny alimony based on all the circumstances.

Illicit sexual behavior is not a defense against the payment of post-separation support (PSS).

15. **Q. WHAT IS A *DEPENDENT SPOUSE*?**

A. A dependent spouse is one who is actually and substantially dependent upon the other spouse for support or who is actually in need of support from the other spouse.

16. **Q. WHAT IS A *SUPPORTING SPOUSE*?**

A. The supporting spouse is one who is actually capable of providing support for the alimony claimant. If there is no surplus left when the reasonable needs of the defendant are subtracted from his net monthly income, then it is arguable that he is not the "supporting spouse." Be careful with this sort of logic, however, since most alimony defendants will claim poverty and proclaim loudly their inability to provide spousal support. It is up to the judge to make a determination of the amount of the defendant's **reasonable monthly needs** so that the court can then find out how much money is "left over" to be used as alimony or PSS.

17. **Q. ARE THERE ANY "ALIMONY GUIDELINES"? HOW IS THE AMOUNT OF ALIMONY DETERMINED?**

    A. The amount of alimony is up to the judge. Although in some cases there may be an award of limited-term alimony, a more likely approach by the judge would be to grant an open-ended award of alimony, reviewable by the court upon a motion alleging grounds for modification, namely, a substantial change of circumstances since the date of the original court order. Unlike the area of child support, there are no clear guidelines as to the amount of alimony. The award is completely in the discretion of the court, subject to the "factors" listed above for alimony.

    As a practical matter, the judge will usually attempt to find out what the **unmet needs** of the claimant are. This is the difference between her reasonable monthly needs and expenses and her net monthly income, if any. This is the "deficit" that must be filled in order to support her properly.

    Next the judge will attempt to find out what the "excess income" of the defendant is. If this exists, it becomes the "surplus," which is applied against the "deficit" in order to support the claimant properly. The judge will often take the deficit of the plaintiff (or the surplus of the defendant) and convert it into the amount of alimony to be paid in a case, although this ignores the tax consequences of alimony set forth below.

18. **Q. HOW CAN ALIMONY BE PAID?**

    A. The law gives the judge the power to order alimony on a periodic basis—which is usually the case, i.e., in a monthly sum paid directly to the claimant or paid through the Clerk of Superior Court. It can also be paid in a lump sum, such as "the sum of $5,000 due on October 1 of this year" or even "the sum of $5,000, due in monthly installments of $500 each for ten months." Alimony can be paid indefinitely or for a specific period of time, such as "for the next 24 months." The judge has these options for PSS also.

19. **Q. WHEN DOES ALIMONY END?**

    A. Alimony ends at the earlier of:

    - the date set by the court for termination, if any;
    - the date of death of either party; or
    - the occurrence of the remarriage or cohabitation of the dependent spouse.

20. **Q. ARE THERE ANY OTHER WAYS TO STOP ALIMONY?**

    A. There are two legal acts that will bar the award of alimony (or PSS) in the first place. One is the granting of a **judgment of absolute divorce** with no claim pending for alimony. One of the effects of absolute divorce is to **bar a claim for alimony** if it has not been **asserted in a pleading before the divorce is granted.** The second bar is found when there has been a **waiver of alimony** in an agreement of the parties. A separation agreement can contain a waiver of alimony, and so can an antenuptial agreement. When a party gives up a right to alimony, she or he may not thereafter go back and retrieve the lost support right.

21. **Q. WHAT IF I HAVE OTHER QUESTIONS?**
    A. Please set up an appointment to see one of our attorneys. They are here to help you.

■■■

Divorce in East Carolina

1. Q. WHAT IF MY SPOUSE WON'T GIVE ME A DIVORCE?

 A. The *judge* is the person who grants a divorce, not your spouse. Once you have filed the divorce complaint at the courthouse, your attorney will serve a copy of the summons and complaint on your spouse, by sheriff or by certified mail. If no answer is filed within 30 days after service, you will probably be granted a divorce by default. If your spouse contests the divorce action by filing an answer denying one or more of the statements in your complaint, a hearing will be set during which the two of you can testify and the judge can decide what the truth is.

2. Q. IS MY DIVORCE FINAL WHEN THE JUDGE SIGNS THE JUDGMENT?

 A. Yes. There is no waiting period after entry of judgment.

3. Q. CAN I RESUME THE USE OF MY MAIDEN NAME AT THE TIME OF DIVORCE?

 A. Yes. You may ask for the right to resume your maiden name in the divorce papers your lawyer files for you. This is routinely granted by the judge. Even if you do not ask for your maiden name back at the time of the divorce, you can file for resumption of your maiden name after the divorce is granted.

4. Q. CAN I USE "MENTAL CRUELTY" OR ADULTERY AS A GROUND FOR DIVORCE HERE?

 A. No. In East Carolina, the only ground for divorce that is ever used is separation for over one year. The other ground, three years' incurable insanity, is almost never used. Most divorces granted on separation grounds are uncontested. This is essentially a "no-fault" divorce, with no proof necessary as to who left whom or what reason was involved. If at least one of the parties has been a legal resident of East Carolina for six months preceding the filing of the divorce complaint and the separation was intended to be permanent, then the court can grant the divorce.

5. Q. IF MY MARRIAGE OCCURRED IN ANOTHER STATE, CAN I FILE FOR DIVORCE IN THIS STATE?

 A. Maybe, depending on whether you or your spouse fulfills the residency requirements of East Carolina law. Our laws state that you may file divorce here if you are a true legal resident of East Carolina and have been living here for at least six months prior to the date of filing the divorce complaint. If your spouse is a legal resident of East Carolina and resides here, you may also file for divorce.

6. Q. DO I HAVE TO HAVE A "LEGAL SEPARATION" TO GET A DIVORCE HERE, OR DO I HAVE TO "FILE FOR SEPARATION" IN EAST CAROLINA?

 A. All you need to do to obtain a divorce in East Carolina is live separate and apart from your spouse for *more than* one year with the intention that the separation be permanent. You will testify to this in divorce court. You do not need to show the judge a copy of a separation agreement, since such a document doesn't necessarily prove that you have indeed separated from your spouse. There is no such thing as "filing for separation" in East Carolina, although there are certain cases in which a judge approved separation, which allows you to live separate and apart from your partner.

7. Q. CAN THE JUDGE IN EAST CAROLINA ORDER A PROPERTY DIVISION AT THE TIME OF DIVORCE?

A. After the divorce has been granted, the judge can divide the marital property of the couple if the divorce decree reserves the authority of the court to decide equitable distribution. The court would not have the power to divide the marital property if neither party asked the court to do so before the divorce judgment was entered or if the parties had already executed a separation agreement that fairly divided their property. You can't get a court-ordered property division if you don't file a claim for equitable distribution before your divorce is granted.

8. Q. WHAT ABOUT ALIMONY? IS THAT COVERED WHEN I GET MY DIVORCE?

A. The same rules apply as in equitable distribution (see above). The claim must be filed with the court, in a complaint or counterclaim, in order to preserve it for a hearing after the divorce decree is signed by a judge. If you haven't asked for alimony in a court paper before you get your divorce and reserved that issue for later ruling of the court in the divorce decree, you *cannot get alimony*.

9. Q. WHO PAYS MY ATTORNEY'S FEES IN A DIVORCE CASE?

A. The law states that each party is expected to pay his or her attorney's fees in regard to obtaining an uncontested divorce.

10. Q. WHEN WILL I GET MY DIVORCE?

A. After the summons and complaint are served on your spouse, he or she has 30 days in which to file an answer. This is the *answer period*. One of the following will occur:

- The spouse will *default*, that is, he or she will file nothing within the following 30 days. In this case, we can set your divorce for a hearing after the expiration of the *answer period*.
- Your spouse will obtain an extension of time for answer. In this case, he or she will file a motion with the clerk to obtain another 30 days in which to answer. These motions are usually granted, and we are not even required to be notified before the motion is made. Thus it will be 60 days, not 30, for the *answer period*. When the answer is filed, we can then proceed to calendar your divorce hearing (so long as your spouse does not contest the divorce and admits all the facts that we allege in the complaint).
- Your spouse will answer the divorce complaint, either admitting all the allegations (in which case we can go ahead and schedule the divorce hearing) or denying at least one of the allegations (in which case we'll have to sit down and discuss our options).
- Your spouse will "speed up" the process by filing a document (with the help of his or her lawyer) that allows us to schedule your divorce hearing before the *answer period* expires. Note that we can't force anyone to do this. A spouse will only do it to get the divorce more quickly.

■■■

Name Changes

1. Q. I RECENTLY MARRIED A WOMAN WHO HAS A MINOR CHILD FROM A PREVIOUS MARRIAGE/RELATIONSHIP. CAN WE GET THE CHILD'S LAST NAME TO MY OWN?

A. This can be done if your wife and the biological father of the child consent to the name change. If the biological father does not consent, you'll need to file suit to terminate the biological father's parental rights. If the biological father's parental rights are terminated, the name change may proceed. If there has not yet been a judicial termination of the biological father's parental rights and the minor child has reached the age of 16, the name change may proceed if:

1. The biological mother consents;
2. The mother has custody of the child and has supported the child; and
3. The clerk of court is satisfied that the bio-father has abandoned the child.

2. Q. I RECENTLY MARRIED A WOMAN WITH A CHILD FROM A PREVIOUS MARRIAGE/RELATIONSHIP. SINCE I AM ADOPTING THE CHILD, WITH CONSENT OF MY WIFE AND THE BIOLOGICAL FATHER, CAN I CHANGE THE CHILD'S LAST NAME TO MY OWN?

A. Yes. Simply let the attorney who is handling the adoption paperwork know. There is an entry on the adoption petition which allows you to request that the child's name be changed.

3. Q. BEFORE MY WIFE AND I GOT MARRIED WE HAD A CHILD. SINCE WE WERE NOT MARRIED AT THE TIME OF THE CHILD'S BIRTH, THE CHILD HAS MY WIFE'S MAIDEN NAME. CAN WE HAVE THE LAST NAME CHANGED?

A. If both you and your wife consent, this can be done by the Clerk of Superior Court. Since both biological parents consent, it is not necessary to go to court in order to make a showing of abandonment or to terminate parental rights. All you need to do is file a petition to legitimate the child and request in the position that the child's name be changed.

4. Q. I WANT TO CHANGE MY OWN NAME. HOW DO I GO ABOUT THIS?

A. You first must be able to supply the names of two citizens of your county who can provide affidavits attesting to your good character. These people should have both resided in the county (which will include paying taxes in the county) and have known you for at least one year.

5. Q. MY WIFE AND I ARE GETTING DIVORCED. CAN LEGAL ASSISTANCE HELP WITH THIS?

A. Yes. It is fairly common for a woman to request the resumption of her maiden name when she gets divorced. Here are the rules to follow:

- If he is the plaintiff, the party filing for divorce, then she can request it in her complaint.
- If you are filing and she is the defendant, she can respond to your complaint by filing an answer and counterclaim requesting the resumption of her maiden name.
- The judgment of divorce signed by the judge will state that she is allowed to resume the use of her maiden name.

- After the affidavits are signed (in front of a notary public), then a petition for name change is prepared; this states the current name you have, the one you propose to adopt, and the reason(s) that you want to use the new name.
- After this, a notice must be posted at the courthouse of the county where you live and remain there for at least 10 days. Then the petition is filed with the clerk, along with the affidavits. A certificate of name change is signed by the clerk.

■■■

Understanding Your Divorce:

Spotlighting the People, the Processes,

and the Possibilities

Studies have shown that for many people, separation and divorce rank second only to the death of a loved one in terms of emotional turmoil, pain, and stress. Not only are separation and divorce accompanied by feelings of guilt, rejection, embarrassment, and anger, but the legal process also triggers feelings of fear and uncertainty. Reserves of inner strength are often as necessary as the financial resources required to get through it intact.

The first step to conquering fear of the unknown is to learn as much as possible about the process. A good lawyer can clarify the legal procedures, help in establishing your goals, and propose a positive strategy to achieve realistic results.

Shown below are some common questions and answers about the separation or divorce process. If you have any additional questions after reading these explanations, don't hesitate to ask your lawyer for more information.

1. Q. WHAT ISSUES ARE INVOLVED IN A DIVORCE?
   A. The breakup of a marriage often involves five issues: property division, alimony, child support, custody/visitation, and divorce. Each of these can be resolved by consent (a negotiated settlement) or contested in court. Let's take a close look at how the process works.

   At the outset, it is important to note that not all states handle divorce in the same way. In some states, such as New York and Wisconsin, divorce is a "package deal." All issues must be resolved by the parties (through agreement) or by the court (through trial) before the divorce is granted. "My wife/husband won't give me a divorce" is sometimes heard in these jurisdictions, because the only alternative to a long, messy, and expensive trial is a settlement driven or guided by the other party. *Divorce* is the end result of the process. When you get your divorce, everything else is already in place. The other issues in the case are raised by law or court rule, and all issues are presented to the court for a decision when one party files for a divorce.

   In other states, such as Delaware and North Carolina, a divorce case is not necessarily joined with other issues. These other issues may be presented to the court before or after the lawsuit for divorce is filed. Custody may be contested or settled in a different lawsuit or joined in the divorce suit. The same applies to child support, alimony (also called maintenance or spousal support), and property division (or equitable distribution).

   In these states, divorce is not necessarily the *end* of the case; it may be the *beginning*. Parties also may resolve other issues through court decision or agreements. Each of these issues can be heard by the court on different timetables, before or after the divorce. Understanding the type of state where your divorce is filed, the timetables, and the deadlines is the first step for the newcomer.

2. Q. WHERE DO I START?

A. Getting the right lawyer is often the first step. Whether the attorney you select has represented you previously or has been recommended by a friend, relative, or bar association lawyer referral service, the important thing is that you communicate well with each other and that you have confidence in his or her ability to handle your case.

You may want to consider hiring a lawyer who specializes in your particular kind of case. Many states allow lawyers to become specialists and list themselves as such if they meet certain qualifications.

What you say to your lawyer is "privileged information." Generally speaking, this means that what you tell your attorney must be held in confidence unless you give permission otherwise. In addition, your attorney has the duty to: (1) allow you to make the major decisions in your case, such as pleading guilty in a criminal case or accepting a compromise or settlement in a civil case; and (2) remain open and honest with you in all aspects of your case, including your chances of success, the positives and negatives of your position, and the time and fee required.

3. Q. HOW MUCH WILL ALL OF THIS COST?

A. Lawyers set fees in a number of ways. The two major types of fees in domestic cases are flat-rate and hourly billing. Thus, many lawyers may use a flat-rate or set fee in uncontested divorces, adoptions, and name-change cases. A flat fee generally is paid in advance and does not vary depending on the time or work involved. No refund is due if the work takes less time than expected, and no additional charges are incurred if the case is longer or more complex.

An hourly rate is most common when the client's work will be substantial, but difficult to estimate. Thus, for example, a lawyer might charge an hourly rate in a contested custody or alimony case. It is fairly common for the lawyer to require part of the fee to be paid in advance, or "up front." This "retainer" is a deposit or down payment to make sure that the client is serious about the case and is financially prepared to cover all costs. The size of the retainer and whether any part of it is refundable will vary from case to case and lawyer to lawyer.

In certain cases, the court may order one party to pay some or all of the other's legal expenses. For example, the court usually can make such an award in cases involving alimony, child support, custody, and paternity. Remember, however, that the award of attorney's fees in such cases is not mandatory or automatic. Such an award depends on a variety of factors, such as good faith, need, lack of adequate support, and so on. The courts see these awards as a way to pay back or reimburse for attorney's fees already paid or presently due. A client will have difficulty retaining a good attorney based on the promise or hope of court-awarded fees. This is especially true because court-ordered fees are not always paid, and additional legal work may be required to secure them.

4. Q. HOW CAN I SELECT A LAWYER WHO HAS ENOUGH EXPERTISE TO HELP ME?

A. Find out from the state bar or bar association if there are "certified specialists" in family law in your state. A majority of states have "specialty" designations for lawyers who concentrate their practices in a particular field, and these lawyers (although charging a premium for their services) will be more likely to be able to handle your case competently than a general practitioner.

You can now use the Internet for referrals using your computer and a modem. To connect to the *Attorney Referral Network Internet Index of Legal Professionals with Websites*, type on your browser http://www.attorney referral.net. Select the state in which you need to find an attorney.

For the *American Bar Association*, use http://www.martindale.com/xp/Martindale/home.xml, and then enter the required information needed, which includes location of desired attorney and type of practice. After entering the information, press "Search" and the information is sent to the database.

Martindale-Hubbell has to be the most popular Internet attorney referral source available. Go to http://www.lawyers.com/ on the Internet browser. After the web page appears, click on SEARCH. When the next page is loaded, enter the information needed and click Enter.

West Legal Directory is also a popular tool. Enter http://lawyers.findlaw.com/, and then enter the information and click on "Go." You can enter the information by *lawyer's name and location* or by *firm and location*.

For help with tough or complex family law problems, take a look at the membership directory of the American Academy of Matrimonial Lawyers at http://www.aaml.org/Directory.htm.

Try the ABA's on-line list of local lawyer referral programs, many of which have family law panels and modest means panels. It's a great way to tap into local lawyer referral networks. Check out the site, which is open to all, at http://www.abanet.org/legalservices/lris/directory.html.

5. Q. **WHAT QUESTIONS SHOULD I ASK THE LAWYER?**
   A. You should ask him or her some background questions to get an idea of whether you'll be getting the knowledge and experience you need for your particular case. Some cases might require a "brain surgeon" for an attorney, while others would not. The client should ask the attorney about his/her experience in the specific area which is involved in the client's case. Here are some examples:

- How long have you been practicing law?
- How long have you been practicing family law?
- Is your practice exclusively family law?
- Which bar association family law sections do you belong to?
- What offices have you held in those organizations?
- Are you board-certified in family law? How long have you been certified?
- Are you a member of the American Bar Association's Family Law Section?
- Are you a Fellow of the American Academy of Matrimonial Lawyers? Since when? Have you held any offices in the North Carolina Chapter?
- What articles have you published, or manuscripts have you presented, in the area of family law? Can I have a copy of those written in the last __ years?

- Are you on any local or statewide boards or committees dealing with family law?
- Have you ever gone up against Lawyer X (opposing attorney) in a trial? What results?
- Tell me about your participation in alternative dispute resolution (arbitration/mediation).
- Are you certified as a mediator? As a family law arbitrator?
- How do you use associates and paralegals to hold down clients' bills and expand your ability to work on cases?
- What client handouts do you have that will help me understand my case and how you can help me with it?

6. Q. HOW CAN I MAKE SURE THAT MY LAWYER IS DOING WHAT I WANT?

A. To ensure that your lawyer understands what you want, ask specifically (1) what will be done in your case, and (2) how much it will cost. If you want these answers included in a written contract between you and your lawyer, ask for one. Then read it before you sign it.

You should also ask for an estimate of the total charges and a list of services covered in the estimate. Inquire about what steps your attorney expects to take and how much time (or expense) they might involve. An experienced lawyer should be able to outline the process for you with a fair degree of accuracy. Although many cases are resolved as standard "uncontested divorces" with no alimony, property, or child-related issues, many others are completely unpredictable. Don't expect a specific dollar amount to be quoted as "the entire fee" in anything but a standard uncontested divorce. In fact, be wary of an attorney who promises to handle your case for a fixed sum, since it is impossible to tell what will occur in all but the most routine, uncontested divorce case—one involving no issues of alimony, property division, custody, or child support; no problems serving divorce papers on the other party; and two parties who want the divorce.

The rules of most state bars require lawyers to communicate regularly with clients and to provide periodic case updates. If this is important to you, ask your lawyer to keep you current and provide copies of the "pleadings"—motions, complaints, counterclaims, petitions—that have been filed in your case, any order or judgment signed by the judge, as well as letters or e-mails exchanged between the lawyers. At the conclusion of your case or upon his or her withdrawal, your lawyer should release your file to you upon request and with reasonable notice.

When you first meet with your lawyer, review the important facts of your case and outline your goals. Although we all have hopes, desires, and dreams, it is vital to keep goals realistic and achievable; don't expect your case to go anywhere if your goals are to embarrass or financially break the other side.

Your lawyer has a duty to be candid with you and explain the pros and cons, the strengths and weaknesses of your case. Do not tolerate failure to return telephone calls; nothing makes a client angrier—and justifiably so—than a lawyer who won't respond to a request for information. Also be careful not to get into a personality conflict with the other side (client or counsel), since your money will be wasted on an unproductive "spitting contest." Armed with the facts, you can then consider your finances and decide "how much case you can afford."

7. **Q. WHAT IS INVOLVED IN "GOING TO COURT?"**
   A. If you must litigate, you need to know something about the process. You can't play ball if you do not know the rules. Litigation always starts with the filing of a complaint or petition along with a summons. The petition states the facts of the case and what relief is requested. The summons specifies that the other side has been sued and has a certain period in which to respond. The other side usually files an answer following the service of these papers.

   Depending on state or local rules, additional documents may have to be filed by the spouses. They include financial affidavits or declarations stating the incomes and expenses of each party, or property inventories showing what each party claims to be marital or separate property and debt, as well as the value claimed for each item. Sometimes courts also require parties to file a copy of tax returns, pay stubs, or other financial documents.

   Contested divorce cases can take a long time to resolve. While the entire case is pending, temporary, interim, or emergency hearings may be requested. For example, a party may ask for an emergency ruling on issues of custody or visitation, especially when the parents are engaged in a "tug of war" or the children are in serious danger. Courts often consider the need for interim spousal support or child support at a temporary hearing in the weeks or months after a case is filed. This is done to protect the financially disadvantaged spouse during the divorce process. Some courts use the time after filing to conduct a hearing on *interim allocation*, which means a temporary division or distribution of marital assets pending the final hearing. This also can be useful in providing each party with sufficient means to pay the lawyers, psychologists, or accountants required to assist in resolving the case or preparing for trial.

8. **Q. I THINK MY HUSBAND IS HIDING INFORMATION, BUT HOW CAN I BE SURE?**
   A. You might find the answer in the "discovery" stage of litigation. Discovery means "finding out information that the other side has." Many state court rules allocate to discovery the first 90–120 days after the lawsuit has been filed. Even more time is allowed in complex cases. This is probably the most important part of trial preparation—finding out what the case is all about from the other side's perspective.

   "Informal discovery" usually means obtaining information from the other side without formal notices or requests. This can be done surreptitiously by making a copy of a spouse's bank statement and then returning the original to the home file. It can also involve getting copies of your joint bank statements or financial statements from the bank, your joint tax return from the tax accountant or IRS, or your joint deed and real estate closing statement from the attorney who closed your home loan. These are quick and inexpensive ways to get the documents your attorney needs.

   Likewise, an attorney can request certain papers, receipts, titles, or deeds from the other side. If the adversaries are friendly and the marital dispute is under control (which often depends on the personalities of the attorneys and the level of animosity between the parties), it is possible to save hundreds or even thousands of dollars by agreeing on a "discovery plan." This allows each party to request in writing relevant documents, within reason, from the other side. Although no penalties or sanctions are incurred for failure to produce or reply (as is the case with formal discovery), considerable time and money can be saved if the parties and their lawyers are willing to cooperate.

Formal or traditional discovery, on the other hand, has structures, deadlines, definitions, and rules that must be obeyed. Here are some examples:

- *Interrogatories* are written questions that are sent by mail to opposing counsel. They must be answered by the opposing party under oath within a certain number of days (usually around 30).
- *Document requests* require the other side to produce documents at a specified place and time for inspection and photocopying.
- A *request for entry upon land* can be used to get into the office or home of the other party to inspect, inventory, and photograph (or videotape) what's there.
- A *deposition* is oral testimony given under oath in front of a court reporter. Generally, the deposition is taken in a lawyer's office and no judge is present. It results in a typed transcript of the testimony, and it can be very useful in exploring what facts or data the other side has, what accusations will be made, and how the other side is thinking about the case. Although generally more expensive than interrogatories, a deposition tends to generate more complete and spontaneous responses. Also, a deposition allows a lawyer to ask "follow-up questions."

9. **Q.** **WHAT WILL HAPPEN IF WE END UP IN COURT?**
   A. Going to trial doesn't just happen. It is the end to a long process that includes meeting with your attorney (rehearsing for the hearing, getting an overview of questions that *will* be asked and that *may* be asked, and reviewing documents that will be introduced as evidence), preparing witnesses and exhibits for introduction, and setting the case on the court's calendar for weeks or even months in the future. Lawyers frequently prepare written briefs that summarize and explain points of law that may be at issue in the case. Sometimes there is a pretrial conference with the judge to organize the case and focus the issues.

   On the day of trial, the judge will usually "call the calendar," which means announcing the names of the cases for that day. Yes, there are *other* people getting a divorce, and yes, they also have *their cases* set on *your day!* It is the job of the judge to figure out which ones can be tried that day and which ones must be rescheduled or "continued." If a continuance is not ordered, your case will be tried. The trial usually consists of several sections:

   - *The plaintiff's (or petitioner's) case* involves his or her testimony, immediately followed by opposing counsel's cross-examination. At this point, the plaintiff's exhibits and documents often are introduced. Then the witnesses for the plaintiff testify and are cross-examined by the other side. Likewise, they may offer documents into evidence.

- *The defendant (or respondent)* has the same opportunity—to give testimony, present evidence, and offer witnesses. Likewise, the plaintiff's attorney may cross-examine.
- *The attorneys* usually do opening and closing statements, or arguments, for their clients.

Most divorce or domestic relations cases are heard by a judge, although occasionally state law allows them to be tried before a jury.

After both sides present their case, each is given the opportunity for rebuttal, which is testimony that denies or contradicts what the other side has presented. The lawyers will have the opportunity for final argument or "closing statement," in which they summarize their evidence and argue for the results they seek.

Then comes the court's decision. This may follow closing statements, or it may come days or weeks after the trial has concluded if the judge takes the case "under advisement."

Once the decision has been made, it is noted in the court record and announced (formally in court or sometimes informally by telephone conference). If the parties do not attend the decision conference, they will be notified by their respective attorneys.

Entry of the order, judgment, or decree is the next stage. Sometimes this is done by the court, but more often than not the attorneys write up a decision for the judge to sign. This often requires meeting together or with the judge while they are preparing *findings of fact* for the judge on contested issues. This process can take days, weeks, or even months in a complex or strongly contested case.

10. **Q. Isn't there any alternative to a long trial?**
    A. Yes. There are several other options worth considering: mediation, collaborative law, arbitration, coaching, and negotiation. If handled correctly, these options generally are less expensive and less time-consuming than a trial. However, these options require that both parties be willing to give a little to get a little. Oftentimes these options will not be available if there has been domestic violence.

    Arbitration is a process by which a neutral third party renders a binding decision on the issue or issues presented—alimony, pension division, child support, etc. The arbitrator acts in much the same fashion as a judge in a civil trial. He or she usually is paid by the parties (in equal shares or not), and the proceedings usually are faster and less formal than a trial. The arbitrator's job is not to choose sides but to listen to the facts of the case and render a decision.

    Mediation is informal dispute resolution in which a neutral third party, a trained mediator, helps you and your spouse reach an agreement. The mediator's role is to assist the parties in resolving their conflicts. Choosing sides or giving legal advice is not a mediator's role. The mediator does not make decisions, but rather encourages both parties to work together to make mutual decisions. Mediation is an increasingly popular option and generally cheaper than a trial. Sometimes a free or inexpensive court-sponsored mediation program is available for part or all of a case.

Every state has its own requirements for mediation. In some states or counties it is optional; in others the court may require it. Independent of the courts, the parties can hire a mediator to conduct a settlement conference if they are willing to share the cost.

A NEGOTIATED SETTLEMENT can be a productive way to settle the parties' dispute. In this scenario, both parties and their lawyers attempt to resolve all or some issues in the case. Taking some of the issues off the table will likely make the trial shorter and the process less expensive and less stressful. It is also a good way to bargain through the items on the table and see if there is room for negotiation.

COLLABORATIVE LAW means agreeing to negotiate a settlement without going to court at all. The parties agree to cooperate fully in the settlement negotiation process and to provide freely and promptly any documents or information requested. The attorneys help to facilitate the negotiations and draft the settlement document, but they cannot go to court; they are dismissed and new counsel hired if litigation is desired by either party.

Coaching involves hiring an attorney to advise you on how to handle your own case without a lawyer. When a case is simple and straightforward, this can save you money while teaching you how to present your case to the judge on your own. If your case is a simple, uncontested divorce without other issues, this could be effective. It could also be useful if your ex-spouse has charged you with missing a child support payment but you have a legal excuse, or if you want to defend yourself on a simple visitation dispute. It is *not* a good idea for complex cases.

Mediation, collaborative law, and negotiation are give-and-take situations. Nothing can be demanded, and usually a good deal of compromise is necessary. It is important to examine exactly what you want to happen in your case and to be aware of your "bottom line." Fair negotiations and an open mind are essential to the success of these alternate resolutions. Bringing your anger over past events into the ring will ensure the failure of any settlement offers.

When will these alternatives work? They work best when both parties are willing to work together to reach an amicable settlement that is in the best interest of all concerned. When are these three options to trial not a good idea? They are less likely to be successful if a case involves physical abuse, substance abuse, persistent anger or passivity, mental health problems for one or both spouses (such as severe depression), or if one spouse wants to use the legal process for "revenge" or to "punish" the other spouse. In these situations, attempting to reach agreement may be a waste of time and money for both parties. During the initial consult with your lawyer, you should discuss all of your options and what may or may not work for your case.

■ ■ ■

For Unmarried Couples

1. Q. WHAT IS THE LEGAL AGE FOR MARRIAGE IN NORTH CAROLINA?
 A. While laws in different states vary, the law in North Carolina requires generally that the parties be at least 18 years of age.

2. Q. WHEN IS CONSENT OF A PARENT NECESSARY?
 A. A couple may marry if one or both are between ages 16 and 18 with parental consent.

3. Q. DOES NORTH CAROLINA RECOGNIZE COMMON-LAW MARRIAGE?
 A. Common-law marriage, which is recognized in some states, involves a couple living together and holding themselves out to everyone as man and wife. Even though there is no marriage ceremony or certificate, this marriage is considered valid in those states that recognize common-law marriage. North Carolina is not one of those states, and no amount of living together in this state can result in a valid marriage without a valid marriage ceremony.

4. Q. OTHER THAN AGE, WHAT DOES THE LAW REQUIRE FOR MARRIAGE IN NORTH CAROLINA?
 A. First, the parties must both be unmarried and no closer than first cousins to each other. Next, they must obtain a marriage license from the Register of Deeds in the county where the marriage is to take place. There is no waiting period and the license is good for 60 days after it is issued.

5. Q. ARE THERE ANY MEDICAL REQUIREMENTS FOR A MARRIAGE LICENSE?
 A. Prior to October 1, 1994, the man and woman needed a doctor's certificate showing that they were mentally competent and free from venereal disease and infectious tuberculosis. Further information is available about these certificates from the Register of Deeds at the county courthouse. After October 1, 1994, health certificates for the issuance of marriage licenses were no longer required.

■■■

Your Divorce Hearing

We believe in *"client preparation"*—telling our clients what to expect in court makes them more comfortable and lets us do a better job. This is the best way to ensure a good outcome for them.

Although there is seldom anything unusual or unexpected in an uncontested divorce case, it must be remembered that many people never go to court in their entire lives. Clients want to "do right" in court but may be nervous or upset on the day of the hearing. A good lawyer takes the time for a "trial run," and that is what we are doing in this handout. Once you have finished reading this, we feel you will have a better idea of how your divorce hearing will proceed.

Summary Judgment Divorces

The first item will be our calendaring of your divorce case for a hearing. No oral testimony is required if we decide to do your divorce by *summary judgment*, which means the filing of a motion on your behalf stating that the divorce is uncontested. If the other party does not contest this motion, then the divorce is granted without your being there to testify. Please ask us about this procedure if you are interested in divorce by summary judgment. The rest of this information letter applies to divorce cases not done by summary judgment.

Hearing and Oral Testimony

If your spouse has filed an *Answer* or *Waiver of Answer* to your *Complaint*, we can then set the hearing on the calendar for court, so long as the divorce is indeed uncontested (i.e., your spouse has not *denied* any of the allegations in the Complaint). We can also set it on the calendar if your spouse has been properly served and has failed to file anything in the 30 days following service.

Uncontested divorce cases are currently set in Courtroom 9-B, Wake County Courthouse, Raleigh, at 10:00 a.m. every Friday. Be sure to dress *appropriately* for your court appearance. You should plan to arrive at the Courthouse by 9:30 a.m. Go directly to Courtroom 9-B.

We make every effort to be on time for our court appearances. If, however, we are not present when the judge calls your case, please answer by saying that your attorney is on the way—we sometimes are "running late" due to conflicts in other courts, last-minute emergencies, telephone calls, children, flat tires, or a host of other reasons. We will do our best to avoid any delay in your case, but please be patient if this occurs.

The Case is Called

When your case is called, we will ask you to "come around," or approach the tables in front of the judge's bench. When you "come around," you will be asked to place your left hand on the Bible and raise your right hand. Then you will be sworn to tell the truth by the clerk (unless you wish to be affirmed instead of taking an oath).

Next you will take the witness stand, which is actually a chair next to the judge's. Take your seat *and relax.*

Your lawyer will inform the judge as to certain preliminaries—the grounds for divorce, the method of serving your spouse, and so on. We will also hand the judge several copies of the divorce judgment that we have prepared.

Questions Asked

We will then begin questioning you to get the testimony needed to establish the grounds for your divorce. As you will observe in other cases that may be called before yours, there are many different questions that may be asked of a client in divorce court.

We believe in asking only—

A. *"Leading" questions*—those which *tell you the answer in advance, such as* "Your name is Pat Brown and you're the plaintiff in this case, right?"

B. *Necessary questions*—you may hear the other attorney asking irrelevant or unnecessary questions ("When were you married? Where? What is your address?"), but we will not do so. The *minimum necessary questions* for an uncontested divorce may vary, but here is an example:

1. "Your name is Pat Brown and you are the plaintiff in this case, right?" *"Yes."*

2. "You are presently married to the defendant and both of you have been citizens and residents of Wake County, North Carolina, for at least six months before you filed this divorce complaint, is that correct?" *"That's right."*

3. "You separated from each other more than a year before the filing of this case and you have continued to live separate and apart since that time?" *"Yes."*

4. "At the time of separation, it was intended to be permanent, right?" *"Yes."*

5. "There are no minor children born of the marriage?" *"Correct."*

OR

6. "The names and ages of the minor children born of the marriage are: Tina Brown, age 10; and Calvin Brown, age 5. Right?" *"Yes."*

When a woman requests the right to resume the use of her maiden name in the Complaint, we will also ask about that in our questions.

When you are answering these questions, please sit forward in the chair and speak clearly into the microphone in front of you. After you have finished answering, the attorney will usually say "No further questions," or "Any questions by the court?" This indicates that our questions are over. You may leave the witness stand and resume your seat in the courtroom when your attorney says, "Please come down from the stand."

After the Questions

While you are leaving the witness stand, the judge is signing the copies of the divorce judgment. Your divorce, of course, is final upon signing by the judge and filing in the Clerk's Office. There is no waiting period afterward.

Your attorney will next approach the clerk to make sure she has all the paperwork in your case. This usually means that she wants the statistical information sheet that our office prepared for you, containing the date and place of marriage, date of separation, and number of minor children. When this is done, we will leave the courtroom and go to the Office of the Clerk of Superior Court on the eleventh floor.

At the Clerk's office, we will file your divorce judgment and get a *certified copy* from the Clerk, so you can use it whenever an official copy is needed, such as for government records or insurance. This is the final step in obtaining your divorce judgment.

Please let us know if you have any questions, comments or suggestions on this information letter.

■■■

Section 7

Property Division

Divorce and Equitable Distribution

East Carolina

1. Q. Do I have to show "fault" to get a divorce in East Carolina?
   A. No. In East Carolina, divorce is "no fault." That means that to get a divorce, you only have to show that you have been living apart from your spouse for over one year and that at least one of you intended that separation to be permanent. No proof is necessary as to who left whom or why. Most divorces granted on the grounds of one year's separation are uncontested.

2. Q. If I just move here from another state, can I file for divorce in this state?
   A. East Carolina law states that you may file for divorce here if you have been living in East Carolina for at least six months prior to the date of filing. You cannot file before then, even if you've been separated for over a year.

3. Q. Do I have to have a "legal separation" to get a divorce here if I have been living in East Carolina?
   A. All you need to do to obtain a divorce in East Carolina is live separate and apart for at least one year and a day, with the intention that the separation be permanent. You do not need to show the judge a copy of a separation agreement, since such a document doesn't necessarily prove that you have indeed separated from your spouse. There is no such thing as "filing for separation" in East Carolina, although there are certain cases in which a judge can grant a "divorce from bed and board," or judge-approved separation, which allows you to live separate and apart from your partner.

4. Q. What if my spouse won't give me a divorce?
   A. The judge is the person who grants a divorce, not your spouse. Once you have filed the divorce complaint at the courthouse, your attorney will serve a copy of the summons and complaint on your spouse, by sheriff or by certified mail. If no answer is filed within 30 days after service, you will probably be granted a divorce after a hearing. Your spouse can only contest the divorce action by filing an answer denying one or more of the statements in your complaint. If that happens, a hearing will be set during which the two of you can testify and the judge can decide what the truth is.

5. Q. Can I get my own divorce without an attorney?
   A. Yes. You can prepare your own summons, complaint, and judgment and go through the steps of filing for divorce and scheduling a hearing. The Wake County Clerk of Court has a "Divorce Kit" which can be purchased for a minimal fee and has sample forms you can use. However, although it is not required that you hire a private attorney, there are many errors and mistakes that can be avoided if you retain an attorney to represent you, especially if you haven't reached a property settlement with your spouse or if you have a claim for alimony. Your claim for alimony or property division will be lost if it's not filed before your divorce is granted.

6. **Q. WHO PAYS FOR MY LAWYER?**
   A. As a general rule, you must retain and pay for your own attorney in a divorce case. There are exceptions, but these are usually in cases involving alimony, custody, or child support, and *not* property division or divorce.

7. **Q. IS MY DIVORCE FINAL WHEN THE JUDGE SIGNS THE JUDGMENT?**
   A. Yes. You are then legally divorced. There is no waiting period after entry of judgment.

8. **Q. CAN I RESUME THE USE OF MY MAIDEN NAME AT THE TIME OF DIVORCE?**
   A. Yes. You may ask for the right to resume your maiden name in the divorce papers your lawyer files for you. This is routinely granted by the judge. Even if you do not ask for your maiden name back at the time of the divorce, you can file for resumption of your maiden name after the divorce is granted.

9. **Q. CAN THE JUDGE IN EAST CAROLINA ORDER A PROPERTY DIVISION AT THE TIME OF DIVORCE?**
   A. The property division is usually done in a separate hearing and not at the divorce hearing. So long as a claim is raised before the divorce judgment is entered, the judge can divide the marital property of the couple either before or after the divorce hearing. The court would not have the power to divide the marital property if neither party asked the court to do so before the divorce judgment was entered or if the parties had already executed a separation agreement that fairly divided their property.

10. **Q. IS THERE SOME PROPERTY THAT THE JUDGE CANNOT DIVIDE?**
    A. The judge in East Carolina cannot divide "separate property," and there are several kinds of separate property. Property acquired by either party before the marriage cannot be divided by the judge. Property acquired by either party by gift or by inheritance is separate property, even if it is later traded or exchanged for another item. Business and professional licenses are also separate property if they cannot be transferred to another individual. For more on pensions and retirement rights, see our client information letter on that subject.

11. **Q. HOW WILL THE JUDGE DIVIDE OUR PROPERTY?**
    A. There is a presumption in East Carolina law that the fairest split would be an equal division of all the marital property, regardless of who has title to the property, who paid for it, and so on. Under certain circumstances, however, the judge might decide that a 50–50 split is not fair to one or both of the parties. The statute has a list of factors that the judge may then use to determine if an unequal division of property between the couple is appropriate. The judge will consider such matters as monetary and homemaker contributions to the marriage by each party, tax consequences of unequal division, whether alimony or child support is presently being paid, source of the property and who purchased it, and so on. Marital fault, such as adultery or abandonment, is not a factor in equitable distribution.

■■■

Your Spouse's "Hidden" Assets Checklist
[adapted from article by Leonard Karp, Tucson, AZ]

In helping you to prepare for your property division settlement or trial, we try not to overlook anything. Please take a moment to help us complete this list of "hidden" assets (or easily overlooked ones) so that we don't miss anything.

✔	Type of Asset	Location of Documents	Notes/Comments
	Frequent flyer mileage		
	Security deposits (e.g., utilities, car lease)		
	Timeshare property		
	Leased vehicles, cell phone, other items		
	Stock options		
	Memberships (e.g., country club)		
	Bond or deposit for country club		
	Unused vacation, sick leave		

✔	Type of Asset	Location of Documents	Notes/Comments
	Patents, copyrights, royalties		
	Income tax refunds		
	Income tax capital loss carry-forwards		
	Income tax charitable contributions carry-forwards		
	Marketable government licenses (radio licenses, commercial fishing quotas)		
	Special retirement benefits ("golden parachutes")		
	Retirement— life insurance benefits		
	Retirement— medical benefits		
	Retirement— survivor benefits		
	Hobby or other collections		

✔	Type of Asset	Location of Documents	Notes/Comments
	Contract rights from marital employment (e.g., insurance renewal payments for agent)		
	Affiliation "rewards" programs (e.g., points or discounts for credit card use)		
	Entertainment tickets, season ticket options		
	Business vehicle for personal use		
	Prepaid rent, leases, subscriptions		
	Burial plots		
	Life insurance cash surrender value (or perhaps death benefit if insured is elderly)		
	Tort, worker's comp claims		
	Stock options		
	Hangar lease (for aircraft)		

✔	Type of Asset	Location of Documents	Notes/Comments
	Hotel or credit card points		
	Cash		
	Small business retained earnings		
	U.S. Savings Bonds, other securities		
	"Hidden value" items—rare items of personal property (e.g., antiques), rare pets, collectibles		
	Options to purchase property		
	Unpaid commissions on deals set to close		
	Referral fees (e.g., for personal injury lawyers)		
	Security or performance bonds posted		
	Car insurance prepaid		
	Taxes prepaid		

■■■

Marital Assets and Finances

Preface

The equitable distribution of marital property is a *no fault* claim. It is essential that all marital assets and liabilities be discovered and evaluated. A list of information and documents to be gathered follows, although it is by no means complete. Rather, it is a point of beginning, and lists documents that are common to many domestic cases. It is intended to be supplemented to obtain additional items that are unique to your particular case.

While *separately-owned* assets and liabilities are not subject to division, it is important to know what they are, and their values, as they may influence how the court divides the marital assets and liabilities.

The values of assets acquired during the marriage should be determined (a) at date of separation, and (b) at present.

The values of separate assets should be determined (a) at date of marriage; (b) at date of separation; and (c) at present.

The following information will help us determine how your marital property may be equitably distributed by the courts or how we might best craft an agreement to divide the marital property on your behalf.

1. **TAX RETURNS.** State, federal, and intangible returns for the previous five years, including all schedules and other attachments to such returns, including, but not limited to, W-2, 1099, and K-1 forms.

2. **FINANCIAL STATEMENTS.** Copies of all financial or net worth statements prepared by you or for you or your spouse in the last five years. List all banks and other institutions (and individuals) to which you have supplied financial statements within the past five years.

3. **RETIREMENT PLANS.** If you are a participant in any profit-sharing, pension, stock purchase, or retirement plan (including any KEOGH or 401(k) plan), copies of all printouts or statements provided to you in the past three years. (Contact the bookkeeper, plan administrator, or person responsible for the maintenance of the plan for copies of the summary plan description, a statement of your current interest in such plan, and its value. You are entitled to this information from your employer upon request.)

4. **RETIREMENT ACCOUNTS.** Verification of any Individual Retirement Accounts (IRAs) which you or your spouse own. Identify the institution where the accounts are maintained and provide the account numbers, names of beneficiaries, and a statement of the balance in each account at separation and at present.

5. **REAL ESTATE.** If you or your spouse have an interest in any real estate (whether marital or separate), provide the address of each parcel and a copy of the deed, notes, deeds of trust, and last paid tax bill for each parcel. This information must include a legal description for each parcel of real estate for use in pertinent legal documents.

    If any real estate or personal property you own (including any owned wholly or in part by any corporation, partnership, or proprietorship in which you have a substantial interest) has been appraised for any reason within the past five years, provide copies of those appraisals.

6. LIFE INSURANCE. The name of each insurance company, the face amount of the policy, a description of the policy (whether whole life, universal life, or term), the policy number, the owner of the policy, the beneficiary, its cash or other value at separation and at present, the annual premium, the terms and conditions of the policy, and the amount and terms of any loans outstanding against it.

7. MEDICAL INSURANCE. The company name, address, policy or group number, and subscriber number of all health, medical, and dental insurance that is maintained for your benefit or for the benefit of any family member. This information is to include a statement detailing coverage for your spouse and children (to include stepchildren) and policy provisions relating to conversion after separation and divorce.

8. OTHER INSURANCE. Copies of all insurance policies which you presently maintain, or which cover property you own, or in which you have a substantial interest, including homeowners, automobile, personal property, and umbrella policies, together with all schedules and riders.

9. BANK ACCOUNTS. Copies of all canceled checks, bank statements, and registers for all checking accounts to which you are a signatory for the last three years, together with records verifying deposits to and withdrawals from any other account at any other bank or financial institution for the last three years.

10. SECURITIES. A list of the stocks or bonds owned, the date of purchase, the purchase price, the current owner, the value at separation, and the present value. Also furnish copies of statements received from any brokerage firm within the past 12 months.

11. BUSINESS INTEREST. If you or your spouse have an interest in any business entity, furnish copies of partnership or corporate state and federal tax returns and all schedules, together with copies of balance sheets and profit-and-loss statements for the past five years.

12. ESTATE OR TRUST INTEREST. Statements providing verification of any interest which you or your spouse has in any trust, estate, inheritance, or other interest which you believe may become your property in the future. If such is the case, furnish a copy of any will, inventory, final accounting, or judgment describing or affecting that interest. If you have an interest in any trust, provide a copy of the trust agreement, the inventory, the most recent annual accounting, and tax returns for the past five years, if any.

13. WRITTEN AGREEMENT. If you or your spouse have entered into any written agreement addressing support, property, or which imposes obligations upon you or confers benefits upon you, provide copies of same.

14. SAFETY DEPOSIT BOX. If you or your spouse have access to a safety deposit box, furnish the location, box number, length of time you have had access to it, and a list of everything the box has contained at any time during the past five years.

15. **LIST OF CREDITORS.** A list of your creditors not covered above, including the name and address of each creditor, the purpose of the debt, the balance at separation, its present balance, the monthly payment, a statement as to what portion of the obligation you consider to be your individual debt, and what portion you consider to be a joint obligation with your spouse.

16. **SALARY AND OTHER INCOME.** Your present annual salary, your pay period, the gross amount you receive for each pay period, and the itemized deductions from the periodic check.

17. **BONUS AND COMMISSION ARRANGEMENTS.** Verification of bonuses and commissions paid by your employer or company, and if you have an employment contract, provide a copy of same. Specify the amount of bonuses or commission for the following 12 months (to include the manner by which it is computed, the time it is earned, and the date it is to be paid).

18. **EMPLOYMENT FRINGE BENEFITS.** A statement of all fringe benefits, including, but not limited to, automobiles, automobile expenses, expense accounts, reimbursements of expenses, life insurance, medical insurance, medical reimbursement (for both you and your dependents), club dues, retirement programs, profit sharing, thrift plan, stock option plan, or pension benefits which are not addressed elsewhere.

19. **GUARANTEE.** A statement of all obligations for which your spouse may be liable, such as guaranty agreements, lines of credit, bank card reserve accounts, and checkline accounts.

20. **CLAIMS.** If you are presently involved in any litigation, state the nature of the litigation, the caption of the lawsuit, the Court in which it is filed, and details of the relief sought. This information should be provided both as to claims made against you and claims brought by you.

21. **WILLS AND TRUST INSTRUMENTS.** Copies of any wills and trust instruments you have executed in the past five years.

22. **CREDIT CARD ACCOUNTS.** Copies of all records, to include receipts, billing statements, charge slips, and the like with respect to any credit card account maintained by you (or by you jointly with any other person, or maintained for your benefit) for the last three years.

23. **RECENT SALES, TRANSFERS, EXCHANGES, OR CONVEYANCES.** The particulars of all sales, purchases, transfers, exchanges, or conveyances of any real or personal property in which you have an interest having a value in excess of $500 at any time within the past five years which are not addressed elsewhere.

■■■

Part IV

General or Federal Law

Section 1

Custody

Advice to Custody Clients

You are in custody litigation. This is intended to give you basic information about what you can, and can't, do with your children . . . if you want to enhance your chances of success.

1. **COMMUNICATION WITH THE OTHER PARENT.** Try to discuss your child's welfare with the other parent. Limit your discussion to the child's welfare. Don't discuss the new boyfriend or girlfriend or your anger with the other parent; it's counterproductive. If you cannot discuss these matters with the other parent, write him or her a letter or memo. Save a copy.

2. **DATING.** This is addressed from a practical, not moral, stance. If you are still married, you will be until the judge dissolves your marriage. Terminate or put on hold any extramarital relationship. If the new boyfriend or girlfriend cares about you enough, he or she will wait for you. If not, so be it. You need to concentrate on maintaining and developing your relationship with your children. You do not have the time or money right now for affairs. That time will come later, after this case is closed.

   If you perceive the extramarital relationship to be a very stable one leading to marriage, and you elect to ignore my advice, remember that you have been warned. Do not involve the paramour in your child's life. Regardless of how much the new love object purportedly cares for your child, limit your contact with the boy/girlfriend to times when the child is with the other parent. Your paramour's lifestyle, behavior, marital status, and indeed relationship with his/her own children will come under scrutiny in your custody case.

3. **MEDICAL CARE.** Elective, non-emergency medical care should be undertaken after consultation with the child's other parent. If the parent refuses to discuss this with you, let that parent know the name of the service provider, the procedures undertaken, and the diagnosis. Don't keep the child's medical care a secret from the other parent.

4. **SCHOOL.** If you're the physical custodian, let the other parent know when parent-teacher conferences are scheduled. Give the other parent a copy of the child's report card. Share the child's schoolwork with the other parent. Discuss homework and school responsibilities the child may have with the other parent.

   If you're the visiting parent, you have the right to contact the school and ask that you be contacted about parent-teacher conferences and the child's school records. Do so. Don't place all of the responsibility upon your spouse to let you know. Take an active part in the child's education.

5. **VISITATION.** If you are the physical custodian, have the children ready for the visit. Have a supply of suitable clothing ready to accompany the child. You don't want the judge to learn that you let your child go off on a weekend visit with the clothes he was wearing and another change in a plastic bag, do you?

   As a single parent, you need a break from the child. And the child needs a break from you. In an intact family, parents relieve each other from the constant demands of the child. In a divorce situation, the appropriate relief is visitation with the other parent.

If you are the visiting parent, pick up the child on time. Return the child on time. If you're going to be unexpectedly late, call. Don't demand that the child keep toys and clothing at your house just because you purchased them. After all, those items are the child's, not yours.

A medical condition short of hospitalization is no excuse for denying visitation. The visiting parent can, and should, assume some of the responsibility of caring for a sick child.

Do not use the child as an intermediary to carry messages between you and your spouse. You're an adult. You know how to communicate.

Visitation is not a time to revisit disputes with your spouse. It's your time with your child. Use it for that. This is not the time to introduce the child to your new love match.

Do not pump your child for information about life in the other parent's home. If it's worth telling, the child will tell you. Did you tell your parents everything that went on when you were 8 or 12 years old? Remember how you replied, "Oh, nothing" to your mother, when she asked you what you did in school?

Do not ask your child to keep secrets about what takes place in your home.

You do *not* have the right to refuse visitation because the other parent hasn't paid child support. The two issues are not related. You have a remedy for nonpayment of child support. You can lose physical care of your child if you deny court-ordered visitation.

Don't get too upset about your child's behavior at the beginning or end of each visit. The child's cries at the end of a visit are perceived by the physical custodian as tears of joy at being reunited with the parent, and the same outburst is viewed by the visiting parent as tears of sadness at the separation. Plan some kind of activity to allow the child to "wind down."

It's not the end of the world if the child misses a Little League ball game or Sunday school because it took place during the other spouse's visit.

6. **CHILD SUPPORT.** If you are ordered to pay child support during the pendency of this action, pay it. If you simply can't make the full payment, at least make a partial payment. The judge will not look kindly upon your claim for increased visitation or physical care when you have failed to contribute to your child's support.

   Child support is money you have paid to the court (if an order has been entered) or money paid directly to the spouse for the child's support. Child support is not a Schwinn bicycle or Nike shoes that you bought the child during the weekend visit. It is the money that puts bread on the table and pays the rent.

7. **COUNSELING.** Divorce is tough. It's kind of like death, only no one sends you a condolence card. It hurts. However, it's not fatal. Go to the mental health professional. It's often easier to discuss your feelings with someone you'll never see again, someone who'll not say, "I told you so." Therapy will not be held against you in court. In fact, in addition to helping you through the anger and sadness of divorce, the fact that you sought therapy can be looked upon as a positive factor by the court.

8. **PARENTING.** You can never learn enough about parenting. It's an ongoing process. Enroll in a parenting class. Read about child care, child development, parenting techniques. Show the judge that you know something about parenting and that you have a willingness to learn.

9. **TELLING THE CHILD ABOUT DIVORCE.** Your child knows more about what's going on in his or her life than you may realize. You do not need to go into details about why the marriage ended with the child. There are a number of children's books, geared to varying age and reading levels, which discuss divorce and single-parenting issues with the child.

10. **ADJUSTMENTS.** Remember when you first became pregnant? You were filled with worry and doubt about what your life was going to be like. Your friends and relatives all gave you advice about what childbirth and the new baby was going to feel like, but when you actually went through these steps, your feelings were unique. Divorce is much the same. While everybody's case has common threads, the actual experience for each is unique.

   You are making the same adjustments in your life day by day as a divorcing parent that you did as a new parent. Be the best parent for your child in all aspects of your life. Your child will undoubtedly divorce, end a relationship, or quit a job sometime in his or her life. The example you give your child as a divorcing parent is as important as the rest of the "good examples" you try to give your child.

■ ■ ■

International Custody Disputes

Preface

Child custody disputes that cross national borders are among the most frustrating of domestic cases. There are remedies available for parents who are left behind and for parents who are denied visitation. There are also steps parents can take to reduce the risk of international child abduction. This Client Information Letter attempts to summarize the law in this area and answer some common questions that arise. It is, of course, impossible to answer all of your questions in a short brochure such as this, so we encourage you to ask other questions of your lawyer at the appropriate time.

1. Q. MY SPOUSE HAS LEFT THE COUNTRY AND TAKEN OUR CHILDREN. WHAT CAN I DO?
   A. The Hague Convention on the Civil Aspects of International Child Abduction and the International Child Abduction Remedies Act (ICARA) provides remedies for a parent whose child or children have been taken to another country. The Hague Convention and ICARA establish the procedure for responding to these cases and the remedies available to the parent who is left behind. The Convention applies to several dozen member nations. The primary objectives of the Convention are to secure the prompt return of children who have been wrongfully removed or retained and to ensure that rights of custody and visitation are respected. The Convention does not apply in all cases. The procedures for obtaining assistance are outlined below.

2. Q. WILL THE COURT ORDER THE RETURN OF MY CHILDREN?
   A. The Convention does not require a court to order the return of children when a parent has consented or acquiesced in their removal or retention. The Convention does not apply to children over the age of 16 or cases where proceedings are filed more than one year after the child is removed. When the child is old enough, the court may refuse to order his return if he does not want to go. The court may also refuse to return a child if the court determines that the child's return would create a grave risk of physical or psychological harm to the child.

3. Q. WHERE WILL THE CUSTODY DETERMINATION BE MADE?
   A. The purpose of the Hague Convention is to ensure that custody and visitation rights are decided by the court in the appropriate country. The selection of the appropriate country requires a determination of which country is the child's place of habitual residence. The term "habitual residence" has been interpreted to mean "ordinary residence" or the child's customary residence prior to removal. Habitual residence is the place where he or she has been physically present for an amount of time sufficient for acclimatization and which has a "degree of settled purpose" from the child's perspective. Application of this standard must focus on the child's circumstances and the parents' present shared intentions regarding their child's presence there.

4. Q. DON'T I HAVE TO HAVE A COURT ORDER OR A SEPARATION AGREEMENT TO KEEP MY SPOUSE FROM LEAVING WITH THE CHILDREN?

A. Rights of custody or visitation may arise from a court order or an agreement of the parties. In the absence of an order or an agreement, custody and visitation rights are determined by the law of the country of habitual residence. In the absence of an order or agreement, in most countries, the parents will have equal rights to custody. When one party removes a child without a court order or the consent of the other parent, or refuses to allow visitation, the removal or retention is wrongful and violates the Convention. The existence of an order or agreement can be very helpful in avoiding the removal of a child or facilitating a child's return.

5. Q. CAN I PREVENT MY SPOUSE FROM LEAVING THE COUNTRY WITH OUR CHILDREN?

A. There are things that you can and should do to reduce the risk of abduction or retention. If there is a substantial risk that your child's other parent will remove a child or refuse to return a child who is visiting in another country, you should obtain a court order or an agreement on custody. The order or agreement should prohibit the child's international travel without your consent or judicial authorization. You may also consider requesting that a bond be posted as a requirement for international travel. You should also contact the organizations listed at the end of this handout for additional information on how you can reduce the risk of abduction and facilitate return.

6. Q. WHAT DO I DO ABOUT THE CHILDREN'S PASSPORTS?

A. A passport is necessary to travel outside the western hemisphere. Information regarding a child's passport is available to either parent, and either parent can apply for a passport. Passports are good for five years for children under age 18 and 10 years for persons over age 18. Information about an adult's passport is available only to law enforcement or by court order. The State Department maintains a passport clearance system. Upon written request, parents may be notified when a passport application is submitted for a child. Passport applications for children may be denied when there is a court order establishing:

- Full custody with one parent;
- Joint custody (permission of both required);
- Limitations on the child's travel; or
- A requirement that both parents, or the court, authorize the issuance of a passport or travel outside the United States.

The State Department cannot revoke a passport that has already been issued to a child. It is also important to remember that these rules have no effect upon rights of dual citizens as established under the laws of another country. You can send a request to the embassy or consulate for that country requesting that a passport not be issued and send a copy to the State Department.

7. Q. CAN I ENFORCE MY RIGHTS TO VISITATION WHEN MY CHILDREN ARE IN ANOTHER COUNTRY?

A. The Convention also addresses visitation (access) rights. It permits, but does not require, the court in the country where the child or children are located to order that they be made available or sent for visitation with the noncustodial parent. It also does not require the parent who has wrongfully withheld access to pay for the innocent spouse's attorney fees and costs. It only requires the court to "take steps to remove, as much as possible, all obstacles" to the exercise of visitation rights. This may mean that the court will enforce visitation rights on the condition that they be exercised within the country.

8. Q. WHAT ABOUT ATTORNEY'S FEES AND TRAVEL COSTS?
   A. Any court order requiring the return of a child pursuant to the Convention must order the other parent to pay the necessary expenses incurred by or on behalf of the innocent parent, including court costs, legal fees, and foster home or other care during the course of the proceedings in the action, as well as transportation costs related to the return of the child. There is no similar authority in visitation cases. However, a state court properly exercising jurisdiction over the custody or visitation issues can impose these requirements.

9. Q. WHOM CAN I CONTACT FOR HELP?
   A. For help with initiating a Hague petition for the return of a child or enforcement of visitation rights, contact: United States Department of State, Bureau of Consular Affairs, Office of Children's Issues, SA-29, 2201 C Street, NW, Washington, DC 20520, 1-888-407-4747 or 202-501-4444, FAX 202-736-9132, e-mail AskCI@state.gov, www.childabduction.state.gov.
   B. For information regarding passports go to http://travel.state.gov/passport/passport_1738.html.
   C. For additional information on how to prepare for the risk of child abduction or search and recovery, contact the Office of Children's Issues and the National Center for Missing and Exploited Children, 699 Prince Street, Alexandria, VA 22314, 1-800-843-5678. http://www.missingkids.com.

■■■

Child Custody Jurisdiction Questionnaire

Due to the requirements of [statutory citation], The Uniform Child Custody Jurisdiction and Enforcement Act, the Court requires certain information in the original pleadings or documents we file in your case regarding custody of a child or children. Without giving this information under oath, our case will be dismissed. Please fill out the information below so that we can accurately report this information to the Court in our pleadings.

Please list:
1. *Full* name of Child;
2. County and State of birth;
3. Street addresses; and
4. Which parent(s) each child has resided with for the past 5 years, beginning with most recent.

Full Name of Child: _____

                                First   Middle   Last

Date of Birth (Mo/Day/Yr): _____

County/State of Birth: _____/_____

1. Address: _____

    From: _____ To (date): _____

    With Whom? _____

2. Address: _____

    From: _____ To (date): _____

    With Whom? _____

3. Address: _____

    From: _____ To (date): _____

    With Whom? _____

4. Address: _____

    From: _____ To (date): _____

    With Whom? _____

5. Address: _____

    From: _____ To (date): _____

    With Whom? _____

Full Name of Child: _____
                    First   Middle   Last

Date of Birth (Mo/Day/Yr): _____

County/State of Birth: _____/_____

1. Address: _____

   From: _____ To (date): _____

   With Whom? _____

2. Address: _____

   From: _____ To (date): _____

   With Whom? _____

3. Address: _____

   From: _____ To (date): _____

   With Whom? _____

4. Address: _____

   From: _____ To (date): _____

   With Whom? _____

5. Address: _____

   From: _____ To (date): _____

   With Whom? _____

Full Name of Child: _____
                    First   Middle   Last

Date of Birth (Mo/Day/Yr): _____

County/State of Birth: _____/_____

1. Address: _____

   From: _____ To (date): _____

   With Whom? _____

2. Address: _____

   From: _____ To (date): _____

   With Whom? _____

3. Address: _____

   From: _____ To (date): _____

   With Whom? _____

4. Address: _____

   From: _____ To (date): _____

   With Whom? _____

5. Address: _____

   From: _____ To (date): _____

   With Whom? _____

Is there, or has there ever been, any legal action as to custody of the child(ren)?
   Yes   □   No   □

If yes, please give details: _____

_____

Have you ever participated as a party, witness, or in any other capacity, concerning the custody of the child(ren)?
   Yes   □   No   □

If yes, please give details: _____

_____

Do you know of any person, other than the opposing party, who has physical custody of the child(ren) or claims to have custody or visitation rights to the child(ren)?
   Yes   □   No   □

If yes, please give details: _____

_____

■■■

Specific Visitation Rights

Although flexible visitation rights are desirable for many parents who are separated or divorced, it usually helps to set out the specific terms for visitation if there is a disagreement or a misunderstanding. This prevents unnecessary trips to court, lost time with children or unmet expectations.

A good separation agreement or custody consent order will usually provide for visitation at such times as are reasonable, mutually agreeable to the parties, and consistent with the children's scheduled activities. In the absence of such agreement, a schedule of specified visitation should be spelled out. Please fill in the blanks below so we can understand your wishes for specific visitation.

Place a checkmark or an X next to the visitation terms that will be mutually agreeable (or draft your own) below:

☐ Weekends: On every other weekend from pick-up at 6:00 p.m. Friday until return at 6:00 p.m. Sunday.

OR

☐ Weekends: _____

☐ Summer: For two weeks, with notice by HUSB/WIF to WIF/HUSB no later than April 1 of each year as to when summer visitation will be.

OR

☐ Summer: For two two-week periods, separated by at least one week, with notice by HUSB/WIF to WIF/HUSB no later than April 1 of each year as to when this period will be.

OR

☐ Summer: For an uninterrupted thirty-day period, with notice by HUSB/WIF to WIF/HUSB no later than April 1 of each year as to when this period will be.

OR

☐ Summer: _____

☐ Christmas holidays: From 6:00 p.m. on the day school ends until noon on December 25 in even-numbered years, and from noon on December 25 until 6:00 p.m. on the day before school resumes in odd-numbered years.

OR

☐ Christmas holidays: From noon on December 25 until 6:00 p.m. on December 31 every year.

OR

☐ Christmas holidays: From 6:00 p.m. on the day school ends until 6:00 p.m. on the day before school resumes in even-numbered years.

OR

☐ Christmas holidays: _____

☐   <u>Easter vacation/Spring break</u>: For this entire period every year.

<small>OR</small>

☐   <u>Easter vacation/Spring break</u>: For this entire period every even-numbered year.

<small>OR</small>

☐   <u>Easter vacation/Spring break</u>: _____

☐   <u>Thanksgiving holidays</u>: At the Thanksgiving holiday period, from 6:00 p.m. of the Wednesday before Thanksgiving until 6:00 p.m. of the Sunday after Thanksgiving every year.

<small>OR</small>

☐   <u>Thanksgiving holidays</u>: At the Thanksgiving holiday period, from 6:00 p.m. of the Wednesday before Thanksgiving until 6:00 p.m. of the Sunday after Thanksgiving every even-numbered year.

<small>OR</small>

☐   <u>Thanksgiving holidays</u>: _____

☐   <u>Other holidays</u>: For the Friday or Monday holiday (i.e., Memorial Day) whenever such a holiday occurs in conjunction with regular weekend visitation, retaining the pick-up and drop-off times set out above.

<small>OR</small>

☐   <u>Other holidays</u>: _____

☐   <u>Mother's/Father's Day</u>: On Mother's Day with the Mother and on Father's Day with the Father, regardless of other scheduled visitation.

☐   <u>Other visitation</u>: _____

Who will be responsible for transportation for visitation?
  a. *Will advance notice of visitation (or of non-visitation) be required? If so, by how much time?*
  b. *Other provisions to include under visitation terms:*

■■■

Section 2

Divorce

Divorce and Domicile

How Your Legal Residence Affects

Your Legal Rights

Many legal issues involve your legal residence, or "domicile." The place where you live and call "home" (or the place to which you intend to return after a temporary absence) is your domicile.

The choice of domicile can determine where you are entitled to vote, where you are liable for state income taxes, and where your children can obtain in-state tuition for college.

In the world of divorces and family law, a person's domicile determines where he or she can obtain a divorce. In general, a valid divorce can only be granted in the state of domicile of the husband or wife. It can also be important in cases involving military pension division and family support.

Use the checklist below to determine the facts which are used by judges in deciding domicile questions. Then consult an attorney to determine the domicile of you and your spouse.

DOMICILE CHECKLIST FOR SERVICEMEMBERS AND SPOUSES

Question or Issue	State(s), Years
For each item below, answer with information covering the last five years (or other period)	
1. Physical location Describe the dates, places, and circumstances of your residing here in State A in the past years on a separate sheet of paper.	
2. Taxation Where have you paid state income taxes? (If applicable) Where have you paid local income taxes? Where have you paid personal property taxes? Where have you paid real property taxes? Where have you paid any other state-related taxes (e.g., intangibles tax)? Which state is shown on DD Form 2058, State of Legal Residence Certificate? Which state have you shown for your address on your Form 1040 (federal income tax return)?	
3. Real estate In what state(s) do you own residential real estate? In what state(s) do you own other real estate?	

Question or Issue	State(s), Years
4. Motor vehicles Where is each of your motor vehicles titled? Where is each motor vehicle registered? Give the state of your driver's license.	_____ _____ _____
5. Banking In what state(s) do you have a checking account? A savings account? A safe deposit box? Other investment accounts?	_____ _____ _____
6. Voting In which state(s) are you registered to vote in state, county, or local elections? In federal elections?	_____
7. Schooling In which state(s) have your children attended school? In which state(s) have you obtained resident tuition for yourself or a family member? Nonresident tuition?	_____ _____

Your Personal Notes

_____

_____

_____

_____

_____

_____

_____

Section 3

Family Support

Child Care Tax Credit

Preface

Tax consequences are an aspect of divorce negotiations and settlement agreements that are often overlooked. Perhaps some of the most confusing aspects for divorcing families are those surrounding child care expense credits. This pamphlet is not designed to take the place of consultation with and advice from a tax professional, such as a certified public accountant. Rather, it is an attempt to answer some frequently asked questions as to whether you may take advantage of the child care tax credit.

1. **Q. WHAT IS THE CHILD CARE TAX CREDIT?**
   A. The child care tax credit is a credit available to taxpayers who incur child care costs while at work or in school.

2. **Q. MY EX-WIFE SIGNED A FORM 8332 ENTITLING ME TO THE CHILD DEPENDENCY EXEMPTION. DOES THIS MEAN I CAN TAKE THE CHILD CARE TAX CREDIT ALSO?**
   A. This depends. Ordinarily the person who has primary physical custody, i.e., the person who has the child more than 50 percent of the time, has the right to take both the child dependency exemption and the child care tax credit. However, when there is a divorce or separation, the primary custodial parent may transfer the dependency exemption to get some other favorable treatment. While generally the dependency exemption and child care tax credit go hand-in-hand, a parent may not claim the child care tax credit unless he or she is the primary custodian. Being the primary custodian means having the child more than 50 percent of the time. There is a special rule for true 50/50 custody, and that is addressed below.

3. **Q. I SIGNED A FORM 8332 GIVING MY EX-HUSBAND THE CHILD CARE EXEMPTION. I HAVE THE CHILDREN MORE THAN 50 PERCENT OF THE TIME. I HAVE TO PUT THE CHILDREN IN DAY CARE SO THAT I CAN WORK. CAN I TAKE THE CHILD CARE TAX CREDIT?**
   A. Yes. A person who is the physical custodian of a child for more than 50 percent of the time may claim the child care tax credit if he or she places a child who is under the age of 13 in day care so that he or she may work or go to school.

4. **Q. MY CHILDREN LIVE WITH ME, BUT MY EX-HUSBAND PAYS FOR THEIR DAY CARE IN ADDITION TO THE CHILD SUPPORT. I HEARD I CAN TAKE THE CHILD CARE TAX CREDIT EVEN THOUGH I DID NOT INCUR THE EXPENSE. IS THIS TRUE?**
   A. No. You cannot take advantage of the tax care credit unless you actually incur the expense.

5. **Q. MY CHILDREN LIVE WITH MY EX-WIFE, BUT I PAY FOR THEIR DAY CARE IN ADDITION TO CHILD SUPPORT. MAY I TAKE THE CHILD CARE TAX CREDIT?**
   A. No. You must be the primary custodian before you can take the deduction. While you meet the requirement of incurring the expense, you fail the second part of the test, which requires the children be in daycare so that you

may work. Since the children do not even live in your house, you may not take the deduction.

6. Q. MY EMPLOYER HAS A FLEX SPENDING ACCOUNT THAT ALLOWS ME TO DEDUCT UP TO $3,000 PER CHILD OR A MAXIMUM OF $6,000 FOR DAY CARE EXPENSES. SHOULD I PARTICIPATE IN THIS PLAN?

A. It depends. If you are the primary custodian, meaning the children live with you more than 50% of the time, then it would be a wise idea to take advantage of the plan. The maximum allowable deduction for the child care tax credit in 2013 is $3,000 per child or a maximum of $6,000 per family. The amount actually allowed for the deduction is prorated. With employer plans, the entire amount is taken out of your paycheck before taxes and is never reported as income; thus you take advantage of the entire amount of $2,500 or $5,000 with no prorated reduction at the end of the year. If you are not the primary custodian, not only is it not a good idea to participate, you *cannot participate*. The purpose of these programs is to allow the parent to work. If the child is not living with you, there is no need for you to put him/her in day care.

7. Q. MY EX-WIFE AND I HAVE EQUAL PHYSICAL CUSTODY OF OUR CHILD. WHICH OF US MAY TAKE THE CHILD CARE TAX CREDIT?

A. As with the dependency exemption, both parents may not claim the child care tax credit. If indeed there is **exactly equal** shared custody—meaning each parent has the child for 182 and a half days per year, then the parents must decide who claims both the dependency exemption and the child care tax credit. When they decide this, one parent signs a Form 8332 releasing the right to claim the exemption and tax credit to the other parent. If one parent has the child 183 days and the other has the child 182 days, the parent having the 183 days is entitled to claim both absent a waiver in the form of a Form 8332 or a separation agreement. Please remember, it is nearly impossible to have **exactly equal** custody, so this problem rarely arises.

■■■

Custody and Child Support:

The Interstate Connection

Custody

1. **Q.** HELP! MY EX-WIFE TOOK OUR CHILDREN FROM TEXAS, WHERE I HAVE AN ORDER GIVING ME CUSTODY, AND DROVE TO NORTH CAROLINA. DO I NEED AN ORDER FROM A TEXAS JUDGE? A PRIVATE ATTORNEY IN NORTH CAROLINA? CAN A SHERIFF'S DEPUTY HELP ME? WHERE DO I GO FROM HERE?

   A. Slow down—that's a lot of questions. We'll try to answer them all, but first you need to know about the Uniform Child Custody Jurisdiction and Enforcement Act. A summary is provided in this "TAKE-1" handout.

2. **Q.** WHAT IS THE STATUTE YOU JUST MENTIONED?

   A. The Uniform Child Custody Jurisdiction and Enforcement Act (UCCJEA) is a law that's found in all 50 states plus the District of Columbia. It is just about the same everywhere, and it provides a lot of protection in cases of child removal or kidnapping. For example, it allows you to register your "foreign custody order" (that's the one from Texas) in North Carolina.

3. **Q.** REGISTER MY TEXAS ORDER? WHAT GOOD WILL THAT DO?

   A. Registering your foreign custody order allows the court in North Carolina to enforce it just as if it had been entered here by a judge in this state.

4. **Q.** SOUNDS PRETTY GOOD. HOW DO I DO IT? DO I HAVE TO FILE A COMPLAINT OR A MOTION TO GET MY PAPERS FROM TEXAS REGISTERED HERE?

   A. "Registration" under the UCCJEA means filing with the court:

   1. A letter or other document requesting registration;
   2. Two copies (including one that is a *certified copy*) of the foreign court order, plus an affidavit that—to the best of your knowledge and belief—your Texas order has not been modified; and
   3. Except as otherwise provided in G.S. 50A-209, your name and address (or that information for the person who is seeking registration) and the same information for any parent or person acting as a parent who has been awarded custody or visitation in the custody order which you want registered.

The specifics are found on page 1 of one of the court forms, AOC-CV-660 (Petition for Registration of Foreign Child Custody Order). Here are the forms from the Administrative Office of the Courts (AOC) which are available for the foreign custody order registration process:

AOC-CV-660	Instructions For Registration Of Foreign Child Custody Order (Side 1)/Instructions For Expedited Enforcement Of Foreign Child Custody Order (Side Two) (New 12/06)	PDF Ready
AOC-CV-660	Petition For Registration Of Foreign Child Custody Order (New 12/06)	PDF Ready (Fillable)

AOC-CV-661	Notice Of Registration Of Foreign Child Custody Order (New 12/06)	PDF Ready (Fillable)
AOC-CV-663	Motion To Contest Validity Of A Registered Foreign Child Custody Order And Notice Of Hearing (New 12/06)	PDF Ready (Fillable)
AOC-CV-664	Order Confirming Registration Or Denying Confirmation Or Registration Of Foreign Child Custody Order (New 12/06)	PDF Ready (Fillable)
AOC-CV-665	Petition For Expedited Enforcement Of Foreign Child Custody Order (New 12/06)	PDF Ready (Fillable)
AOC-CV-666	Order For Hearing On Motion For Expedited Enforcement Of Foreign Child Custody Order (New 12/06)	PDF Ready (Fillable)
AOC-CV-667	Warrant Directing Law Enforcement To Take Immediate Physical Custody Of Child(ren) Subject To Foreign Child Custody Order (New 12/06)	PDF Ready (Fillable)
AOC-CV-668	Order Allowing Or Denying Expedited Enforcement Of Foreign Child Custody Order (New 12/06)	PDF Ready (Fillable)

They are available from the website of the AOC at this address: http://www.nccourts.org/Forms/FormSearchResults.asp

5. Q. WHAT DOES THAT MEAN—THE PART ABOUT G.S. 50A-209?

   A. G.S. 50A-209 says you don't have to provide this information if you state in your affidavit that the health, safety, or liberty of the child/children would be endangered by disclosure. In that situation, the information must be sealed and may not be disclosed to the other party or the public unless the court, after a hearing, orders it in the interest of justice.

6. Q. WHAT HAPPENS NEXT?

   A. One copy of the registration petition and one copy of the registration notice must be served upon the defendant (that's your ex-wife) and any other person listed in paragraph 3 of the Petition for Registration of Foreign Child Custody Order. Instructions regarding service are found in the "Notice to Plaintiff" section of the Notice of Registration, AOC-CV-661. Then the court determines whether to confirm the order or not. There must be a hearing to determine whether the order is confirmed. The notice states that a registered order is enforceable as of the date of the registration just as if it had been entered by a judge here. Also, the notice states that a hearing to contest the validity of the registered order must be requested within 20 days after service of notice; if the other side doesn't contest the registration, this will result in confirmation of the custody order.

7. Q. WHAT CAN MY EX-WIFE DO WHEN NOTIFIED ABOUT THE REGISTRATION?

   A. The other side can do nothing, which usually means that the foreign order will be confirmed by the judge here, or else the other side, your ex-wife, can contest the registration, which means challenging the validity of the Texas custody order. If the other side files a motion to contest the validity of the foreign order, you will receive a copy of the motion and a notice of hearing informing you of the date and time the court will hear the matter. If no one files a motion to contest the validity of the foreign child custody order, the clerk of court will mail you a copy of the Order Confirming Registration. If there is a question about the existence of a custody order, or the authority of the court to exercise custody jurisdiction, that question, by law, must be given priority on the court's calendar and handled expeditiously.

8. **Q.** **SO A FOREIGN CUSTODY ORDER MUST BE REGISTERED IN EVERY CASE BEFORE NORTH CAROLINA WILL ENFORCE IT?**

   A. No. A foreign child custody order IS NOT required to be registered before it can be enforced in North Carolina. If you are seeking immediate enforcement of a foreign child custody order, see Instructions for Petition for Expedited Enforcement of a Foreign Child Custody Order, Form AOC-CV-665. If you want law enforcement officers to immediately pick up the children, you must check the box before paragraph 10. A warrant directing law enforcement to pick up the children immediately can be issued only by a district court judge, and the warrant is available only if the judge determines that the children are in danger of immediate serious physical harm, or there is an immediate danger of their being removed from the state. You must testify to the judge, or produce another witness to testify, that there is a need for law enforcement to get the children immediately. You will also need to complete portions of Form AOC-CV-667, which is the warrant form. If the warrant is not issued, the judge will consider your request for custody of the children at the hearing that will be set when you file the Petition for Expedited Enforcement of Foreign Child Custody Order.

9. **Q.** **WHEN WILL THE JUDGE HEAR MY CASE?**

   A. After you file the Petition for Expedited Enforcement of a Foreign Child Custody Order, the court must issue an order stating the hearing date. A judge must consider your request for enforcement of the child custody order on the next judicial day after the Petition for Expedited Enforcement is served upon the other side. If your hearing date arrives and the other side hasn't been served, the judge will probably continue the case so that service can be had on the other party, your ex-wife, or any other person who has, or claims to have, custody of the children.

10. **Q.** **SO THERE'S NOTHING THAT MY EX CAN DO TO CONTEST THE PETITION?**

   A. There are several defenses available to her. The instructions on the expedited enforcement order state that custody will be granted to you at the conclusion of the hearing unless she appears at the hearing and is able to prove one of these:

1. The foreign custody order has been stayed, vacated or modified, or was entered by a court that didn't have jurisdiction to do so; or
2. The foreign order has not been confirmed, and the other party was entitled to receive notice before it was entered.

If a defense is proven to the court, then the order will not be confirmed, and the registration will be vacated.

11. Q. ONCE I HAVE GOTTEN CONFIRMATION OF MY TEXAS CUSTODY ORDER HERE IN NORTH CAROLINA, CAN I FORGET ABOUT HEARINGS ON CUSTODY OR VISITATION BACK THERE?

A. Not at all. Texas still has original jurisdiction. Unless at some future time the case gets fully transferred to North Carolina for misconduct by one of the parents or because North Carolina is a more convenient forum, Texas remains the court with the primary responsibility regarding child custody in your case.

Child Support

12. Q. I NEED SOME HELP WITH CHILD SUPPORT. I HAVE A COURT ORDER AGAINST MY EX-HUSBAND FOR CHILD SUPPORT. IT WAS ENTERED IN IOWA. CAN I REGISTER IT HERE FOR ENFORCEMENT?

A. UIFSA (the Uniform Interstate Family Support Act) is the law in all states. It provides that a child support order (or an income withholding order in a support case) issued by another state may be registered in North Carolina for the purpose of enforcing the order against the payor.

13. Q. WHAT'S INVOLVED IN REGISTERING A FOREIGN CHILD SUPPORT ORDER?

A. To register your Iowa order, which is known as a "foreign child support order," you need to file:

1. a letter of transmittal requesting registration of the order for enforcement;
2. two copies, including on certified copy, of the order for which registration is sought, and copies of all orders modifying the order;
3. certification of the amount of any arrearage under the order;
4. the name of the obligor (that's your ex-husband), his address (if known), his Social Security number, the name and address of his employer, the source of any other income of his, and a description and location of any available property which he owns in this state; and
5. your own name and address, as well as the agency or person to whom support payments are to be sent.

14. Q. CAN I ALSO FILE A MOTION FOR ENFORCEMENT OF MY IOWA ORDER?

A. A motion seeking enforcement of a registered order may be filed at the time the order is registered for enforcement or after a registered support order is confirmed. The petition must state the grounds for the remedy that is being sought.

15. Q. IT SOUNDS LIKE THERE ARE TWO THINGS GOING ON HERE—REGISTRATION AND CONFIRMATION. WHAT'S THAT ABOUT?

A. Registration occurs when you submit your order to the court with the above documents and information. Then the notice of registration, AOC-CV-505, is sent to the other side. It warns him about the registration process, what it involves, and the results of ignoring the notice.

16. **Q. What does the notice say?**

    A. The Notice of Registration states that:

    *If you want to contest the validity or enforcement of the registered Foreign Support Order, you **must** file a written request for hearing asking the Court to vacate registration of the order, asserting any defense regarding alleged noncompliance with the order, or contesting the amount of arrears allegedly owed under the order or the remedies that are being sought to enforce the order. Your request for hearing must be filed with the Clerk of Superior Court within twenty (20) days after the date of mailing or personal service of this notice. **Failure to contest the validity or enforcement of the registered Foreign Support Order in a timely manner will result in confirmation of the order and the alleged arrears, and precludes further contest of the order with respect to any matter that could have been asserted.***

    At the hearing, the payor (your ex-husband) may ask the judge to vacate the registration. He may contest the amount of back support that you are requesting. He may contest the enforcement remedy being sought (such as seizure of property or garnishment). And he may assert a defense against his alleged noncompliance with the order. He cannot, however, challenge the fundamental provisions of the registered order; that is available only in the original court where the order was entered. Nor may he ask the court to modify the registered order unless he meets certain requirements of the law. There are only a limited number of defenses available to him for challenging registration. If he does not succeed in challenging registration, then the order is confirmed.

17. **Q. Will the judge treat a registered order from Iowa just like a North Carolina order for enforcement?**

    A. No. The order must be confirmed, not just registered. Then, upon confirmation, the judge can grant you any remedies that a child support order entered in North Carolina would allow.

18. **Q. Does that mean that the judge can order payments through the court?**

    A. Payments no longer go "through the court." The agency that collects child support and sends it to the parent with custody is called "Centralized Collections." This agency will also keep records of payments received, in case there is a dispute about child support payments. The judge will often use this agency as the collection mechanism for child support.

19. **Q. What about direct payments from my ex-husband? If that's ordered, I'm afraid that he won't make them on time in the full amount.**

    A. Good point. In North Carolina, the rule is that payments must be made by garnishment from his employer unless the two of you agree otherwise, or unless the court is convinced that an alternative means is available to guarantee payment of child support to you. When payments are made directly to you by the other side, there's always the risk that they won't be made in the full amount, they will be late, or the check will "bounce" when you try to deposit it at the bank. Some non-custodial parents also think that they can make deductions from child support for things that they provide for the children, or to punish the custodial parent for something she has done. Garnishment and using Centralized Collections are the best ways to ensure proper accountability for the payment of child support.

20. Q. Can I speed up the child support hearing process at all? I'm afraid that it'll take three or four months to get a hearing date!

A. The law in North Carolina (N.C. Gen. Stat. 50-32) states that child support is supposed to be on a fast track when there is a motion or complaint pending for establishment of support. This is known as "Expedited Process." The statute says that:

Except where paternity is at issue, in all child support cases the district court judge shall dispose of the case from filing to disposition within 60 days, except that this period may be extended for a maximum of 30 days by order of the court if:

(1) Either party or his attorney cannot be present for the hearing; or

(2) The parties have consented to an extension.

21. Q. So once I have gotten confirmation of my child support order here in North Carolina, I can forget about hearings on child support back in Iowa?

A. Not at all. Iowa still has original jurisdiction. Unless at some future time the case gets fully transferred to North Carolina for specific reasons set out in the statute, Iowa is the court with the primary responsibility regarding child support in your case.

■■■

How to Fill Out Your Financial Affidavit

INTRODUCTION

Why an Affidavit?

In any case involving support (and this means child support as well as spousal support), the court will require you to submit a financial affidavit. This is because the statutes require the judge to consider the incomes, assets, and reasonable monthly expenses of the parties and the child or children, if any, before support may be ordered.

In any case that we handle for you, even if it involves a separation agreement or consent order, instead of a contested trial, we want you to prepare and sign a financial affidavit with this same information—assets, income, needs, expenses, and debts. We do this for several reasons.

We want you to assess your monthly budget and to have your eyes open concerning your expenses, income, and disposable cash each month. It's important for you to know how much money it takes to meet your reasonable monthly needs. A thorough evaluation of these items will help us know what kind of a settlement would be fair, adequate, and reasonable for you. It will be harder for a party or a judge to overturn such a settlement if there has been an honest appraisal and full disclosure of these matters prior to final settlement. And, if the case can't be settled and has to be tried, you will be that much more prepared if you've taken the time to do your financial affidavit properly.

Some Guidelines for You

There are no court-approved guidelines for preparing your financial affidavit. Thus, it is important to follow these directions closely and to keep a copy of them for future reference. Sometimes the judge will want to know how you arrived at a certain dollar amount for one of your expenses—a copy of these instructions plus your own notes and calculations will help you to explain. On occasion, the other attorney will disagree with one of your financial affidavit figures. If we are negotiating a settlement, we may get a phone call and may need to provide an answer immediately. If we are in a trial, the opposing lawyer might try to cross-examine you on the witness stand about the amounts you've set out in the affidavit. We want you to be prepared. We strongly suggest that you take notes while completing the financial affidavit. These notes might show, for example, how you figured your monthly light bill or car expenses. Save them. They are invaluable in helping you remember facts and figures that you may have reviewed months ago. Amending and updating your affidavit from time to time will show the court, the opposing party, and the opposing attorney that we are honestly and openly trying to provide the most recent and accurate figures available.

Completing this Form

Be sure to use pencil on your affidavit. Once you complete your affidavit, we will enter it into our computer. This will make it easier to edit in the future, should the need arise.

We want you to start the work yourself on the affidavit. It takes a significant amount of time for you to get your bills, budget, expenses, and estimates together. You might want to make a rough draft before printing a final copy. It will be faster and less expensive for you to do the draft before returning the affidavit to us.

Once you have finished, call us for an appointment. We always have a paralegal sit down with you to go over the final draft, check the figures, ask you how you arrived at certain items, and notarize your signature. In case you are cross-examined on the affidavit, we'd better ask those questions first. You're always better prepared if your own law firm is the first to ask you the hard questions and to cross-examine you on your testimony.

Honest Estimates

Your figures for expenses need only to be good-faith estimates within a reasonable degree of certainty. Use averages whenever possible for greater accuracy—the longer the time period, the better. For example, take figures for your electric bill over at least a six-month period (preferably a year) so that you'll include some warm and some cool months in the averaging. If you don't know an answer or a figure, explain why you can't put down an amount or else make as accurate a guess as possible, putting "(EST.)" after the figure in the margin or at the bottom of the page (with a footnote or asterisk). When you are going to move to a new residence or if you have just done so, make as close a guess as possible regarding your monthly expenses there. If you are to pay a fixed sum to your parents, for example, for room, board, and all other household expenses while living with them, show that sum on your affidavit and explain it in a footnote. If you've just moved to a new apartment, get the utility company, your neighbors, and/or the management to give you estimates for your affidavit on such things as electric bills, gas or heating, maintenance, and other fees.

Errors and Discrepancies

If you've made an error, correct it or explain it as quickly as possible. If we are negotiating for you, let us know immediately and we'll make the corrections on your affidavit. If we're in court for you and you're testifying, stop and correct yourself as soon as you realize that you've made a mistake or miscalculation on your financial affidavit. In this way, you will be able to set the record straight, prevent the opposing attorney from exploiting a discrepancy or possible weakness in your testimony, and persuade the judge that you're trying to be honest and straightforward.

Expenses and Needs

Quite often, you'll find that there's a difference between actual expenses and reasonable needs. The affidavit, as you will see, only asks for your *expenses* each month. Your needs, on the other hand, may be quite a bit more for a particular item than what you may now be spending on it. In addition, the statutes and cases concerning support consistently stress that *needs* are what must be determined and these needs must be reasonable.

How to solve the dilemma? The answer lies in the use of footnotes and explanatory sheets to help point out the difference to your own lawyer, the court, or the other side.

Let's take an example. You have a low-paying job and are not getting enough support from your spouse for your two children. As a result, you can only budget $10 a month for clothing for each child, or a total of $240 for both per year. This is what you actually spend. You can't afford to spend more or you won't be able to pay your other bills. You know that $10 a month per child is accurate because you've gone over 10 months of bills, check stubs, and charge card receipts and the total averages out to this figure.

Still, you need more support and the kids need new clothes. In this situation, you might use a footnote at the bottom of the page to explain what you have estimated you would *need* each month for clothes, either as a new total per child or as an additional amount over and above what you stated earlier in the text of the affidavit.

Remember that your needs estimates must be *reasonable*. They need not be the same as the present monthly expenses for clothing if those clothes are already too small or worn out. It cannot, however, be grossly inflated to allow the children to buy a new set of "designer jeans" every month. Your estimate should be based on the reasonable and accustomed standard of living for you and the children. In most cases, this means that you don't have to reduce yourself to poverty but you also can't use the other parent to support you or the children in "high style."

When in doubt, be conservative in your estimates. It is better to be on the low side than on the high side if you must make a calculated guess. Just make sure you identify the figure (by footnote, on an accompanying analysis sheet that you prepare or during your oral testimony) as a "low estimate." That way, the judge will know what you're doing in the financial affidavit and the other side won't have a chance to "trip you up" by claiming that you're exaggerating or inflating the actual amount of certain expenses or needs.

Some Final Notes

Remember that you don't have to have bills and receipts for every item, but it helps if you have reviewed such things as charge card statements and check stubs before you start work on your affidavit. Try to have a good, solid basis or reason for every figure you put down on paper.

Don't be surprised if your expense totals at the end are greater than your income from all sources. This happens often, and there is usually a good explanation. Sometimes a client will indeed be spending beyond his or her means for basic living expenses, in which case this will show up under "Debts" on the second page of the financial affidavit. In other cases, a parent or friend will be helping the client to meet monthly needs, such as by providing a room rent-free or by buying food or clothes occasionally. Be sure to note and explain this. In any event, whenever your monthly expenditures are more than your income, be sure to double-check your figures for accuracy.

We know it takes time and effort to read these instructions, prepare and verify the financial affidavit by yourself, and then come back to our office with a final copy for us to review. So, we urge you to call us if you have any questions while you are completing the form. We value our clients too much to give you inadequate assistance on filling out a financial affidavit. We hope you understand and appreciate the importance of our lawyer/client partnership in this regard.

* * * * * * * * * *

SPECIFIC INSTRUCTIONS

The information below is meant to apply to those items designated by the companion heading on the financial affidavit labeled "Affidavit of Plaintiff/Defendant."

Detail of Monthly Gross Income

1. MONTHLY GROSS WAGES: Divide annual gross by 12; if employed less than a year or paid over 9 or 10 months instead of 12, divide gross wages since employment by applicable number of months and put that info in a note at right margin.
2. INVESTMENT INCOME: Divide this annual income by 12.
3. BONUS/COMMISSIONS: All bonuses, commissions over last 12 months divided by 12; if employed less than a year, divide these amounts since employment by number of months employed.
4. ALIMONY, CHILD SUPPORT: Total received over prior 12 months divided by 12.
5. OTHER: Identify other sources of pay, compensation, income; provide monthly average.

[Note: For these and all other affidavit calculations, retain all records, documents, data, checks, receipts, and other evidence in one folder; in another, keep all the papers upon which you perform the calculations, clearly identified to show what is being computed and how.]

6. MANDATORY MONTHLY DEDUCTIONS: Self-explanatory.
7. VOLUNTARY MONTHLY DEDUCTIONS: Show monthly average amounts for last 12 months, or shorter period if applicable; for health insurance items, note how many people are covered in the right margin.

Regular Recurring Monthly Expenses

[most of these are self-explanatory; notes for specific items are below]

1. RENT OR MORTGAGE PAYMENT: Put note in right margin for amount of annual property tax included in escrow; to find out, check payment coupon or annual statement, or call lender. Also, list here any Home Equity Line/Loan or Line of Credit information; use margin for details.
2. RENTERS/HOMEOWNERS INSURANCE: List this here even if paid into escrow with monthly in mortgage payment; review your payment coupon or call the lender to break out this figure—remember, monthly, not annual figure goes here.
3. TAXES NOT INCLUDED IN MORTGAGE: This could be property tax from another state; vehicle taxes are below.
4. ROUTINE HOUSE AND APPLIANCE REPAIR/MAINTENANCE: These expenses are generally self-explanatory. However, with regard to "House Maintenance," you should estimate the yearly costs of maintenance for your residence. If you live in rental property, this may be nothing, or it may include an occasional visit by a plumber or carpet-cleaner. If you own your home, consider the annual costs of plumbing, yard work, roofing, carpentry, painting, furnace/air conditioning repairs, etc. then divide by 12.

[Note: Sometimes maintenance costs include a major expense or capital improvement (such as a new roof or a paint job) with a lifetime of more than one year. If so, be sure to spread out the cost over the number of years of its life (or else you'll be awfully embarrassed when the other attorney asks you, "Do you put on a new roof every year?") If a new roof costs $12,000 and is good for 10 years, then divide $12,000 by 10 to get $1,200 per year, which is $100 per month. A good source of data for life spans of things around the house is the report, "Study of Life Expectancy of Home Components 2007," found at the website of the National Association of Home Builders, www.nahb.org under Reports For Consumers, Home Maintenance. This is currently found at: www.nahb.org/fileUpload_details.aspx?contentID=99359, although URL's and websites change from time to time.]

5. ELECTRICITY: Divide electric bill by 12 months; if not available, divide by highest number of months you have been billed; call electric company to verify.
6. GAS, HOME HEATING FUEL, OIL: Self-explanatory.
7. WATER: Self-explanatory.
8. GARBAGE: Self-explanatory.
9. CABLE, DIGITAL TELEVISION: Self-explanatory.
10. TELEPHONE: Break out monthly flat payment and monthly long-distance average in note at right margin.
11. INTERNET SERVICE: Self-explanatory.
12. YARD MAINTENANCE: Self-explanatory.
13. HOME SECURITY SYSTEM: Self-explanatory.
14. HOUSE CLEANING SERVICE: Self-explanatory.
15. PEST CONTROL SERVICES: Self-explanatory.
16. AUTOMOBILE PAYMENT: Self-explanatory.
17. AUTO INSURANCE: Self-explanatory.
18. GASOLINE (AUTO): Self-explanatory.
19. AUTO REPAIR/MAINTENANCE, REGISTRATION, TAXES: This item includes estimated repairs and maintenance on a monthly-average basis. If in doubt, check with your car mechanic as to items such as oil changes, shock absorbers, tire replacement and rotation, tune-ups, valve jobs, new batteries, etc. Take the projected annual total and divide by 12 to get a monthly estimated total. If you include major expenses, items with a life of over one year, be sure to spread the cost out over the expected lifetime. For example, if you paid $360 for a new set of tires with a life expectancy of three years, then you would divide $360 by 36 months, not 12 months.
20. FOOD AND HOUSEHOLD SUPPLIES: Self-explanatory.
21. PETS (insurance, vet, food, kennel).
22. OTHER.

Individual Monthly Expenses

Show the names and ages of the children (if any) involved in this case.

[Note: All items below are average and estimated amounts, calculated on a *monthly* basis. Round off all figures to the nearest dollar.]

1. MEDICAL INSURANCE PREMIUM: In note at margin or bottom of page, state number of people covered by insurance and cost for self if no dependents.

2. DENTAL/VISION INSURANCE PREMIUM: In note at margin or bottom of page, state number of people covered by insurance and cost for self if no dependents.

3. UNINSURED MEDICAL EXPENSES (CO-PAYS, DEDUCTIBLES): Average out-of-pocket costs over 12 months. Allocate on a per-person basis those out-of-pocket medical and/or dental expenses you incur on average each month. Be sure you show only those amounts not covered or reimbursed by any health insurance policy. Be sure to count the initial deductible amount. Use the last six- or 12-month period for averaging unless you can fairly and accurately estimate these expenses for the future (as is the case when a child will soon need braces, for example).

4. UNINSURED PRESCRIPTION & OTC DRUGS & MEDICATION: Enter the average per month figure for those drugs (prescription or otherwise) that are not reimbursed by medical insurance and are not included (such as aspirin) in your monthly "market basket" totals. Allocate the sums to each individual involved to the best of your ability.

5. WORK-RELATED CHILD CARE EXPENSE, INCLUDING SUMMER CAMPS: Show amounts for day care, pre-school and after-school care, and summer camp if necessary due to work.

6. PERSONAL UPKEEP: This means haircuts, hair-do's, and other professional grooming.

7. LAUNDRY/DRY CLEANING: This means dry-cleaning and laundry and should not include costs for detergent, bleach, etc., purchased in the "market basket." It *does* include the monthly average cost of a coin-operated washer/dryer, if applicable.

8. ENTERTAINMENT: Estimate and allocate the monthly amount for this item, both as to yourself and as to a child or children (if applicable). Examples include going out to or renting movies, concerts, plays, etc.

9. RECREATION: Once again, estimate and allocate the monthly amount for this item, both as to yourself and as to a child or children (if applicable). Examples include any fees required or equipment purchased to participate in a recreational activity (i.e., golf, baseball, soccer). Be sure not to duplicate these expenditures with those for "Vacation" or "Entertainment."

10. READING MATERIALS: Self-explanatory. Make sure you include newspapers, professional periodicals, and any books/magazines for children.

11. CHURCH DONATIONS: Self-explanatory. If you give to a church each Sunday, remember that there are 4.3 weeks in a month.

12. GIFTS (HOLIDAYS, BIRTHDAYS): Under your own column, show a monthly average of all gift expenses you incur each year (meaning gifts you give to others, outside of your children, at holidays, birthdays, and on other occasions). If there are children, indicate under each one's column the total of gifts that you give them each year (divided by 12) and the monthly total of gifts you provide them to give to others (such as friends and relatives at holidays or birthday parties).

13. CLUB DUES: Self-explanatory. For children, remember to include expenses you pay for band, scouts, etc.

14. EDUCATION: Self-explanatory. For children, remember to include expenses you pay for textbooks, tuition, summer school, tutoring, field trips, etc.

15. ANNUAL VACATION: Divide total cost for travel, lodging, meals, and entertainment by 12.

16. RETIREMENT: Amount set aside monthly for these; do not double-count with *Voluntary Monthly Deductions* for Retirement.

17. SCHOOL & WORK LUNCH: Enter the average monthly amount for school and/or work lunches for you and each child, if applicable. Note that there are about 20 school days and work days each month.

18. MEDICAL/DENTAL: Allocate on a per-person basis those out-of-pocket medical and/or dental expenses you incur on the average each month. Be sure you show only those amounts not covered or reimbursed by any health insurance policy. Be sure to count the initial deductible amount. Use the last six- or 12-month period for averaging unless you can fairly and accurately estimate these expenses for the future (as is the case when a child will soon need braces, for example).

19. DRUGS: Enter the average per month figure for those drugs (prescription or otherwise) that are not reimbursed by medical insurance and are not included (such as aspirin) in your monthly "market basket" totals. Allocate the sums to each individual to the best of your ability.

20. CLOTHING, ACCESSORIES: The best way to arrive at this figure is to estimate *yearly* clothing costs for each person and divide by 12.

21. ALLOWANCES FOR CHILDREN: Self-explanatory.

22. ANNUAL VACATION: Enter the amount you actually budget or spend each year.

23. EATING OUT: Estimate and allocate the monthly amount for this item, both as to yourself and as to a child or children (if applicable). Your own total, under "SELF," should not reflect lunch at work, but should reflect any other meals eaten out each month. Remember that "School & Work Lunch" is shown above and should not be included here.

24. OTHER: This is an opportunity for you to enter additional monthly expense items not shown above. For example, you might show here the cost of furniture/TV rental (if you do not own these items) or storage expenses, post-office box rental, or monthly bank fees. Since the above is a very generalized list, be sure to include here any items of monthly needs/expenses that might have been overlooked in the above list.

Debts

List all unsecured debts, such as credit cards, amounts due to finance companies or credit unions, or loans being paid back to parents; secured loans, such as mortgage and car payments, should already be shown above. Be sure to contact creditors for DOS and present balances; if no info available, use most recent info and annotate accordingly in margin.

■■■

Your Rights under C.O.B.R.A.

1. Q. WHAT IS C.O.B.R.A.?
  A. C.O.B.R.A. stands for the Consolidated Omnibus Budget Reconciliation Act of 1985. The Act was passed by Congress in 1986, and it requires certain employers to provide, at group rates, continued health insurance coverage for up to three years for divorced persons, widows, spouses of retiring workers, and their children. These benefits must also be provided for workers and their dependents when the worker is terminated (for reasons other than gross misconduct) or has a reduction in hours.

2. Q. ARE ALL EMPLOYERS AFFECTED BY C.O.B.R.A.?
  A. No. The Act affects employers who:

  a. have 20 or more employees; and
  b. are not covered by governmental or church plans.

3. Q. HOW LONG WILL COVERAGE UNDER C.O.B.R.A. LAST?
  A. If you and your spouse are divorcing, you can remain covered by your ex-spouse's employer for up to three years. Widows, spouses of retiring workers and children who are no longer dependent can also be covered for up to three years.

4. Q. WHAT KIND OF COVERAGE CAN I OBTAIN?
  A. C.O.B.R.A. requires that employers offer identical coverage to C.O.B.R.A. recipients as is provided to any other beneficiary. If the plan has "core" or "basic" coverage and also options that may be added (such as dental coverage), you may elect to receive only the core coverage or as many additional benefits as you wish.

5. Q. HOW DO I GET COVERAGE UNDER C.O.B.R.A.?
  A. If you and your spouse are divorcing, and your spouse is employed by a company that is affected by C.O.B.R.A., you are a "qualified beneficiary." It is your or your spouse's responsibility to notify the plan administrator of your divorce within 60 days of the date of the final divorce decree. Once you have notified the plan administrator, the company has 14 days to send you information describing your rights under C.O.B.R.A. You will then have 60 days to decide if you want to be covered under C.O.B.R.A. Other qualified beneficiaries include dependent children, spouses of retiring employees, and widows of previous employees. All qualified beneficiaries are subject to the same rules.

6. Q. WHO WILL PAY THE PREMIUMS?
  A. The employer will no longer pay your premiums once you elect C.O.B.R.A. coverage. You or your ex-spouse will have to pay these premiums, and this may well have an effect on how much coverage you want beyond the basic or core coverage. The employer will charge you the same group rate that an employee must pay. However, a maximum surcharge of 2 percent can be charged to you by the company for administrative costs. The employer also has to allow you to pay the premium in monthly installments if you would like.

7. **Q. IS THERE ANY WAY THAT MY COVERAGE CAN TERMINATE BEFORE THE THREE YEARS?**
   A. Yes. In the following circumstances, your coverage would terminate:

   a. If the employer should decide not to offer a group health plan to *any* employee;
   b. If you or your ex-spouse fail to pay your premium;
   c. If your ex-spouse gets another job; or
   d. If you become eligible for Medicare or certain Social Security benefits.

8. **Q. IF I REMARRY, WILL I LOSE MY C.O.B.R.A. HEALTH INSURANCE?**
   A. It depends. If you remarry but do not receive coverage under your new spouse's group health plan, you may retain your C.O.B.R.A. coverage. To lose your C.O.B.R.A. coverage you must remarry AND become covered under another group plan.

9. **Q. ARE THERE ANY SPECIAL CONDITIONS THAT MIGHT EXCLUDE ME FROM COVERAGE?**
   A. Usually not. In most cases, you are not required to have a physical exam. If your deductible has been met for that year, it will carry over to your separate policy. Also, you will not lose coverage due to preexisting conditions. This means that any ongoing illness or condition you have that was covered *prior* to divorce will still be covered by your policy under C.O.B.R.A.

∎∎∎

Section 4

Last Will and Probate

Choosing an Executor

One of the hardest decisions to make when preparing a Last Will and Testament is who to choose as your executor. This information letter should guide you in your search for the right person. Your attorney cannot make this decision for you, but he or she can make you aware of some important considerations as you make this choice.

The executor will be the person to make important decisions regarding your estate and to ensure that your loved ones are protected, so do not make this choice lightly. This pamphlet should be used along with our Will Questionnaire, Client Information Letter #41, to assist us in drafting your Will. Feel free to contact our office and schedule an appointment with one of our attorneys if you have other questions about your Will or estate.

Since choosing an executor is one of the most important decisions that you will make when preparing a Will, please carefully consider the suggestions listed below.

1. Q. WHAT QUALITIES SHOULD I LOOK FOR IN AN EXECUTOR?
   A. The person that you choose must be at least 18 years of age and a U.S. citizen. An executor cannot be a convicted felon. He or she must be able to communicate well with others as well as understand the financial aspects of your estate. Your executor will have a big responsibility. Therefore, the person you choose must be very reliable, stable, and financially trustworthy. Paying bills and getting reimbursement from insurance companies can be a tedious process, so perseverance and patience are essential.

2. Q. WHEN DOES MY EXECUTOR'S JOB BEGIN?
   A. Many executors begin with tasks outside the formality of the job, helping to plan the funeral and reimburse or advance funds to family members who pay for it. Your executor should also ensure the safety of your home and property during and after the funeral. However, your executor cannot exercise any official rights as executor until the court establishes that you left a valid will and then issues "letters testamentary," which formally name your executor.

3. Q. I WANT TO NAME MY BROTHER AS MY EXECUTOR. WHAT WILL HE HAVE TO DO?
   A. Beyond any informal tasks your executor may attend to, your brother's formal job responsibility will be managing your estate through probate, which is the court process wherein the validity of a Will is decided and your estate is administered. An inexperienced executor may choose to obtain help from a personal legal advisor or hire legal counsel for the estate. Generally, routine tasks can be adequately handled by a lawyer's staff. Once the executor is qualified before the court and the Will is found to be valid, the distribution of property according to the Will is supervised by the court.
      Your brother, as the executor, may be asked to perform the following duties:
      1. Determining what the deceased owned and collecting any money due on the decedent's estate. Locating property may involve a little detective work, as property includes not just the obvious, such as real estate or bank accounts, but also pensions, insurance benefits from employers, and old insurance policies that never lapsed. There may even be accounts in many banks or safe deposit boxes in other states.

2. Gathering assets and gifts for distribution to the beneficiaries once all property has been located.
3. Providing legal notice to creditors.
4. Paying all debts against the estate, including state and federal taxes.
5. Selling estate items to pay any claims or debts against the estate.
6. Applying for a taxpayer ID number from the IRS, which acts as their notification of his appointment as executor.
7. Hiring professionals to deal with the financial and legal aspects of settling the estate (if necessary).
8. Preparing an inventory and filing an accounting of the handling of assets from the estate with the court.
9. Having the property appraised (if necessary). Property appraisals may help in the decision to give the property to the heirs directly or sell it and divide the proceeds among the heirs.
10. Mortgaging, leasing, buying and selling real estate or other assets. If not specified in the Will, this ability is often limited by law.

4. **Q. WHEN DOES MY EXECUTOR'S JOB END?**
   A. Until final settlement of the estate, your executor is responsible for keeping the estate in good order, protecting tangible assets, and investing the estate's funds safely.

5. **Q. CAN I CHOOSE MORE THAN ONE PERSON AS EXECUTOR?**
   A. You can appoint co-executors if you want to split the duties between two people, especially if they have expertise in different areas. You must be careful if you're thinking of choosing this option. There may be a disagreement between them and no way to break the "tie vote." Keeping this in mind, be sure to choose two people who will cooperate and work well together.

6. **Q. DOES MY EXECUTOR HAVE TO LIVE IN THIS STATE?**
   A. You should choose an executor that lives in the state where the property is located, or else the estate may be required to post a bond. To make the executor's job easier and to save expense, we recommend that you choose a resident of North Carolina if your property is in North Carolina.

7. **Q. WHAT HAPPENS IF MY EXECUTOR CANNOT FULFILL THE JOB?**
   A. It is also very important to choose an alternate executor in case the primary executor is unwilling or unable to accept the task. Choose the executor carefully, as if you were choosing an employee for an important position. Whoever you choose will be the one to settle all of your affairs and carry out your wishes. This is an important decision, and you should consider all of your options carefully.

8. **Q. WHAT CAN I DO IF I HAVE OTHER QUESTIONS?**
   A. Please feel free to ask your lawyers for help and assistance. They are here to help you.

■■■

Client Asset Inventory

CLIENT: _____

SOCIAL SECURITY NUMBER: _____

EMPLOYER: _____

ADDRESS: _____

_____

MY VALUABLE PAPERS AND ASSETS ARE STORED IN THESE LOCATIONS:

A. RESIDENCE: _____

_____

LOCATION: _____

_____

B. SAFE-DEPOSIT BOX:

BANK: _____

ADDRESS: _____

_____

C. OFFICE: _____

ADDRESS: _____

_____

LOCATION: _____

_____

D. _____

_____

E. _____

_____

ITEM LOCATION
(Refer to previous page)

MY WILL (original)	A	B	C	D	E	F
MY WILL (copy)	A	B	C	D	E	F
POWERS OF ATTORNEY	A	B	C	D	E	F
MY BURIAL INSTRUCTIONS	A	B	C	D	E	F
SPOUSE'S WILL (original)	A	B	C	D	E	F
SPOUSE'S WILL (copy)	A	B	C	D	E	F
SPOUSE'S BURIAL INSTRUCTIONS	A	B	C	D	E	F
DOCUMENT APPOINTING CHILDREN'S GUARDIAN	A	B	C	D	E	F
HANDWRITTEN LIST OF SPECIAL BEQUESTS	A	B	C	D	E	F
TRUST AGREEMENTS	A	B	C	D	E	F
LIFE INSURANCE, group	A	B	C	D	E	F
LIFE INSURANCE, individual	A	B	C	D	E	F
OTHER DEATH BENEFITS	A	B	C	D	E	F
PROPERTY & CASUALTY INSURANCE	A	B	C	D	E	F
HEALTH INSURANCE POLICY	A	B	C	D	E	F
CAR INSURANCE POLICY	A	B	C	D	E	F
EMPLOYMENT CONTRACTS	A	B	C	D	E	F
LIST OF CHECKING & SAVINGS ACCOUNTS	A	B	C	D	E	F
BANK STATEMENTS, CANCELED CHECKS	A	B	C	D	E	F
LIST OF CREDIT CARDS	A	B	C	D	E	F
CERTIFICATES OF DEPOSIT	A	B	C	D	E	F
CHECKBOOKS	A	B	C	D	E	F
SAVINGS PASSBOOKS	A	B	C	D	E	F
STOCK CERTIFICATES & OTHER SECURITY RECORDS	A	B	C	D	E	F
INCOME & TAX RETURNS	A	B	C	D	E	F
TITLES & DEEDS TO REAL ESTATE & LAND	A	B	C	D	E	F
TITLE INSURANCE	A	B	C	D	E	F
NOTES & OTHER LOAN AGREEMENTS, INCLUDING MORTGAGE	A	B	C	D	E	F
AUTO OWNERSHIP RECORDS	A	B	C	D	E	F
BIRTH CERTIFICATE	A	B	C	D	E	F
MILITARY DISCHARGE PAPERS	A	B	C	D	E	F
MARRIAGE CERTIFICATE	A	B	C	D	E	F
CHILDREN'S BIRTH CERTIFICATES	A	B	C	D	E	F
DIVORCE/SEPARATION DOCUMENTS	A	B	C	D	E	F
NAMES & ADDRESSES OF RELATIVES/FRIENDS	A	B	C	D	E	F
KEYS TO SAFE DEPOSIT BOX	A	B	C	D	E	F
OTHER: _____	A	B	C	D	E	F
_____	A	B	C	D	E	F
_____	A	B	C	D	E	F

IMPORTANT INFORMATION

MY DOCTOR: _____

ADDRESS: _____

_____

PHONE NUMBER: _____

MY LAWYER: _____

ADDRESS: _____

_____

PHONE NUMBER: _____

MY ACCOUNTANT: _____

ADDRESS: _____

_____

PHONE NUMBER: _____

MY MINISTER: _____

ADDRESS: _____

_____

PHONE NUMBER: _____

■■■

Estate Planning Simplified

If you think that your family's future is completely protected simply because you have a will in place, think again. It's true that having a will drafted is the first step in preparing for an unforeseen calamity. However, you should not stop there.

What else should you do? **Plan ahead**. For example, a will won't do your family much good if they can't locate assets such as bank accounts, retirement plans, and insurance contracts. Proper planning now can ensure that the decisions expressed in your will are carried out. It may also protect your family from unscrupulous advisers who prey on widows, widowers, and other heirs. Finally, planning ahead can save your family money in the long run.

Here are some of the steps you can take now that may benefit your family in the future:

- MAKE AN INVENTORY OF ALL YOUR ASSETS. For instance, you might list any bank accounts (IRAs), pension and profit-sharing plans, broker accounts, mutual funds, annuities, etc. Don't forget about pensions from previous jobs. This "inventory" should include an estimate of the value of each item. *Important*: state where the assets are located so they can be easily found.

- PREPARE EMERGENCY INSTRUCTIONS. Your family must notify certain people in case of a tragedy, such as your boss at work, your attorney, and other key advisers. In addition, you may have to provide for someone to watch small children on a short-term basis. Don't overlook such "trivialities" as where the spare keys for the house and car are located.

- UPDATE YOUR WILL. A will spells out who will receive your property at the time of your death, who will be the executor of your estate, and who will serve as guardian to your children. It ensures that your assets are distributed according to your wishes. It is important to review your will periodically to make sure that it addresses any changes in your life, such as the death of a spouse, the birth of a new child or grandchild, or a second marriage. Also, check with your accountant to find out if any tax-law changes necessitate changes in your will.

- PROVIDE COPIES OF DOCUMENTS. Be sure to make at least two copies of important documents (i.e., your will, birth certificate, and powers of attorney). Keep them in your safe deposit box, your file cabinet, or your safe. Be sure they are clearly labeled.

- REVIEW THE BENEFICIARIES ON YOUR ACCOUNTS. You may need to update some accounts as a result of a change in circumstances. For example, you might delete the name of a deceased relative or an ex-spouse or add a newborn child or grandchild. After a divorce or upon separation from your spouse, you might want to change the beneficiary designation on your IRA or life insurance.

- ESTIMATE YOUR FAMILY'S NEEDS. What with medical expenses, burial costs, and other necessary expenses, cash on hand can disappear quickly for a bereaved family. If survivors do not have access to bank accounts, they may need to tap into other sources. One possibility: increase the amount of your **life insurance**

protection. In general, the money is available to survivors within a short time after the death of the insured.

- **GET INVESTMENT ADVICE.** It doesn't have to be written in stone, but you can provide investment guidance—especially for the short term. It is helpful if you have a trusted, reliable financial adviser. **Note:** your spouse may be able to avoid current tax on a payout from a retirement plan by rolling over the funds into an IRA or another eligible plan within 60 days.

- **DO SOME TAX PLANNING.** Uncle Sam allows everyone to get a unified tax credit that, in effect, lets $5,250,000 (in 2013) pass to your heirs tax-free. This tax exemption will increase in the next few years up to $3,500,000 in 2009. You can transfer an unlimited amount of assets to your spouse tax-free. However, doing so may not always be beneficial to your family. Such transfers can boost the surviving spouse's assets over the $5,250,000 threshold and result in increased estate taxes when he or she dies. As soon as your estate exceeds this amount, you're subject to federal estate taxes, which can be up to 40 percent. You may also be subject to state estate taxes. Keep in mind that it is easier to exceed the $5,250,000 threshold than you may think. That's why it's important to review your total assets periodically to determine how much you need to remove from your estate to minimize or avoid the estate tax.

- **PREPARE AND SIGN A "LIVING WILL."** This document, a declaration of your desire to die a natural death, can save thousands of dollars in medical expenses and hospital bills. It will also relieve your next of kin of the burden of deciding whether to prolong your life with artificial life support systems.

- **EVALUATE YOUR ESTATE.** To assess your estate's worth, remember to consider the value of your home, insurance policies, investments, business interests, personal property, and future holdings. In addition, you should subtract any liabilities, which may include your mortgage, other personal or business debts, charitable bequests made in your will, money allocated for funeral and burial expenses, and the costs of administering your estate.

- **TAKE CARE OF FUNERAL ARRANGEMENTS.** You should let your family know how elaborate or simple you prefer a funeral to be.

- **CONSIDER FAMILY GIFTS.** One way to remove money from your estate is by making large gifts. The IRS allows you to make annual gifts of up to $14,000 of property per individual—$28,000 if you are electing to make a joint gift with a spouse—without any tax ramifications and without reducing your unified tax credit. Gifts that are larger than these amounts are generally subject to gift tax.

It may be difficult to consider all the implications of estate planning. That is why it is often put off until it is too late. Having a will drafted is a good start. By making other provisions, you can help ease your family through a difficult time.

WE CAN HELP! Our firm provides questionnaires for basic wills, general powers of attorney, and living wills. We can also prepare special (or limited) powers of attorney, trust agreements, and wills with trusts.

■■■

Your Last Will and Testament

1. Q. **WHAT IS A LAST WILL AND TESTAMENT?**
   A. A Last Will and Testament is the legal document which controls the disposition of your property at death and may provide for guardianship for your children after your death. A will is not effective until death. As long as you are living, your will has no effect and no property or rights to property are transferred by it.

2. Q. **CAN MY LAST WILL AND TESTAMENT BE CHANGED?**
   A. Yes. Changes to a will are made by drafting a new will and destroying the old one, or by adding a "codicil." A codicil is a legal document which must be signed and executed in the same manner as your will. *NEVER MAKE ANY CHANGES TO YOUR WILL* without consulting an attorney. Changes on the face of your original may make it invalid.

3. Q. **WHAT IS MY LEGAL RESIDENCE?**
   A. Your legal residence is the state in which you have your true, fixed, and permanent home and to which, if you are temporarily absent, you intend to return. Voting, paying taxes, owning property, motor vehicle registration, and so on are some indicators of one's legal residency in some state. You cannot be a citizen *at large*. If you are a naturalized U.S. citizen, you are considered to be a resident of the state in which you were naturalized.

4. Q. **IS MY LEGAL RESIDENCE IMPORTANT WITH REGARD TO MY WILL?**
   A. Yes. Your legal residence may affect where your will is probated and the amount of state inheritance or estate tax that may be paid at death.

5. Q. **WHAT IS MY ESTATE?**
   A. Your estate consists of all property and personal belongings which you own or are entitled to possess at the time of your death. This includes real and personal property, cash, savings and checking accounts, stocks, bonds, real estate, automobiles, etc. Although the proceeds of insurance policies may be considered part of your estate in some states, a will does not change the designated beneficiaries of an insurance policy. The proceeds of an insurance policy, although part of your estate for tax purposes in North Carolina, will normally pass to the primary or secondary beneficiary designated on the face of the policy.

6. Q. **TO WHOM SHOULD I LEAVE MY ESTATE?**
   A. A person who receives property through a will is known as a *beneficiary*. You may leave all of your property to one beneficiary, or you may wish to divide your estate among several persons. You may state in your will that several different items of property or sums of money shall go to different persons. In any event, you should decide on at least two levels of beneficiaries: *PRIMARY BENEFICIARIES*—those who will inherit your property upon your death; and *SECONDARY BENEFICIARIES*—those who will inherit your property in the event the primary beneficiaries die before you.

You may even want to select a third-level beneficiary in the event that both the primary and secondary beneficiaries die before you.

7. **Q. May a person dispose of his property in any way?**

    A. Almost, but not quite. For example, in North Carolina, a married person cannot completely exclude a spouse. Generally, you are free to give your property to whomever you desire. However, most states have laws which entitle spouses to at least part of the other spouse's estate. This *statutory share* ranges generally from one-third to one half of the other spouse's estate. Some states, such as Louisiana, also provide shares of the estate to children of the decedent. Insurance proceeds and jointly owned property may be controlled by other provisions of the law. If you have questions concerning the statutory share law in your home state, you should ask a legal assistance attorney.

8. **Q. Should I name a guardian for my children in my will?**

    A. Yes. A guardian should be named in a will to ensure that the children and their estates are cared for in the event that both parents should die. Your guardian should be chosen with extreme care, as this person will be charged with the duty of raising your children and managing their legal affairs. Do not automatically assume that your parents or any other relative will be suitable guardians. Such factors as the age of the guardian, age of the children, religion, social status, economics, and relation of the proposed guardian to the children, if any, should be considered in making your decision. Additionally, a substitute guardian should be chosen with the same care as the primary guardian just in case the primary guardian cannot serve in that capacity.

9. **Q. I want my parents to be the secondary guardians of our children and my spouse disagrees. Do we have to agree on the appointment of a secondary guardian?**

    A. It depends. The guardianship provision is normally effective when both parents die at or about the same time. As an example, if the husband's will nominates his parents and the wife's nominates her parents, and both husband and wife die at or about the same time, then *the court* will have to decide who is the proper party to be the children's guardian. That will cause undue hardship on all parties concerned as well as considerable unnecessary expense, a large part of which your estate will have to pay. On the other hand, if the parties die several years apart from one another, the guardianship clause in the second will to be probated is the only one that would be effective, so there would really be no conflict between the two wills if different secondary guardians were chosen by the husband and wife.

10. **Q. What is an executor?**

    A. An executor (executrix, if female) is the person who will manage and settle your estate according to the will. You should also consider naming a substitute executor in the event that the named executor is unable or unwilling to act as the executor of your estate. By the wording of your will, you can require that your executor or substitute executor be required to post bond or other security, or you can waive this requirement, thereby saving expense to your estate. The choice is yours.

11. Q. **WHAT IF I WANT TO SET UP A TRUST?**
    A. The resources available in this office permit the drafting of simple trust agreements. Consult with your legal assistance attorney for further details.

12. Q. **HOW LONG IS A WILL VALID?**
    A. A properly drawn and executed will remains valid until it is changed or revoked. However, changes in circumstances after a will has been made, such as tax laws, marriage, birth of children, or even a substantial change in the nature or amount of a person's estate can affect whether your will is still adequate or whether your property will still pass in the manner you chose. All changes in circumstances require a careful analysis and reconsideration of the provisions of a will and may make it wise to change the will, with the help of your legal assistance attorney.

13. Q. **DOES A WILL INCREASE PROBATE EXPENSE?**
    A. No. It usually costs less to administer an estate when a person leaves a will than when there is no will. A properly drafted will may reduce the expense of administration in a number of ways. Provisions can be placed in wills that take full advantage of the federal and state tax laws. Drawing a will can avoid the expense of posting bond or appointing a guardian for your children. A will can save money for you and your family if it is properly drafted.

14. Q. **HOW LARGE AN ESTATE IS NECESSARY TO JUSTIFY A WILL?**
    A. Everyone who owns any real or personal property should have a will regardless of the present amount of his estate. Your estate grows daily in value through the repayment of mortgages; appreciation of real estate, stocks, and other securities; inheritances from relatives; and other factors.

15. Q. **WHAT HAPPENS WHEN YOU DON'T MAKE A WILL?**
    A. When a person dies without a will (or dies *intestate*, as the law calls it), the property of the deceased is distributed according to a formula fixed by law. In other words, if you don't make a will, you don't have any say as to how your property will be divided. Take the case of a North Carolina resident dying without a will. If this person dies leaving children, the surviving spouse would share the estate with the children. With no will, the surviving spouse receives the first $30,000 of personal property and half of the remaining estate when there is only one child; if there were two or more children, then the widow or widower would get $1/3$ of the remainder and the children $2/3$. Now, usually a person would prefer that all of his estate, if it is not large, go to the surviving spouse. If there are any children under 18, the property cannot be delivered to them and a guardian must be appointed for them. A guardian will require considerable expense and could create legal problems that might have been avoided with a will. Most important for mothers and fathers, however, is not the disposition of their property after their death but rather the proper care and custody of their minor children. Grandparents, other family members, and godparents do not auto-

matically receive custody of children who do not have a surviving parent. Your will should specify the individual, as well as an alternate, you would like to designate as the guardian of your children. This decision on your part will be of great assistance to the court in determining who will receive custody of your children.

16. Q. WHAT HAPPENS TO PROPERTY HELD IN THE NAMES OF BOTH HUSBAND AND WIFE?
  A. Joint bank accounts and real property held in the names of both husband and wife with right of survivorship usually pass to the survivor by law and not by the terms of the deceased's will. There are many cases, however, in which it is not to your advantage to hold property in this manner.

17. Q. IS A LIFE INSURANCE PROGRAM A SUBSTITUTE FOR A WILL?
  A. No. Life insurance is only one kind of property that a person may own. If a life insurance policy is payable to an individual, the will of the insured has no effect on the proceeds. If the policy is payable to the estate of the insured, the payment of the proceeds may be directed by a will. The careful person will have a lawyer and life insurance counselor work together on a life insurance program as one important aspect of estate planning.

■■■

Your Letter of Instruction

In addition to your will, you'll need to prepare a Letter of Instruction. This document provides your family with the information necessary to locate your assets, carry out funeral arrangements, and collect any survivor's benefits or life insurance proceeds. The letter isn't a legal document, meaning it can't be legally enforced, but it can be the guide your family needs to close your affairs.

Write the letter clearly so even a stranger could understand it, and check with your attorney to be sure it agrees with the terms of your will. Give copies of the letter to your executor and your closest beneficiaries. Because the letter describes your finances in great detail, the original and copies should be kept in a safe place.

When writing your Letter of Instruction, provide in detail (that includes names, addresses, and telephone numbers) such information as the following:

A. DIRECTIONS AND REQUESTS

NOTIFICATIONS. Instruct that these people and institutions be notified of your death: employer, banks and financial institutions, pension plans, trustees, next of kin, accountant, stockbroker, insurance agents, and Social Security office. List your Social Security number and give the location of your card.

FUNERAL ARRANGEMENTS. Describe arrangements you have already made or want your family to make. Include a reminder to ask the funeral director for at least six copies of the death certificate. They'll be needed to collect insurance and other benefits.

B. LISTS & LOCATIONS

PERSONAL PAPERS. Give the location of your personal documents—will, birth and marriage certificates, military papers, and other documents.

BANK ACCOUNTS. List your checking and savings accounts by name of institution, address of the office where the account is located, type of account, and account number. Also give the location of canceled checks and statements.

CREDIT CARDS. List by name of card, bank, and card number.

SAFE DEPOSIT BOX. Give the location of the box, location of the key, and a list of contents.

HOMEOWNER RECORDS. Note the location of the deed and mortgage papers and provide information on taxes, liens, leases, etc.

INSURANCE. List all life, auto, home, veterans', medical, and credit insurance policies you have. Name the agents and give the location of all the documents needed to process claims. Also, describe any loans you have taken out against your insurance policies and haven't yet paid.

VEHICLES. Tell where the registration, title, and other papers can be found.

TAXES. Give the location of your federal and state income tax returns for the past five years.

INVESTMENTS. List stocks, bonds, and other securities by certificate number, issuer, and cost. Tell where they're located, and identify your stockbroker(s).

TRUSTS. List the type and size of any trust you've established and give the name and address of the trustee.

LOANS. List loans and other accounts payable by lender and give full information on terms, payments, collateral, etc.

ACCOUNTS RECEIVABLE. List all debts owed to you, giving the same specifics as for loans and other accounts payable.

SURVIVOR'S BENEFITS. List possible sources of benefits not named in your will—Social Security, veterans, employee, fraternal association, etc.—and how much to expect from each source.

OTHER. Give the location of receipts. Explain any unusual provisions of your will, such as disinheritance of a child.

C. **MEMORANDUM OF SPECIFIC REQUESTS**

State your wishes here as to small items of sentimental value or gifts of personal property. This is not binding on your executor and it does not override the provisions of your will. It does, however, give valuable guidance as to your wishes and intentions for your next of kin and heirs.

■■■

Section 5

Property and Pension Division

Separation and Divorce—
The Bible for Business Clients

1. **Q.** "HELP! MY HUSBAND JUST LEFT HOME LAST WEEK AND TODAY HE FILED A MOTION TO GET A RESTRAINING ORDER. HE WANTS TO STOP ME FROM SPENDING ANY MONEY IN MY BUSINESS. CAN A JUDGE DO THAT?"

   A. Emergency orders are available to the court in unusual circumstances, such as to prevent waste or dissipation of assets; they are not meant to tie up a business so that it cannot operate on a day-to-day basis. The judge will not restrict the normal payment of expenses and receipt of income if there is no harm to the non-owner by the conduct of the owner. If you are continuing to operate the business just as before your separation, you have nothing to fear. If you're about to take some unusual step, then you should immediately check with your lawyer to see if it could be interpreted as dissipation or waste of assets by the court.

2. **Q.** "WHAT'S A TRO?"

   A. A TRO, or temporary restraining order, is granted by the judge when there is an immediate danger of irreparable harm. It must be backed up with an affidavit (a sworn declaration by someone with personal knowledge) as to the facts which justify it, and often it is issued without a hearing. It must be followed up by a hearing within 10 days to allow the other party his day in court. This allows him to testify and produce evidence that it should not be extended into a temporary injunction.

3. **Q.** "I DON'T NEED TO HIRE A CPA TO EVALUATE MY BUSINESS. WE ALREADY HAVE AN ACCOUNTANT WHO CAN EASILY DO THAT."

   A. Business valuation is one of the trickiest parts of "equitable distribution," or the division of marital property. It can easily cost $5,000 to $20,000, depending on the nature and complexity of the business involved. The company's accountant (or CPA, for that matter) is just not in a position to provide the required information to the court and the opinion testimony to link that information to a fair market value. Just as you wouldn't want a car mechanic to give the value of your roadster to the judge, you don't want a company accountant to be the expert you call for business valuation. You'd want a CPA or economist who is skilled in establishing value for the divorce court, one who knows the valuation rules that operate there. The expert will, for example, need to give testimony—in pretrial depositions and at court—regarding such matters as good will, marital and separate components of the company, discount rates, normalized cash flow, and so on. Your divorce lawyer will be able to give you the names of several CPAs who have such experience and are recognized by the court as experts who can be believed in valuation matters.

4. Q. "DON'T WE VALUE A BUSINESS ON *BOOK VALUE*? WHY GO TO ALL THE TROUBLE OF HIRING A CPA? IN FACT, JUST LAST MONTH MY PARTNER AND I JUST AGREED ON A VALUE FOR BUY-SELL PURPOSES. SURELY ONE OF THESE WOULD BE BETTER THAN SPENDING ALL THAT MONEY ON AN EXPERT TO PUT A VALUE ON THE BUSINESS!"

A. The book value or the value in a buy-sell agreement may be relevant to proving the value of the partnership or corporation. Either one may, in fact, be the *best value* that can be put on the business entity. But neither one of them is the *only value* that is applicable. Your own trial expert—the CPA whom you hire—may very well come up with a *lower value* than the one your own buy-sell agreement states! And no valuation that we arrive at will prevent the other side from doing their own valuation if they don't agree with *our value.* So the answer is, tighten your seat belt—you might need to contend with *four valuations*, not just one or two: the buy-sell value, the book value, that placed on the business by your expert, and that placed on it by the opposing party's expert. Unfortunately, these entities are not easy to evaluate, and it's not uncommon for Expert A to put a value of $80,000 on Business X, while the other expert places a value of $250,000 on it. We have even had cases in which *our own experts* differed wildly in the valuation process. In a 1989 case involving a medical practice, for example, the other side's five experts all said, "No more than $60,000, *period!*" Our firm's expert said $250,000. The client went out to find her own expert, thinking that her husband's medical practice *must be worth more* than $250,000. Her new expert, who was completely ignored by the judge, put the value at $750,000!

5. Q. "I DON'T HAVE ANY EXTRA MONEY TO PAY ALIMONY. ALL OUR PROFITS AT XYZ INC. GO BACK INTO THE BUSINESS SO WE HAVE MONEY FOR NEEDED PURCHASES AND SERVICES."

A. This might be the way that you operate XYZ Inc., but it won't be the way that the judge looks at support, whether it's alimony or child support. The court is required to look at the funds that are reasonably available to you in XYZ Inc. when you subtract ordinary and reasonable business expenses from gross revenues. Whether you pack away all your income into retained earnings or spend it as quickly as it comes in, in the form of draws or salary, the judge will need you to account for actual income and, in the case of retained earnings, for potential income in determining a level of support to be paid.

6. Q. "I KNOW WHAT I'LL DO! I CAN MAKE SURE THAT WE DON'T SELL *ANY WIDGETS* FOR THE NEXT SIX MONTHS. THAT WAY, THERE'LL BE NO INCOME FOR THE JUDGE TO USE IN AWARDING ALIMONY!"

A. Not so fast. The judge has the power to award support based on earning capacity, not actual income, when there has been a voluntary reduction of income done in bad faith. This means that, even if you don't actually earn the money, you can be ordered to pay support as if you had.

7. **Q.** "HOW IS IT THAT MY WIFE CAN GET A SHARE OF MY BUSINESS? I STARTED IT! ALL THE STOCK CERTIFICATES ARE IN MY NAME! SHE DOESN'T HAVE ANY CLAIM TO IT BECAUSE SHE DIDN'T CREATE IT AND SHE'S NOT ON THE TITLE!"

   A. In equitable distribution cases, that's not how it works. The rule that the courts and our legislature have created can be put quite simply: *Title doesn't matter.* Whether an asset is in the name of husband, wife, or both, the court only looks at whether the asset was obtained, created, or purchased during the marriage, which makes it marital property (as opposed to separate property, that which came before the marriage or is a gift or inheritance).

8. **Q.** "WHAT I MEANT WAS, I STARTED IT *BEFORE WE WERE MARRIED.* I THOUGHT THAT MADE IT MY OWN PROPERTY!"

   A. Yes, that makes at least part of it separate property. Your lawyer and the CPA will need to do some work, however, in tracing the portion of the present value that is attributable to separate funds or assets coming into the business before the marriage. In a notable case several years ago, the owner of the Charlotte Motor Speedway lost the right to claim any part of his pre-marriage assets as his *separate property* since he couldn't trace them out of his current holdings; he'd commingled the funds and assets and the CPA couldn't follow the trail backwards to prove what was his separate property.

9. **Q.** "I DON'T HAVE ANY PERSONAL EXPENSES FOR TRANSPORTATION AND MEALS. I WRITE IT ALL OFF FOR BUSINESS."

   A. This could be a problem. The judge will want to see income and expense figures to determine such issues as spousal support and business value. Reasonable and ordinary business expenses do not include *all your mileage* charged against the business, or all meals taken as business expenses. The other side's expert—and your own expert, as well—should remove the personal component of these business write-offs and add it back into your income.

10. **Q.** "I DON'T THINK THAT MY WIFE SHOULD GET MORE THAN HALF OF THE VALUE OF THIS BUSINESS. CAN THE JUDGE AWARD HER MORE?"

    A. There is a statutory presumption of an equal division; that is, the law says that the usual or assumed split is 50-50. However, the judge can apply numerous factors to result in an "equitable" split—that is, one which is other than equal. The factors are many, such as the tax consequences of a division, the incomes and expenses of the parties, the health of the parties, the length of the marriage, and the contributions of your spouse to the acquisition of the business. Any of these, standing alone, can tip the scales to create an unequal division.

11. **Q.** "I DON'T HAVE THE MONEY NEEDED TO BUY OUT MY HUSBAND'S INTEREST IN MY BUSINESS. THE CASH JUST ISN'T THERE! HOW WILL I BE ABLE TO SETTLE MY CASE?"

    A. The term is "distributive award." It's a cash payment over time, usually six years as the maximum, which allows one party to pay the other in what appears to be a lopsided property division in which one side has most of the assets locked up in a valuable business that cannot be sold off or liquidated.

12. **Q.** "OUR SETTLEMENT JUST GAVE MY WIFE SOME RENTAL PROPERTIES THAT WE OWNED. DOESN'T THAT MEAN THAT THE JUDGE WILL REVERSE THE ORDER GRANTING ALIMONY TO MY WIFE?"

   A. Maybe. The court, if requested, must revisit a property division when the issue of alimony or child support is involved and the support recipient has received income-producing property that wasn't there at the time of the initial support award.

13. **Q.** "I CAUGHT MY WIFE COMMITTING ADULTERY. SURELY THAT'S ENOUGH FOR THE JUDGE TO ALLOW ME TO KEEP MY OWN BUSINESS!"

   A. Marital fault is not a relevant factor in the equation of an equitable distribution case. If she committed adultery before the date of separation, that might be useful in an alimony case, but the only fault that equitable distribution cases recognize is "economic fault"—that is, a party's wrongful conduct to damage, dissipate, waste, or destroy marital property.

14. **Q.** "WILL I HAVE TO PROVIDE MY HUSBAND AND HIS LAWYERS WITH INFORMATION ABOUT MY BUSINESS?"

   A. Yes—lots of it! The process is called "discovery," and it involves written questions (interrogatories), document requests, and possibly a visit to the site of the property or business under Rule 34. Either side can demand, as well, to hear oral testimony about business matters under oath (a "deposition"). The other side can demand that you designate someone who is particularly skilled in the giving of answers in certain areas, such as financial operations.

15. **Q.** "I DON'T WANT MY ENTIRE CASE EXPOSED IN A COURTROOM BEFORE A BUNCH OF STRANGERS. WE HAVE TRADE SECRETS, COMPENSATION DATA, AND PROPRIETARY INFORMATION THAT NEED NOT BE MADE PUBLIC. HOW CAN WE AVOID A MESSY PUBLIC TRIAL?"

   A. In family law cases, the parties can agree (but the court cannot mandate) the use of arbitration. This means that the case is contested in a conference room, not a courtroom. The parties' attorneys will select the arbitrator, usually a skilled family law attorney, and the parties are responsible for paying the fees charged by the arbitrator, either 50-50 or in such other ration as agreed upon. The parties' attorneys will sit down with the arbitrator and set up the dates and times for arbitration and the rules to be applied.

16. **Q.** "CAN'T WE TRY TO SETTLE THE CASE BEFORE LITIGATION?"

   A. Yes—you should. The rules of court here in Wake County require that all equitable distribution cases must proceed to mediation before they can be calendared for trial. A skilled mediator—who is often an attorney specializing in family law—can often broker a compromise between the parties which will keep the case out of court and will cost a lot less than a contested trial.

17. **Q.** "CAN'T I GET A PRE-NUP TO AVOID THIS MESS?"

   A. Yes—if you're not already married! An antenuptial agreement, also called a "pre-nup," will allow you to specify what is marital, what is separate, and what happens if one of you dies or if the two of you go through a divorce. You can also make provisions for alimony—or a waiver of alimony—in a pre-nup.

18. Q. **"HOW DO I FIND A LAWYER WHO CAN HELP ME THROUGH THIS MESS?"**

A. A good family law attorney is your best bet—one who works in this field most (or all) of the time. There are more than 100 lawyers in East Carolina who are recognized as "board-certified" in family law; they have had to meet the high standards (an initial examination, recommendations from other lawyers, annual continued education, and re-certification every five years) of the East Carolina State Bar's Board of Legal Specialization. The listing of all such lawyers, arranged by county, is found at [website]. You can also choose an East Carolina lawyer who has been selected as a Fellow of the American Academy of Matrimonial Lawyers, a small and select group of distinguished lawyers in the area of family law; there are only about 30 such family law leaders in the state. The website listing all Fellows in the state is [website]. There are photographs, profiles, and samples of professional writings there as well.

■■■

Uniformed Services Former Spouses' Protection Act (USFSPA)

1. Q. **What is *USFSPA*?**
   A. USFSPA is a law passed by Congress in 1982 to offer some financial protection to certain former spouses of servicemembers (SMs). It allows states to divide military disposable retired pay as marital property upon divorce. It allows some former spouses (through a court order) to be awarded a share of *disposable retired pay* by direct payment from the retired pay center. For most servicemembers (SMs) and retirees from the uniformed services, this center is DFAS (Defense Finance and Accounting Service). Other federal laws provide for former spouse coverage under the Survivor Benefit Plan, as well as medical care and certain other benefits.

2. Q. **What is *disposable retired pay*?**
   A. Disposable retired pay is the total monthly pay to which a retired SM is entitled, minus most disability pay, federal debt repayments, fines, forfeitures, and Survivor Benefit Plan premiums.

3. Q. **Can I get child support or alimony taken out of my spouse's retired pay and sent directly to me?**
   A. Yes. To get direct payment from DFAS for alimony or child support under the Act, you will first need to get a court order requiring the payment of child support or alimony. The court order should state that the award is made as direct payment of retired pay. The court order and/or other documents served with the court order must identify the SM concerned and, *if possible*, state his or her Social Security number.

4. Q. **If part of the retired pay is awarded as marital property upon divorce, how do I obtain direct payment from *DFAS*?**
   A. You must meet the "10-year test" to receive direct payment under the Act. You, the former spouse, must have been married to the SM for at least 10 years, during which the member performed at least 10 years of creditable service for retirement purposes. Further, if you meet the test, you must get a *court order* specifically stating that the award shall be made as direct payment of retired pay. If these conditions are met, then you can get monthly checks from DFAS.

5. Q. **Do all states allow military retired pay to be divided as marital or community property?**
   A. Yes. Only Puerto Rico bars the division of military pension upon divorce. All states have one method or another of granting the division of military pensions as marital property, although some states have conditions which must be met for military pension division. You should check the laws of the state where you're a legal resident, as well as the "home state" (or domicile) of the SM. You should also consult a military legal assistance attorney or civilian lawyer as to pension division in specific states. An overseas

court, however, cannot grant military pension division; DFAS will only honor orders regarding division of retired pay from U.S. courts, not those of foreign countries.

6. **Q. IF STATE LAW ALLOWS THE RETIRED PAY TO BE DIVIDED, HOW WILL THE DIVISION TAKE PLACE?**

   A. The rules for retired pay division vary from state to state. For example, the court can divide the pension by ordering that a portion be paid to the non-military spouse upon the SM's retirement. This would be paid on a monthly basis as long as the retiree receives payments. The payments could come from the retiree or, if the "direct payment" conditions in #4 above are met, directly from DFAS so long as it is contained in a court order (not just in a separation agreement).

7. **Q. IS THERE ANY WAY THE COURT CAN DIVIDE THE RETIRED PAY SO I DON'T HAVE TO WAIT UNTIL MY HUSBAND RETIRES?**

   A. Some states, such as California, allow payments to be made under court order while the member is still on active duty. Most states, however, do not. In all states, however, the law allows the present value of the pension to be used as a set-off or trade against other property that the nonmilitary spouse will receive. Thus the retired pay might be traded against the marital residence if the values of each were roughly equal. If the values were not equal and the SM received "too much" of the marital property, the judge could order him or her to transfer other property to the nonmilitary spouse, or to make regular payments to the other party (called a "distributive award") until the shares of the parties were adjusted as the judge ordered.

8. **Q. HOW CAN I FIND OUT WHAT STATE COURT CAN DIVIDE MY HUSBAND'S PENSION?**

   A. The answer to this question depends on your husband's **legal residence** (or domicile). A state has jurisdiction over the husband's military pension if:
   - He is a legal resident of this state; **or**
   - He is residing in that state for reasons other than military assignment; **or**
   - He consents to the jurisdiction of that state's courts over the division of his retired pay in a property division lawsuit.

   If none of the above conditions apply, then that state's courts cannot divide his retired pay.

9. **Q. HOW MUCH OF HIS RETIRED PAY WILL BE DIVIDED OR AWARDED TO ME?**

   A. The court can only divide the "marital portion" of the pension, that is, the portion that was earned during the marriage. The rest of the pension (that earned before marriage or after separation or divorce) is his separate property. In addition to this, the Act says that no more than *half* of the pension can, under most circumstances, be divided. Many states presume an equal division of all marital property, including retirement rights. Other than this, there is no way of telling how much marital property will be awarded or how much of the pension will be granted to you.

10. **Q.** IF I DIE, WHAT HAPPENS TO THE PENSION DIVISION AWARD?
    A. Under USFSPA, your rights to a portion of military retired pay end upon your death. Payments cannot be made to your estate, survivors, or heirs.

11. **Q.** IS THERE ANY WAY THAT I CAN STILL CONTINUE TO RECEIVE PAYMENTS AFTER MY HUSBAND DIES?
    A. Yes. Federal law states that, in the event the SM dies, the person receiving the award shall receive no further benefits unless the Survivor Benefit Plan (SBP) has been elected by the SM. Payments will continue if SBP coverage has been chosen (but not necessarily in the amount of payments under USFSPA). The court can order a spouse to provide SBP coverage for the former spouse.

12. **Q.** IS THERE A MAXIMUM AMOUNT THAT I CAN RECEIVE UNDER **USFSPA**?
    A. Yes. USFSPA limits pension division awards to 50 percent of the net retired pay, regardless of whether the pay is awarded as child support, alimony, or marital property to be directly paid from the finance center. There are certain exceptions in the event of multiple court orders involving different spouses. Ask your attorney about these exceptions.

13. **Q.** WHAT CAN I DO IF MY HUSBAND IS ORDERED TO PAY MORE THAN THE MAXIMUM ALLOWABLE AMOUNT UNDER **USFSPA**?
    A. If this happens, DFAS cannot help you. If there is no exception in USFSPA, then you will need to take action directly against your husband through the courts for amounts in excess of 50 percent of his disposable retired pay.

14. **Q.** BESIDES RETIRED PAY, WHAT OTHER BENEFITS CAN I RECEIVE UPON DIVORCE?
    A. If you are a former spouse and meet certain requirements, you may be able to receive full or partial medical, dental, commissary, and post exchange benefits.

15. **Q.** HOW CAN I RECEIVE *FULL* MEDICAL BENEFITS?
    A. You can receive *full* benefits (including medical care on a "space-available" basis and TRICARE coverage) if you meet the "20/20/20 test." This three-part test requires that you must have been married to the SM for at least *20 years*. The SM must have performed at least *20 years* of creditable service toward retirement. Finally, at least *20 years* of the marriage must overlap at least 20 years of active service. You must meet *all three parts* of the test.

16. **Q.** DOES THE DATE OF THE DIVORCE DECREE MATTER IF I MEET THE *20/20/20 TEST*?
    A. No. If you meet the test, you are eligible to receive full benefits regardless of the date of the divorce decree.

17. **Q.** IF I DO NOT MEET THE *20/20/20 TEST* FOR FULL BENEFITS, ARE THERE OTHER BENEFITS AVAILABLE?
    A. Yes. You may be able to receive permanent medical benefits if the divorce decree was final before April 1, 1985, and you meet the "20/20/15 test."

18. Q. **WHAT IS THE *20/20/15* TEST?**
    A. You must have been married to the SM for at least *20 years* and the SM must have performed at least *20 years* of creditable service towards retirement. Finally, at least 15 years of the marriage must be during military service. Again, as with the "20/20/20 test," you must meet all parts of the test.

19. Q. **IF I RECEIVE FULL BENEFITS, CAN I BE COVERED BY OTHER MEDICAL INSURANCE?**
    A. Under either test, if you receive full benefits you cannot be covered by any type of employer-sponsored medical coverage. However, you can refuse your employer-sponsored medical benefits and retain the military medical benefits. You would also be disqualified if you have individually obtained medical insurance.

20. Q. **MAY I RETAIN FULL BENEFITS IF I REMARRY?**
    A. No. You must remain unmarried under either test. Any subsequent remarriage eliminates the benefits, *even if you are widowed or divorced later.*

21. Q. **IF I MEET THE *20/20/15* TEST, BUT MY DIVORCE DECREE IS FINAL AFTER *APRIL 1, 1985*, AM I STILL ELIGIBLE FOR SOME BENEFITS?**
    A. Yes. You are entitled to one year of transitional benefits, after which you have the right to convert to a private health plan set up by the Defense Department. However, you must remain unmarried and not be covered under employer-sponsored medical coverage.

22. Q. **ARE THERE ANY OTHER ASPECTS OF MILITARY BENEFITS THAT I SHOULD KNOW?**
    A. Yes. Remember these points:
    - If the former spouse for some reason loses eligibility to medical care, he or she may purchase a "conversion health policy" under the DOD Continued Health Care Benefit Program (CHCBP). CHCBP coverage must ordinarily be purchased within 60 days of the divorce or end of military service, and it's usually available for 36 months. CHCBP is *not* part of TRICARE. For further information on this program, contact a military medical treatment facility health benefits advisor, or contact the Humana Military, Attn: CHCBP, P.O. Box 740072, Louisville, KY 40201-7472 (1-800-444-5445). You can visit CHCBP's website at http://www.humana-military.com.
    - A former spouse may also obtain *indefinite* medical coverage through CHCBP (under 10 U.S. Code 1078a) if she or he meets certain conditions. The former spouse:
      • Must be entitled to a share of the servicemember's pension or SBP coverage;
      • May not be remarried if below age 55;
      • Must pay quarterly advance premiums; and
      • Must meet certain deadlines for initial application.
      Details regarding application for this "CHCBP-indefinite" coverage may be found at www.tricare.mil/welcome/specialprograms/chcbp/chcbp claims.aspx. The coverage is the same as that for federal employees, and the cost is the sum of the following: premium for a federal employee, plus premium paid by the federal agency, plus 10%. This amounts to around $400 per month as of 2013.

▸ A former spouse who qualifies for any of these benefits may apply for an ID card at any military ID card facility. He or she will be required to complete DD Form 1172, "Application for Uniformed Services Identification and Privilege Card." The former spouse should be sure to take along a current and valid picture ID card (such as a driver's license), a copy of the marriage certificate, the court decree, a statement of the SM's service (if available), and a statement that he or she has not remarried and is not participating in an employer-sponsored health care plan.

▸ The benefits we're discussing *are statutory entitlements*; they belong to the nonmilitary spouse if she or he meets the requirements as set out above. They are not terms that may be given or withheld by the SM, and thus they should not ordinarily be part of the "give and take" of pension and property negotiations, since the SM has no control over these spousal benefits.

23. Q. ARE THERE ANY CIVILIAN AGENCIES AVAILABLE TO HELP ME?
    A. EXPOSE is an organization that has been lobbying Congress for increased military benefits for ex-military wives. EXPOSE can be reached at (703) 941-5844, Post Office Box 11191, Alexandria, VA 22312-0191, and http://EX-POSE.org. The American Retirees Association (ARA) is an organization that serves divorced SMs—active-duty, Guard/Reserve, and retired. The ARA can be reached at 700 E. Redlands Blvd, Ste U-307, Redlands, CA 92373-0781 (703-527-3065), and http://www.americanretirees.org. The ARA has also published a book, *Divorce and the Military II*, that covers in depth most of the issues discussed here.

24. Q. GOD BLESS AMERICA! THIS STUFF IS SO DARNED COMPLEX THAT I CAN'T FIND A GOOD CIVILIAN ATTORNEY WHO KNOWS ANYTHING ABOUT *USFSPA* AND MILITARY PENSION DIVISION. HOW CAN I GET A GOOD, COMPETENT LAWYER TO HELP ME?
    A. That's a very good question. There are lots of military cases where rights and advantages have been lost because of the attorney's lack of knowledge of the subject matter. As a practical matter, there are very few attorneys in any given state (and even fewer overseas) who know much about this little-known corner of the law—USFSPA and the division of military retirement benefits. And since you only get *one chance* to do it right, it makes sense to find the right lawyer right off the bat! Here are a couple of tips to help you:

    ▸ Ask a military legal assistance attorney to help you; they will sometimes know local lawyers near the military base who specialize in "military divorce" cases.

    ▸ Ask a friend who's been through this already; if he or she has had a good attorney, this kind of "word-of-mouth" advertising may help you hook up with the right attorney.

    ▸ If you already have a lawyer, ask him (or her) how much experience he has in the area of military pension division. A good lawyer should never hesitate to answer a question like this; an honest attorney will not flinch at giving you a straightforward answer. Be careful if your lawyer is "offended" or becomes defensive, however.

▸ If you're generally satisfied with your current lawyer but she needs some help, don't hesitate to suggest that another attorney be hired *to act as co-counsel* in the area of USFSPA and military pension division. The code of ethics in virtually every state requires attorneys to be competent in the area in which they practice or else to associate competent co-counsel. Maybe if your lawyer has a "silent partner" to help out when the going gets rough, your case will be settled (or tried) more effectively and fairly.

▸ Try to get a Reservist who practices in the field of family law as your attorney. Members of the Reserves are frequently the ones who are the most "up to speed" on current law and regulations in this area.

▸ Find out from the state bar or bar association if there are "certified specialists" in family law in your state. A majority of states have "specialty" designations for lawyers that concentrate their practices in a particular field, and these lawyers (although charging a premium for their services) will more likely be able to handle your case competently than a general practitioner.

▸ Contact the family law section of your state's bar association or the American Bar Association to see if they can recommend the names of some attorneys who've spoken or written in the area of military divorce law.

■■■

The Survivor Benefit Plan

1. Q. What is the survivor benefit plan, and how does it work?

A. The Survivor Benefit Plan (SBP) is an annuity paid to the surviving spouse or family member of a deceased servicemember. It's similar to insurance in that it enables retired military personnel to provide monthly income to beneficiaries after the retiree's death. The beneficiary of your SBP can be your spouse, former spouse, dependent children, or any other person with an insurable interest in your life.

2. Q. How do I decide how much my beneficiary will receive?

A. To determine how much the beneficiary will receive, you must first designate a "base amount," and this is based on your retired pay. The minimum base amount is $300 per month, but you can select any greater amount up to the full monthly amount of your retired pay.

The annuity for your spouse or former spouse is 55% of the designated base amount. For example, if the designated base amount is $2,000, then the monthly annuity payment to the beneficiary will be $1,100. Your cost for the annuity depends on who your beneficiary is and what base amount you select. Former spouse coverage, for example, costs 6.5% of the selected base amount. The annuity cost is deducted from your gross retired pay.

3. Q. Do I *have to* sign up? Or do I have a choice?

A. SBP participation is optional, but if you are on active duty and married, you will not be able to reject full spousal SBP coverage without your spouse's consent. There is also a Guard/Reserve SBP program; once enrolled, a member of the Guard/Reserve must elect the maximum coverage for the spouse unless the spouse consents to a lesser amount. The options are set out in the "20-year letter."

4. Q. When do I have to decide?

A. There are three points to remember:

- If you are married and on active duty, you must make your SBP election when you retire. If you elect to participate, you cannot cancel the SBP coverage later, except under very limited circumstances. If you decline to participate, this decision is irrevocable absent an Open Enrollment period established by Congress. There hasn't been one, though, since 2006.
- If you are a Guard or Reserve member, you have two chances to select SBP coverage—first when you complete 20 years of service and again when you turn 60. However if you elect to participate at the 20-year point, you cannot "unenroll" at age 60.
- You are allowed only one adult SBP beneficiary. You can't reserve part for a present or future spouse and part for a former spouse. Multiple beneficiaries are permitted only if you choose "child coverage" and there is more than one child, or "spouse and child coverage."

5. Q. IS THIS *REALLY* A GOOD DEAL?

   A. SBP is generally a good plan, but there are some situations in which it may not be the most economical plan. For example, the minimum SBP plan premium for $300 per month as the base amount is cheaper than almost every private insurance program. But at larger amounts, SBP coverage may be more expensive than commercial insurance. Also, if you're going through a divorce and the SBP has not been designated for your soon-to-be-ex, consider "saving" the SBP for a future spouse if your soon-to-be former spouse is likely to remarry before 55, thus losing eligibility for coverage.

   Commercial life insurance or a private annuity may also provide better or cheaper protection for a younger surviving spouse. But SBP is a lifetime annuity and it will never become "too expensive," as might be the case with life insurance and rising premiums. For better comparison information on life insurance, check with an insurance agent who is familiar with the costs and benefits of SBP, such as a military retiree or an agent who is in the Reserves or the National Guard. The bottom line here is, "Shop around!"

SBP CHECKLIST

This attorney checklist will help to explain the SBP and coverage for the nonmilitary spouse.

✔	Action or issue	Comments
	SBP is a unitary benefit; it cannot be divided between current spouse and former spouse.	
	Election: Servicemember on active duty is automatically covered; at retirement an election must be made, and spouse concurrence is necessary if member chooses no SBP, child-only coverage or coverage at base amount less than his/her full retired pay.	
	Election—Guard/Reserve: There is one opportunity to make election at the 20-year mark (after 20 years of creditable Guard/Reserve service). At time of application for retired pay (about a year before member turns 60), he/she is given another opportunity if he/she deferred election at the 20-year mark. Spouse concurrence as above.	
	If representing the nonmilitary spouse, be sure to mandate former spouse coverage with member selecting full retired pay as base amount.	SBP benefit payments equal 55% of the selected base amount, which can be from $300 up to the full retired pay.

✔	Action or issue	Comments
	If representing the member/retiree, make sure that the base amount selected yields an SBP payment not to exceed the amount of retired pay awarded to the former spouse, so that spouse doesn't profit by retiree's death.	Selection of a base amount lower than full retired pay means that the death benefit payments from SBP can be about the same as the lifetime spousal payment. This "mirror benefit" approach may be very difficult to calculate before retirement, depending on what the rules of pension division are in the state involved.
	If representing the member/retiree, try to negotiate a reduction of the spouse's share of the military pension to reflect the additional cost of the SBP premium, which is taken out of the retired pay.	For former spouse coverage in retirement from active duty, SBP premium is 6.5% of selected base amount, payable out of retired pay, and it is "taken off the top" and deducted before division of disposable retired pay, so the default is that both parties pay in same shares as their respective shares of the retired pay.
	If member/retiree is to submit SBP election to DFAS, make sure this is done within one year of divorce unless the divorce is before retirement, in which case the SM must set up SBP at retirement; enclose divorce decree and SBP application form titled Survivor Benefit Plan (SBP) Election Statement for Former Spouse Coverage (DD Form 2656-1).	
	If spouse/former spouse applies, be sure to enclose copy of divorce decree, order for SBP coverage and "deemed election request" within one year of order granting SBP coverage [different deadline from one year after divorce, in some cases].	Use DD Form 2656-10 for deemed election request.
	If above deadlines are exceeded, apply to the appropriate Board for the Correction of Military Records for relief. Deadline in most cases is 3 years from discovery of problems. Relief may be available if retiree has not remarried, or if new spouse consents.	
	Send SBP documents to: Defense Finance and Accounting Service, U.S. Military Retirement Pay, P.O. Box 7130, London, KY 40742-7130 (if retired or in a pay status).	It is recommended to send by certified mail, return receipt requested. See DD Form 2656-10 for other addresses to use if not an active duty SM or a retiree already in a pay status.
	SBP is reduced by Dependency and Indemnity Compensation in certain circumstances.	For information, go to **http://www.vba.va.gov/ bln/21/Milsvc/Docs/DICDec2002Eng.doc**, or call toll-free 1-800-827-1000.

6. **Q.** I'M GOING THROUGH A DIVORCE FROM MY HUSBAND. IS THERE ANYTHING I SHOULD KNOW ABOUT HIS **SBP** COVERAGE FOR ME?

   A. Yes. Here are the most important points:
   - First of all, it's not automatic. You must ask for it, and the two of you must agree on this coverage (or the judge must order it) for SBP to be effective.
   - Secondly, it must be included in a court order and sent to DFAS (Defense Finance and Accounting Service) or other applicable retired pay center if you want to be sure that this option will be honored. And the order must be sent to DFAS *within one year of the divorce* (if by the retiree or service-member) or within a *year of the SBP order* (if by the spouse). If divorce happens prior to retirement, the SBP Election needs to be made at retirement, even if it occurs before the 1-year window expires.
   - Finally, if retirement is approaching soon, see an SBP counselor, a person from the Retirement Services Office on base, or a legal assistance attorney now, so you can make an informed decision.

7. **Q.** WON'T THIS BE TAKEN CARE OF WHEN MY DIVORCE GOES THROUGH?

   A. Not necessarily. If your divorce is in an overseas court—Germany, Japan, etc.—then the court *cannot do anything* about military retirement benefits, including retired pay and Survivor Benefit Plan. No order from an overseas court will be obeyed by DFAS regarding SBP. You'll have to ask a court in the U.S. to make provisions for SBP if you want to be covered.

   On the other hand, you may be proceeding with a divorce in an American court. In this case, you should ask your civilian attorney to be sure to include a request for *property division* in the divorce papers you file with the court. Your papers should specifically ask for division of any military pension rights and coverage under the Survivor Benefit Plan in case your spouse dies. If DFAS is served with a proper SBP order by the spouse or former spouse within the appropriate deadlines, then it will honor that request, even if the servicemember or retiree refuses to sign an application to that effect.

   ■■■

Section 6

Separation and Negotiation

Financial Checklist

Financial preparation for divorce

If you and your partner are just thinking about divorce:

- Start putting away savings in an account of your own. This will give you ready cash in case your spouse suddenly stops contributing to household bills.

- If you do not have credit in your own name, get it. Apply for credit cards and, if necessary, have someone other than your spouse co-sign a small bank loan.

- Make an inventory of all separately and jointly held assets, including investments, cars, and furniture. This tally, along with a list of outstanding debts, may be necessary to determine a division of property. Have your bank verify a list of contents of any joint safe deposit box.

Once you have decided to separate

- Notify banks and brokerages where you and your spouse have joint accounts of your intent to divorce. Ask that no brokerage transactions be carried out without the written approval of both you and your spouse. Keep a record of the date, the time, and the person with whom you speak.

- Close out joint accounts or, if you wish to keep the accounts open, notify the creditors in writing that you will no longer be responsible for your spouse's purchases.

- Try to negotiate an agreement with your spouse on the division of assets, child support, and visitation rights. If you want child support or alimony, prepare a list of your monthly and yearly expenses so your lawyer can see what you need. Also, in cases where child support or alimony is an issue, obtain copies of state and federal income tax returns for previous years to show at least an approximation of your spouse's income. Make copies of your spouse's most recent paystubs. This can eliminate a lot of time and expense in lawyer fees trying to prove your spouse's income.

- You will also need to decide who leaves or who remains in the marital residence. In making this decision, you should remember that only the spouse who stays in the home may take the federal and state deductions for mortgage payments.

■■■

Property Division Financial Checklist

Please give us, on a separate sheet of paper, your answers to the following questions so that we can better help you in regard to property division:

1. Describe your assets and liabilities, both jointly and separately owned [see attached form].

2. Give your estimation of values, as well as any appraisals of any significant property, both real and personal, including the marital residence, contents, and personal possessions.

3. Which assets did each of you own at the time of the separation?

4. For all those assets or debts existing at the date of separation, did you or your spouse possess them at the date of marriage? If so, indicate what portion existed at date of marriage, as well.

5. Did you receive any assets by gift or inheritance? If so, have any such assets been used regularly for the common benefit of the family? If so, what is the status of those assets?

6. Describe each liability, i.e., in whose name, the purpose or use of the borrowed funds, etc. [see attached form].

7. Describe the educational and employment history of you and your spouse, including employability, comparison of salaries, and future prospects.

8. List all cash assets, i.e., IRAs, money market funds, certificates of deposit, pension plans, etc., owned by you and your spouse, jointly or separately [see attached form].

9. Describe your direct and/or indirect contributions to the financial status of the marriage. Describe your spouse's contribution, e.g., who paid what bills and for how long that has been the case.

10. What would you consider to be a fair settlement?

11. Is there any item or issue that will be a deal-breaker for you? For your spouse?

12. List and provide copies of any documents or other materials that support any claim or desire you have expressed.

LISTING OF ASSETS & LIABILITIES [use additional sheets of paper if necessary]		
	DESCRIPTION	**MARITAL OR SEPARATE** [IF SEPARATE, STATE WHY— e.g., PRE-MARITAL, INHERITANCE, GIFT]
A	REAL PROPERTY:	
B	MOTOR VEHICLES:	

LISTING OF ASSETS & LIABILITIES [use additional sheets of paper if necessary]	
NET ASSET VALUE (OR DEBT BALANCE) AT DATE OF SEPARATION [SHOW FULL FAIR MARKET VALUE, THEN SHOW ANY LIENS OR MORTGAGES; SUBTRACT THE LATTER FOR NET]	COMMENTS

	LISTING OF ASSETS & LIABILITIES [use additional sheets of paper if necessary]	
	DESCRIPTION	**MARITAL OR SEPARATE** [IF SEPARATE, STATE WHY— e.g., PRE-MARITAL, INHERITANCE, GIFT]
C	STOCKS, BONDS:	
D	RETIREMENT BENEFITS:	

LISTING OF ASSETS & LIABILITIES
[use additional sheets of paper if necessary]

NET ASSET VALUE (OR DEBT BALANCE) AT DATE OF SEPARATION [SHOW FULL FAIR MARKET VALUE, THEN SHOW ANY LIENS OR MORTGAGES; SUBTRACT THE LATTER FOR NET]	COMMENTS

LISTING OF ASSETS & LIABILITIES
[use additional sheets of paper if necessary]

	DESCRIPTION	MARITAL OR SEPARATE [IF SEPARATE, STATE WHY— e.g., PRE-MARITAL, INHERITANCE, GIFT]
E	BANK ACCOUNTS, OTHER FINANCIAL ASSETS:	
F	ARTWORK, COLLECTIBLES:	

LISTING OF ASSETS & LIABILITIES	
[use additional sheets of paper if necessary]	
NET ASSET VALUE (OR DEBT BALANCE) AT DATE OF SEPARATION [SHOW FULL FAIR MARKET VALUE, THEN SHOW ANY LIENS OR MORTGAGES; SUBTRACT THE LATTER FOR NET]	**COMMENTS**

LISTING OF ASSETS & LIABILITIES
[use additional sheets of paper if necessary]

	DESCRIPTION	MARITAL OR SEPARATE [IF SEPARATE, STATE WHY— e.g., PRE-MARITAL, INHERITANCE, GIFT]
G	HOUSEHOLD FURNISHINGS:	
H	BUSINESS INTERESTS:	

LISTING OF ASSETS & LIABILITIES	
[use additional sheets of paper if necessary]	
NET ASSET VALUE **(OR DEBT BALANCE)** **AT DATE OF SEPARATION** [SHOW FULL FAIR MARKET VALUE, THEN SHOW ANY LIENS OR MORTGAGES; SUBTRACT THE LATTER FOR NET]	**COMMENTS**

LISTING OF ASSETS & LIABILITIES [use additional sheets of paper if necessary]	
DESCRIPTION	MARITAL OR SEPARATE [IF SEPARATE, STATE WHY— e.g., PRE-MARITAL, INHERITANCE, GIFT]
I LIFE INSURANCE:	
J MISCELLANEOUS ASSETS: [NOT OTHERWISE LISTED]	

LISTING OF ASSETS & LIABILITIES [use additional sheets of paper if necessary]	
NET ASSET VALUE (OR DEBT BALANCE) AT DATE OF SEPARATION [SHOW FULL FAIR MARKET VALUE, THEN SHOW ANY LIENS OR MORTGAGES; SUBTRACT THE LATTER FOR NET]	COMMENTS

LISTING OF ASSETS & LIABILITIES [use additional sheets of paper if necessary]	
DESCRIPTION	**MARITAL OR SEPARATE** [IF SEPARATE, STATE WHY— e.g., PRE-MARITAL, INHERITANCE, GIFT]
K DEBTS: [IN WHOSE NAME? INCURRED FOR WHAT PURPOSE?]	
WHICH ASSETS DID EACH OF YOU OWN AT THE TIME OF THE MARRIAGE?	

LISTING OF ASSETS & LIABILITIES
[use additional sheets of paper if necessary]

NET ASSET VALUE (OR DEBT BALANCE) AT DATE OF SEPARATION [SHOW FULL FAIR MARKET VALUE, THEN SHOW ANY LIENS OR MORTGAGES; SUBTRACT THE LATTER FOR NET]	COMMENTS

Separation Agreement Survival Guide

Preface

The purpose of this handout is to assist you in answering questions that you may have regarding separation agreements. It is, of course, impossible to answer all of your questions in a short brochure such as this, so we want to encourage you to ask other questions of your lawyer at the appropriate time. Feel free to take this handout with you so that you may refer to these answers from time to time and have a better idea of how your case is being handled.

1. **Q. Do I have to have a separation agreement?**
   A. No law requires a separating couple to execute a separation agreement, but it is a wise idea if there are debts, children, support claims, or property involved, and the parties want to settle these matters in writing. Oral promises between spouses are worthless and unenforceable.

2. **Q. What is a separation agreement?**
   A. A separation agreement is a contract between a husband and wife in which they resolve such matters as property division, debts, custody, and support when they separate from each other.

3. **Q. Who prepares a separation agreement?**
   A. It is best to have your own attorney prepare it for you. The separation agreement is not valid in North Carolina unless both parties have signed, and their signatures are notarized. Never try to prepare such a complex and important document yourself—this is a job for a specialist.

4. **Q. Can we divide our property in a separation agreement?**
   A. Yes. A couple that is separating can agree on a division of property in their separation agreement, and that agreement will be binding on them. The property to be divided consists of real property (such as land and the buildings on it), tangible property (cars, jewelry, and furniture, for example), and intangible personal property (such as bank accounts, stocks and bonds, pensions, and life insurance).

5. **Q. Is my spouse required to sign a separation agreement?**
   A. No. "Agreement" means that *both parties sign voluntarily.* You cannot compel your spouse to sign a separation agreement or to agree to the terms you wish to impose on him or her in the agreement.

6. **Q. Does a separation agreement help me to get a divorce?**
   A. A separation agreement is not "proof" that you have been living separate and apart from your spouse. It does not make divorce in North Carolina easier or more difficult to obtain.

7. **Q. Can our separation agreement settle who claims the tax exemption for our children?**
   A. Yes. The 1984 Tax Reform Act allows the parties to agree on who can claim the children as exemptions for income tax purposes. Without a written agreement, the parent who has physical custody of the child for more than half the year will get the dependency exemption.

8. **Q. WHAT ARE THE FACTORS I SHOULD CONSIDER IN TRANSFERRING THE EXEMPTION?**

   A. Consider these issues:

   a. Should the dependency exemption be *traded,* instead of *given,* to the noncustodial parent in exchange for an increase in child support? Even a small increase in child support would help offset the tax increase paid by the custodial parent, and the other parent can better afford such an increase due to the taxes he or she saves by claiming the exemption on federal and state tax returns.

   b. Should you alternate the tax exemption between parents? For example, the father could claim the exemption in even-numbered years (1996, 1998, and so on) and the mother could do so in odd-numbered years. Or the father could claim one child and the mother could claim the other. Such alternation would lessen the impact of higher taxes on the custodial parent.

   c. Should you condition the transfer on the noncustodial parent's regular and full payment of child support? Instead of transferring the exemption permanently without regard to payment of child support on time, some custodial parents agree to transfer of the dependency exemption only if the other parent is current (not in arrears) on child support payments by December 31 of each year.

9. **Q. CAN I GET MY HUSBAND FOR CONTEMPT OF COURT IF HE BREAKS THE PROMISES IN THE SEPARATION AGREEMENT?**

   A. No. Contempt of court is the failure to obey a court order without legal justification. It is not contempt of court to violate a separation agreement unless the agreement has been made a part of a court order. You may, however, sue your spouse for breach of contract if he or she violates the separation agreement.

10. **Q. WILL A SEPARATION AGREEMENT FREE ME FROM PAYING DEBTS FOR WHICH I HAVE SIGNED ALONG WITH MY SPOUSE?**

    A. No. A separation agreement is a contract between spouses. *It cannot bind third parties* (such as banks or finance companies) *who have not signed it.* If, however, one spouse promises to pay a bill and then breaks that promise resulting in your having to pay, you can sue your spouse for breach of contract for the amount of money you had to pay.

11. **Q. WILL A SEPARATION AGREEMENT STOP MY SPOUSE FROM HASSLING ME?**

    A. While separation agreements usually have a non-harrassment clause in them, you should understand that no piece of paper—be it agreement or court order—is going to stop a person from doing something he or she wants to do. If the problem is one of physical violence, a court order would be better than a separation agreement and could be used to punish the wrongdoer if he or she violated the order. If there is only an agreement, a lawsuit for breach of contract is one possible remedy for breaking the promise of not hassling each other.

12. **Q. IS A COURT BOUND BY WHAT WE PUT IN THE SEPARATION AGREEMENT ABOUT OUR CHILDREN?**

    A. No. The terms you include for child support, custody, and visitation can always be modified by the court in the best interest of the children. In the absence of proof to the contrary, however, there is a presumption that the terms concerning support for the children in your agreement are fair, reasonable, and necessary for the best interest and welfare of the children.

13. **Q.** CAN THE COURT MODIFY THE TERMS WE INCLUDE IN A SEPARATION AGREEMENT CONCERNING OURSELVES?

   A. Unlike the terms concerning children, which are always modifiable by the court, the terms that pertain to adults cannot be modified by the court except in very limited circumstances. For example, if the separation agreement has been incorporated into a court decree, then the court has the power in North Carolina to modify the alimony terms based on a substantial change of circumstances. If the terms involve property division and the agreement has been incorporated, the court can only modify it if it is executory in nature (i.e., it has not yet been completed, such as the transfer next year of a car title to a spouse), as opposed to those items that are already executed by the parties (such as the deed to the house that was signed over to a spouse at the same time the separation agreement was signed). The court can overturn a separation agreement if it was signed due to fraud, coercion, ignorance, or lack of mental capacity. In most cases, however, this is difficult to prove.

14. **Q.** CAN WE PROVIDE FOR COLLEGE EDUCATION FOR OUR CHILDREN IN A SEPARATION AGREEMENT?

   A. Although a North Carolina judge cannot order you to pay child support for your child in college, you may make provision for college expenses in a separation agreement, and it will become a binding, enforceable contract which the court can require each of you to perform. Since college is less of a luxury and more of a necessity these days, it would be a good idea to consider whether you want to provide in writing for your child's/children's college education.

15. **Q.** WHAT POINTS SHOULD WE REMEMBER IN DECIDING ABOUT COLLEGE EXPENSES?

   A. Here are some of the items that a good separation agreement will address:

   a. *How long should the obligation last?* 4 years? 4½ years? Until the child attains age 23? Some ending point should be set.

   b. *What costs will be covered?* The usual ones are room and board, books, tuition, and fees. Some parents also agree on a monthly allowance for spending money for the child.

   c. *What are the spending limits?* Few parents want to agree to finance a college education for a child at *any* college or university. The cost of some private colleges and universities would bankrupt the average parent. It is reasonable to put a ceiling or "cap" on the college expenses, such as by specifying that the maximum shall be "the then-prevailing rate at N.C. State University" or some other nearby public institution. Such a provision is fair to everyone and does not force either parent to go broke paying for college.

   d. *What other limits do you want to set?* For example, some agreements require that the child will be:

      i. attending an accredited institution;

      ii. in pursuit of a generally recognized undergraduate degree;

iii. on a full-time basis; and

iv. while maintaining at least a "C" average.

e. *How much should you pay?* Be sure to set a specific amount or percentage for yourself and your spouse; don't just say, "a reasonable share." Should it be 50 percent? Two-thirds of the cost? Be sure to spell it out specifically!

16. Q. SHOULD WE PROVIDE FOR ALIMONY IN OUR SEPARATION AGREEMENT?

A. Alimony is spousal support—it is money paid by one spouse to the other to help with support, maintenance, and living expenses. It is not the same thing as child support. If the two of you have agreed on an amount of alimony, you should definitely put that in the separation agreement. Such a provision might state, for example, that the husband shall pay the wife alimony of $1,500 per month until he or she dies or until she remarries, or it could state that the wife shall pay the husband alimony of $900 per month for a total of 60 months, at which time it will terminate forever. These are just examples; your attorney will advise you about the applicability of alimony in your particular case.

17. Q. IS ALIMONY TAX-DEDUCTIBLE?

A. If the agreement is drafted properly, the alimony can be made to be deductible for the payor and therefore taxable to the payee. It is also acceptable to make the alimony nontaxable to the payee if it is nondeductible for the payor. This is a particularly important term and it should be spelled out clearly in the agreement how the alimony payments will be treated for tax purposes.

18. Q. WHEN DOES ALIMONY END?

A. The usual times alimony ends are at the death of the husband, the death of the wife, the remarriage of the recipient, or upon the recipient's cohabitation (i.e., living with another person on a regular basis as if they were husband and wife). Some clients specify that alimony will end on a particular date or after a specified period of months or years. It is very important that your agreement set out specifically all of the terminating events for alimony that should apply.

19. Q. WHAT SHOULD WE DO IF WE HAVE AGREED THAT NO ALIMONY WILL BE PAID?

A. It is always best to put such a term in the agreement. Don't just leave it out or let the agreement be silent on this issue. This waiver of alimony is such an important term that it should be clearly spelled out in the agreement so that there is no misunderstanding.

20. Q. HOW DO I KNOW IF I AM ENTITLED TO ALIMONY?

A. Your attorney who prepares the separation agreement will explain alimony to you. In North Carolina, alimony may be granted by the court if:

a. You file a lawsuit requesting alimony;

b. You are financially dependent on the other party or in need of support from him/her;

c. The other spouse is the supporting spouse; that is, he or she is able to provide reasonable spousal support to you; and

d. An award of alimony is equitable (or "fair") under all the circumstances.

An absolute defense to an alimony case exists when the parties have waived alimony in a separation agreement, when a divorce has been granted before an alimony claim is asserted in court, or when the dependent spouse has committed adultery or some other form of illicit sexual behavior.

21. Q. **How much alimony should I get?**

 A. This question is impossible to answer. There are no guidelines for alimony in North Carolina, so there is no way of predicting what the court would have done to set an alimony award if the case had gone to court. Alimony awards of $500–1,000 per month are not uncommon, and some spouses who make a great deal of money could pay as much as $4,000 per month or more in alimony. The best way to figure how much alimony a client needs is to calculate the difference between her reasonable monthly needs and her current net income, and then to compare this figure to the difference between the other party's net income and reasonable monthly expenses. Your gap is "unmet needs" and should be equivalent (under ideal circumstances) to the "extra" money he has left over from his paycheck after he pays for his own reasonable monthly expenses. Since these "gaps" seldom exist in reality and everyone is usually spending a lot more than he or she is making, it is often a question of haggling, discussion, and bargaining as to how much alimony should be paid in any individual case. For a more detailed discussion of alimony, see our Client Information Letter on this subject.

22. Q. **How should we divide our property in the separation agreement?**

 A. In North Carolina, there is a strong presumption that all marital property is divided on a 50-50 or equal basis. This is presumed to be fair. Other divisions, such as 60-40 or 75-25, are certainly legal if the parties agree that the division is fair and equitable. And on rare occasions, they are granted in court after a long and contested trial. In North Carolina, *marital property*, with certain exceptions, is anything acquired during the marriage. The exceptions are *separate property*—that is, property acquired by either party before their marriage or property acquired at any time by gift (from someone other than the spouse) or inheritance. The title to the property—that is, whose name is on the deed or title—is not the deciding factor in determining what is separate and what is marital property. Rather, when the asset was acquired (i.e., before or during marriage) and how it was acquired (i.e., by use of marital funds or separate funds, by gift or inheritance, etc.) is the important consideration.

23. Q. **What about the increase in marital property after the separation— can that be divided?**

 A. It depends. The "passive" appreciation or depreciation, such as market growth or loss, is a kind of property called "divisible property" that should be divided between the spouses. For example, if your money market account has earned interest or your house has increased in value simply due to the market and not because of the active efforts of either spouse since the separation, that passive change in value should be divided along with the marital property.

24. **Q. WHAT ABOUT PENSIONS AND RETIREMENT BENEFITS—ARE THEY DIVISIBLE?**
    A. Pensions and retirement rights acquired during the marriage are marital property even if they are not vested. Often, a spouse's pension is the most valuable asset of the entire marriage, and this should certainly be considered when doing a separation agreement. If there is to be no division, the agreement should so specify. If the decision on pension division is to be put off or deferred because there is no present agreement, that also should be stated clearly. Make sure your agreement is very specific and plain in this area as to your intent on dividing the pension; a poorly worded agreement may be challenged as vague and unenforceable. The division of pension rights in a separation agreement can be done in two ways: a *present-value offset* or a *future percentage of payments*. The former of these involves calculating the present value of the pension right now and setting it off (or trading it) against the value of another item, such as the other spouse's pension or the marital residence. The second of these approaches would postpone the division until whenever the employed spouse starts receiving the pension payments, at which time the nonpensioned spouse would receive a share of each check equal to one-half (or some other portion) of the portion acquired during the marriage. Most pension or retirement benefits require a court order, such as a Qualified Domestic Relations Order, to divide. This order can often be entered by consent. The division of retirement benefits can be complicated, and your attorney can assist you with how to properly divide the benefits in your case.

25. **Q. DO WE ALSO DIVIDE DEBTS IN THE AGREEMENT?**
    A. You should set out a list of who pays what debt in your separation agreement, including the creditor's name, account number, purpose of the debt, approximate balance, and monthly payment amount. This will not stop the creditor from suing both of you if payments are not made by a spouse and both of your names are on the obligation, but it allows you to ask the court to hold your spouse accountable and to reimburse you for any payments you have had to make for the debt distributed to your spouse in the agreement.

26. **Q. HOW SHOULD WE DIVIDE OUR DEBTS?**
    A. There is no "right" answer to this question. In one case, the husband may take on payment for all the debts because he is the sole source of income in the family or because he created the debts in the first place. In another case, the wife may take over certain debt payments for things she charged or purchased or for things that she is being given in the property division. For example, if the husband is getting the station wagon and the wife is getting the washer and dryer, they might decide that each should assume the debt payment for the items he or she is receiving. It is often wise to have the spouse with the greatest incentive for making sure the debt is paid be responsible for that debt. For example, the spouse driving a particular car would want to make sure the loan for that car is paid promptly so the car does not get repossessed. Therefore, it makes sense for that spouse to have the responsibility for that debt in the separation agreement.

27. **Q.** I WANT TO MAKE SURE I CAN "DATE" AFTER WE GET THE SEPARATION AGREEMENT SIGNED. CAN I HAVE MY ATTORNEY PUT IN A "DATING CLAUSE"?

    A. It all depends on what you mean. If you mean the freedom to associate with anyone you wish to see, then it will be covered in the standard language found in your agreement. Most separation agreements contain a clause that allows each spouse to be left alone as if single and unmarried and forbids each spouse from harassing, molesting, or interfering with the other. But if you mean sexual relations with another before you're divorced, don't even think about it! There is no such thing as a separation agreement "dating clause" that allows adultery. Any sexual relations with a person who is not your spouse is adultery in the eyes of the law, regardless of the words in a separation agreement. There can be serious criminal and civil consequences for these, and no "dating clause" will serve to make legal something that is illegal. It is best not to take any chances and refrain from sexual relations until after the divorce is final.

28. **Q.** SHOULD WE ALSO PROVIDE FOR HOW WE FILE FOR TAXES IN THE AGREEMENT?

    A. Yes. This is a very important provision that can save you and your spouse a lot of money in taxes if prepared properly. A good example would be a clause that required the parties to file jointly so long as they are eligible to do so (which is up until the year they are divorced) and to divide the refund or liability for taxes in a specified way, such as 50-50, or 75-25, depending on the incomes of the parties.

29. **Q.** CAN A SINGLE ATTORNEY DO THE SEPARATION AGREEMENT FOR ME AND MY SPOUSE?

    A. It is best to have two attorneys involved, one to advise each spouse. In this way, the husband and the wife both know that they have received independent legal advice for their individual situations from lawyers who do not have a conflict of interest in trying to represent two clients with different goals and needs. The attorneys in our offices will prepare a separation agreement on behalf of only one spouse and not for both parties.

30. **Q.** WHAT IF I HAVE OTHER QUESTIONS?

    A. Please ask us. We're here to help you. If a question comes up between office visits, just call or e-mail us and we'll try to answer it for you.

■■■

Separation Agreement Checklist

We have prepared this list of provisions for separation agreements for you to consider in the preparation of your Separation Agreement. You may wish to review and discuss these terms with your spouse. Using this checklist, which is not all-inclusive by any means, you can help us to prepare a Separation Agreement that will best cover and protect your interests and concerns.

Standard Clauses

1. RIGHT TO LIVE SEPARATE AND APART AS IF SINGLE AND UNMARRIED
2. MUTUAL NON-HARASSMENT PROVISIONS
3. NO MODIFICATION OF AGREEMENT EXCEPT IN WRITING
4. MUTUAL RELEASE OF ALL CLAIMS AND MARITAL RIGHTS
5. RULES FOR INTERPRETING AND ENFORCING AGREEMENT
6. ATTORNEY'S FEES RECOVERABLE IF ONE SPOUSE BREACHES AGREEMENT
7. REPRESENTATION OF PARTIES BY ATTORNEYS (OR NOT)

Optional Clauses

(depending on particular circumstances of spouses)

8. ALIMONY PROVISIONS
   A. Waiver of alimony (spousal support)—this is permanent, even if there is later reconciliation.
   B. Amount of alimony—flat amount or modifiable according to some standard (i.e., income of payor or payee, Consumer Price Index for each year, or flat percentage)
   C. Tax consequences (ordinarily taxable to payee and deductible to payor, unless agreed otherwise)
   D. Medical insurance for spouse/ex-spouse
   E. Unreimbursed health care expenses for spouse/ex-spouse (see 10.c. below)
   F. Termination of alimony based on death of either spouse, payee's remarriage (or payee's cohabitation)

9. CHILD CUSTODY
   A. Joint legal custody—shared decision-making for major choices in child's life (i.e., religion, non-emergency health care, private/public school, tutoring)
   B. Sole custody
   C. Visitation rights by non-custodial parent (NCP)
      1. "Reasonable visitation" unstructured, left to consent of spouses with reasonable advance notice
      2. "Structured visitation" specified times (i.e., one-half Christmas and summer vacation, every other weekend during school year, plus half of each year's major holidays)

10. CHILD SUPPORT BY NCP
    A. Cash amount of support per week, month, etc. (considering North Carolina Child Support Guidelines)
    B. Medical insurance for child—who pays premiums?
    C. Uncovered health care expenses—who pays for what, or for what portion? (i.e., routine physicals, eyeglasses, prescription drugs, psychological/psychiatric treatment, initial deductible amount for insurance, remaining percentage uncovered)

11. ADDITIONAL CHILD-RELATED TERMS
    A. Annual modification—"escalator clause" (see 8.1.b. above)
    B. College expenses
    C. Maintain life insurance for benefit of child (if NCP dies before child support obligation ceases)
    D. When child support ends—age 18, graduation from high school, or emancipation (if earlier)
    E. Dependency exemption for each child for federal and/or state returns (generally this belongs to the parent with custody for over 50% of the year unless agreement states otherwise) and child tax credit

12. TAX ISSUES
    A. Filing status of parties
    B. Dependency exemption (see 4.e above)
    C. Taxes due—who pays? Refunds—who receives?

13. PAYMENT OF DEBTS—HOW MUCH AND BY WHOM?
    A. Property division
       1. Real property (land and buildings)
       2. Tangible personal property:
          a. Division of household furnishings
          b. Personal effects of each spouse
          c. Books, tools of a trade, business equipment
          d. Motor vehicles (cars, boats, planes, motorcycles)
          e. Collections, jewels, china, silver

■ ■ ■

Matters to Decide for Your Separation Agreement

    I. HOME (assuming home has both names on deed):
      A. If the home is to be sold to one spouse or put up for sale:
        1. If sold to one spouse:
          a. How much will buyer pay seller?
          b. When will payment be made?
        2. If put up for sale:
          a. When will it be put up for sale?
          b. Who will choose the real estate firm?
          c. How will the proposed sale price be set?
          d. After all sale expenses and payoff of home, will balance be divided equally?
          e. Who will stay in home while it is up for sale?
          f. Who will pay the home payments, the taxes and insurance while it is being sold?
          g. Who will pay for major home repairs while it is being sold?
          h. Who will pay for minor home repairs while it is being sold?
          i. Major home repairs are those over what dollar amount?
        3. If the house is not to be sold at the present time:
          a. Who will move out and when?
          b. Who will pay the home payments, the taxes and insurance while it is being sold?
          c. Who will pay for major home repairs while it is being sold?
          d. Who will pay for minor home repairs while it is being sold?
          e. Major home repairs are those over what dollar figure?
        4. Will the spouse who moves out agree not to reenter the home without the permission of the party who stays there?

   II. FURNITURE, FURNISHINGS, AND ACCESSORIES:
      A. How will they be divided?
        1. Will each spouse take (or has each spouse already taken) his or her share and the spouses agree to that division? or
        2. Will all items be listed on two separate lists, one for each spouse?
        3. When will the spouse who is moving remove his or her property?
        4. What payment, if any, is due from one spouse to the other as a result of this division?
      B. List all motor vehicles by name(s) on title, year, make, model, and lienholder (this is company to which payments are made).
        1. Who will own each?
        2. Who will pay balance due (if any) on each?
        3. Where should payments be made?

  III. DEBTS:
      A. For debts already owed:
        1. Who will pay for debts made just in one spouse's name?
        2. Who will pay for debts made in joint names?

3. Is it necessary to list debts? (If so, list name, account number, name and address of creditor, amount presently owed, and who will pay for each debt.)
B. For debts made after separation, will each spouse be responsible for all debts made by that spouse:
   1. After their separation, or
   2. After this agreement is signed?
C. If one spouse has co-signed a loan but the other spouse used the proceeds, will that spouse agree to ask the lender to release the other from liability on that loan?

IV. CASH, STOCKS, BONDS, AND BANK ACCOUNTS, ETC.:
A. List all cash, stocks, bonds, savings accounts, checking accounts, savings certificates, and credit union balances, and state the location of each.
B. Who will own each? If an item is to be divided, state in what shares or prepare a list for each spouse.

V. RETIREMENT:
A. If either spouse has a retirement benefit or pension or profit-sharing plan:
   1. What is the name and address of administrator of the plan?
   2. What is the percentage or dollar amount of each party's pension that is to be given to the other spouse?
B. What agreement has been reached about a joint and survivor annuity in the event of the pensioner's death:
   1. Before retirement?
   2. After retirement?

VI. SUPPORT:
A. Spousal support:
   1. Will one spouse pay support to the other? If so:
      a. State amount and whether payments will be made weekly, every other week, twice a month, or monthly;
      b. On what day or date will support be paid?
      c. On what date will it start?
      d. Where will it be paid?
      e. Will support cease if the supported spouse lives with an unrelated person of the opposite sex or upon remarriage?
      f. Upon death of the paying spouse, will his or her estate continue payments as long as funds are available in the estate?
      g. Upon the paying spouse's death, will the surviving spouse receive life insurance death benefits?
   2. In addition to the above, will the paying spouse also be responsible for the medical, dental, hospital, drug and optical expenses of the other spouse? If so, what percentage or amount of these expenses?
   3. If there is a health insurance policy now in force:
      a. Will insured provide comparable coverage if it is canceled or dropped?
      b. Is it with employer or privately owned?
      c. What is the name and address of insurance company?

B. Child support:
   1. Will one parent pay support to the other for child support? If so:
      a. State amount and whether payments will be made weekly, every other week, twice a month, or monthly;
      b. On what day or date will support be paid?
      c. On what day will it commence?
      d. Where will it be paid?
      e. Upon death of the paying parent, will his or her estate continue payments as long as funds are available in the estate?
      f. Will support cease or be prorated if the child visits with the paying parent for extended periods?
   2. In addition to the above, will paying parent also be responsible for the medical, dental, hospital, drug, and optical expenses of the child? If so, what percentage of these expenses?
   3. If there is a health insurance policy now in force:
      a. Until what age will it cover the child?
      b. Will insured provide like coverage if it is canceled or dropped?
      c. Is it with employer or privately owned?
      d. What is the name and address of insurance company?
   4. Will support continue after each child turns 18 if he or she is still enrolled in school? If so, will it stop:
      a. after the child reaches a certain age;
      b. when the child completes a certain amount of education;
      c. when the child marries, or
      d. when the child joins the armed forces?
   5. If the child goes to college or vocational school:
      a. Who will choose the school?
      b. What will be paid?
         (1) room and board?
         (2) books?
         (3) tuition?
         (4) fees?
         (5) transportation home at break?
         (6) food/eating out allowance?
      c. For how long will expenses be paid?
      d. Will there be any change in the amount of support when child is away and living at school?

VII. CUSTODY AND VISITATION:
   A. Will custody be:
      1. Solely with one parent? Which one?
      2. Joint physical custody? If so:
         a. With whom shall the child reside and for what periods?
         b. What effect will this have on child support, if any?
      3. Joint legal custody? If so:
         a. What will happen if the parents cannot agree on any specific major decision regarding the child?
            (1) Who will be the tie-breaker?

    B. Visitation
        1. Will this be defined as "at reasonable times" or will there be a schedule?
        2. Will advance notice be required for nonscheduled visits, and if so, how much?
        3. Will there be special arrangements (such as alternating every other year or half days each year) for special occasions?
            a. child's birthday
            b. Christmas holidays
            c. Thanksgiving
            d. Easter
            e. Father's Day/Mother's Day
        4. Will there be special arrangements for:
            a. school vacation periods
            b. each parent's vacation times
            c. school activities
            d. other opportunities (athletics, dance, music, etc.)
        5. Will there be any limitations on where the noncustodial parent can take the child during visits? If so, what are they?
        6. Any provision about removal of residence from area, and if so, does that affect visitation or support?
        7. Any rights of visitation for grandparents or other relatives?

VIII. INCOME TAXES:
    A. File jointly or separately for the current tax year? [parties entitled to file as "married" if they are not divorced by last day of the calendar year]
    B. If filing jointly, how will any tax refund be divided?
    C. If filing jointly, how will any tax liability be divided?
    D. Who will get the dependency exemption and child tax credit for each of the children?

IX. LIFE INSURANCE:
    A. Give company name/policy number.
    B. On life of either spouse or on child:
        1. Who will be the beneficiary of each policy?
        2. Who will pay the premiums?
        3. Who will be the owner of each policy?

X. ATTORNEY'S FEES:
    A. Who will pay each spouse's attorney?
        1. For work done on this agreement if either side needs services of private attorney?
        2. For any future divorce?

■■■

Separation Agreement Questionnaire

Preface

Please take the time to read this Separation Agreement Questionnaire closely. It will help us prepare a Separation Agreement for you and your spouse that accurately reflects your promises and intentions. Be very careful in preparing this Questionnaire and be sure to read this entire PREFACE before you complete the items below.

Perhaps you don't agree with your spouse on a possible term or clause to be included in or left out of a Separation Agreement. This doesn't mean you should give up or forget about such a provision. Your attorney may need to negotiate some of these terms for you or go to court on your behalf.

Please remember that the promises set out in a Separation Agreement are, for all practical purposes, permanent and binding. They usually cannot be changed by the courts. They *may be changed* if both of you agree and consent to the change, if you put down the change in writing, and then if you properly sign this writing as an amendment to your Separation Agreement before a notary public.

For this reason, your Separation Agreement is very important to us. We want to prepare a Separation Agreement that is fair for you and your spouse (and your children if there are any). You shouldn't rush into the signing of a Separation Agreement. We want to make sure all assets and relevant information are given by you and your partner so the Separation Agreement we prepare will be fair and accurate.

Obviously, your Separation Agreement is also very important to you. You need to have a good agreement, one that is fair and can be enforced. Please read carefully the questions and instructions below so we can help you make such an agreement.

Be fair to yourself. Be reasonable. Don't give in on non-negotiable matters. This is *your agreement*, and we want it to be fair to you and everyone concerned—your spouse and your children (if any). Be sure you are satisfied and *in agreement with* the terms of your Separation Agreement. *It's your Separation Agreement.*

* * * * * * * * * * * * *

HERE ARE THE QUESTIONS WE NEED YOU TO ANSWER.

1. FULL NAME OF HUSBAND:
2. FULL NAME OF WIFE:
3. COUNTY AND STATE WHERE HUSBAND RESIDES:
4. COUNTY AND STATE WHERE WIFE RESIDES:
5. DATE OF MARRIAGE:
6. DATE WHEN YOU SEPARATED:
7. FULL NAMES AND DATES OF BIRTH OF ALL CHILDREN BORN (OR ADOPTED) DURING THIS MARRIAGE:
   a.
   b.
   c.
   d.

8. PAYMENT OF DEBTS BY HUSBAND:

Name of Creditor	Acct. No.	Purpose of Debt	Balance of Debt as of DOS	Monthly Payment
_____	_____	_____	$_____	$_____
_____	_____	_____	$_____	$_____
_____	_____	_____	$_____	$_____
_____	_____	_____	$_____	$_____
_____	_____	_____	$_____	$_____

9. PAYMENT OF DEBTS BY WIFE:

Name of Creditor	Acct. No.	Purpose of Debt	Balance of Debt as of DOS	Monthly Payment
_____	_____	_____	$_____	$_____
_____	_____	_____	$_____	$_____
_____	_____	_____	$_____	$_____
_____	_____	_____	$_____	$_____
_____	_____	_____	$_____	$_____

10. DIVISION OF PERSONAL PROPERTY (this is everything except land and buildings)
   A. HOUSEHOLD FURNISHINGS AND PERSONAL EFFECTS. Choose one:
      ___ Each spouse keeps what he or she now has (you can only choose this if you are already living apart from each other); or
      ___ Husband shall have the following furnishings and personal effects (be specific):
      -or-
      ___ Wife shall have the following household furnishings and personal effects (be specific):
   B. DIVISION OF MOTOR VEHICLES. Choose one:
      ___ Each spouse keeps what vehicle(s) he or she now has and parties will transfer titles, if necessary, at time of signing Separation Agreement (you can only choose this if you are already living apart from each other); or
      ___ Each spouse keeps what is titled in his or her name and there are no jointly titled vehicles.
      -or-
      ___ Husband gets the following:

Year	Make/Model	Serial No.	Name(s) on Title Now
____	_____	_____	_____

      ___ Wife gets the following:

Year	Make/Model	Serial No.	Name(s) on Title Now
____	_____	_____	_____

      (NOTE: Please list who will be responsible for car payments at No. 8 & No. 9 above.)
   C. DIVISION OF FINANCIAL ASSETS (stocks, bonds, bank accounts, accounts, certificates of deposit, etc.). Choose one:
      ___ Each spouse gets all the assets in his or her own name and we have no jointly titled assets; or

___ Each spouse gets all the assets in his or her own name and we divide equally all jointly titled assets;

-or-

___ Husband gets the following assets:

Name of Asset	Description of Asset	Account No.	Location of Asset	Value of Asset
_____	_____	_____	_____	_____
_____	_____	_____	_____	_____

___ Wife gets the following assets:

Name of Asset	Description of Asset	Account No.	Location of Asset	Value of Asset
_____	_____	_____	_____	_____
_____	_____	_____	_____	_____

   D. DIVISION OF OTHER INTANGIBLE PERSONAL PROPERTY (such as cash value of life insurance, vested pension rights, etc.)
Husband gets the following: _____
Wife gets the following: _____

11. DIVISION OF REAL ESTATE (i.e., land and buildings). State what will happen to any real estate that may be owned by either or both of you, such as "Husband gets full ownership and possession of house and lot at 124 Green Street, Apex, North Carolina" or "Husband and Wife shall immediately sell house at 124 Brown Street, Raleigh, North Carolina; net proceeds of sale to be divided equally."

(NOTE: We will need a copy of your *deed* and *deed of trust* to transfer real estate.)

12. CHILD CUSTODY. If there are any minor children of the marriage, please fill in the following information:
    A. Who will have legal custody of the child/children? Choose one:
    ___ Husband   ___ Wife
    B. What visitation rights will the noncustodial parent have?
    ___ Reasonable visitation rights (unspecified and by agreement)
    ___ Specific and structured visitation rights, such as "every other weekend from 6:00 p.m. Friday to 6:00 p.m. Sunday, plus four weeks every summer and one week at Christmas vacation" or other specific language.

13. CHILD SUPPORT (MONETARY): If there are any minor children of the marriage, please complete:
    A. Total amount of child support per month, to be paid to parent with custody:
    B. Day of each month when child support is due:
    C. Address to which child support payments are to be sent:
    D. Child support amount per child (if more than one child):
    E. Child support for each child will end upon the first of the following incidents to occur: the death of the child, the marriage of the child, the emancipation of the child, or the child's moving away, indefinitely or permanently, from the home of the custodian. Outside of these conditions, however, please indicate which of the following you prefer for termination of child support:

___ When each child turns 18 years of age, regardless of whether that child is still in high school; or

___ When each child turns 18 years of age, unless that child is still in high school at that time, in which case child support continues until that child graduates from high school, so long as the child is under 20 years of age.

14. MEDICAL EXPENSES: Who will be responsible for providing and paying for a policy of medical insurance on the child?
___ Husband   ___ Wife   ___ Other

15. UNCOVERED HEALTH CARE EXPENSES. There are certain medical expenses which must be paid out-of-pocket and which are not covered or reimbursed. Examples of these are the initial deductible amount under the policy, the percentage of medical costs that is not covered after the initial deductible amount is met, and the costs of such things as routine physicals or orthodontic work. Who will pay the cost of the uncovered health care expenses? (Choose one.)
___ Husband   ___ Wife
___ Both parties equally up to a maximum of $_____ per year, after which the _____ shall pay all remaining costs not covered by insurance.
___ Both parties in the following ratio:
___ Husband = _____%, Wife = rest

16. TAX EXEMPTION. If there are minor children of the marriage, the tax exemption or credit (federal and state) is an important financial consideration. Under current tax laws effective January 1, 1986, unless there is a written agreement otherwise, the custodian of the children is allowed to claim this. The custodian is the parent with whom a child lives for more than half the year. Please indicate your choice below:

Name of Child	Parent to get Exemption (federal taxes)	Parent to get Exemption (state taxes)
_____	_____	_____
_____	_____	_____
_____	_____	_____
_____	_____	_____

Do you want this conditioned on the noncustodial parent being current with his or her child support duties under your Separation Agreement as of the end of the tax year? Yes   No ___

17. COLLEGE EDUCATION. College is not a luxury today; it is, in many cases, a necessity for a child. No court in North Carolina can force you, without your consent, to provide or assist in providing a college education for a child of yours, but you may agree in a Separation Agreement to help with college expenses for a child. If you cannot reach agreement on such assistance, skip the rest of this question. If you have reached agreement, please answer the following *for the noncustodial parent*:
A. What expenses for college will you pay?
___ Room, board, books, tuition, and fees? YES ___ NO ___
___ If others, please specify: _____

B. For how long in each child's case will the assistance be provided?
    4 years? ___   Other? ___
C. Will you require the child to be enrolled full-time? YES ___   No ___
    ___ At an accredited institution? YES ___   No ___
    ___ In pursuit of a recognized undergraduate degree? YES ___   No ___
    ___ Maintaining at least a "C" average? YES ___   No ___
D. Do you want to put a limit or a "ceiling" on the amount to be paid? If so,
    which of the following do you want?
    ___ 1. All college expenses will be paid by the noncustodial parent.
    ___ 2. Each of us will pay one-half of the college expenses.
    ___ 3. All college expenses will be paid by the noncustodial parent, but
            this obligation shall not in any event exceed the then-prevailing rate
            at the state college/university technical institute nearest to the
            child/children.
    ___ 4. Other:

18. LIFE INSURANCE: If one parent dies before a child reaches 18, there will often be
    no source of support for the child from the estate of a deceased parent. For this
    reason, parents want to provide life insurance as a way of financially caring for
    a child after their death. If you have reached agreement on this, please com-
    plete the following:
    A. What amount of life insurance is to be provided?
        $50,000 ___ $75,000 ___ $100,000 ___   Other ($ _____).
    B. Will both parties agree to pay for and provide life insurance or will just one
        agree to do so?
        ___ Both parents   ___ Husband only   ___ Wife only
    C. If individual (not group) life insurance is involved, will each parent agree
        to name the other as owner of the policy for as long as a child support obli-
        gation exists? YES ___   No ___. (This is very important). The owner of the
        policy is the only one who can cancel the policy or change the beneficiary.
        The owner is the one who must be informed of a missed premium payment
        that might cause the policy to be canceled. Each parent should try to get the
        other parent to allow a transfer of ownership [or an irrevocable choice of
        beneficiary] for at least as long as the child support obligation exists. If
        there is no change of ownership of an individual, one parent might attempt
        to cancel a policy or change the beneficiary in violation of the promises set
        out in the Separation Agreement. If this were done, the other parent would
        have no way of knowing that the policy had been canceled or the benefici-
        ary changed. Transfer of ownership is one good way of protecting against
        this. Transfer of ownership cannot be done with group insurance plans, but
        it can always be done with individual insurance policies. With a group pol-
        icy, you can still execute an irrevocable assignment of beneficiary.

19. ALIMONY:
    ___ A. Waiver of alimony. **PLEASE NOTE CAREFULLY:** If you waive or give up
            alimony, this waiver is, for all practical purposes, *permanent*.
    ___ B. Payment of alimony. Alimony will be paid as set forth below:
            1. Who will be the payor?   ___ Husband   ___ Wife
            2. Amount of alimony per month: $ _____

3. Day of month when each payment is due:
4. When will the alimony payments end? They must end on the death of the payee/recipient; they may also end upon the happening of the following events. Please check which ones you wish to apply:
___ Upon the death of the payor
___ Upon the remarriage of the payee/recipient
___ Upon the regular cohabitation of the payee/recipient with an unrelated person of the opposite sex
___ At the following date: _____, 20

(NOTE: Unless specified otherwise, alimony is taxable to the recipient and deductible for the payor.)

21. MEDICAL EXPENSES FOR SPOUSE: The spouse of a person with medical insurance will ordinarily be entitled to medical benefits until divorce. Whether or not you have agreed to alimony, you may agree to have some of the following items in your Separation Agreement:
A. Who will pay the uncovered health care expenses?
___ Husband   ___ Wife
___ Both in equal shares
___ Husband = _____%, Wife = rest
B. When will payment of uncovered medical expenses end?
___ Upon divorce
___ Upon divorce of dependent spouse, death of supporting spouse, or remarriage of dependent spouse, whichever comes first
___ Other (please specify _____)

■■■

Tax Considerations

Preface

The tax considerations of divorce negotiations and settlement agreements are often overlooked. This pamphlet is not designed to take the place of a consultation with and advice from a tax professional, such as a certified public accountant. Rather, it is an attempt to identify some issues relating to taxes you may want to consider in your domestic situation.

1. Q. MY HUSBAND AND I ARE SEPARATED BUT NOT DIVORCED. DO WE HAVE TO FILE A JOINT TAX RETURN?

   A. No, even married taxpayers who are living together are not required to file joint returns, but only married taxpayers are eligible to file joint returns if they so desire. For tax filing purposes, you are considered unmarried if a final divorce decree was entered by the last day of the tax year. There may be both advantages and disadvantages to filing separately. For example, spouses who file separate returns report their own incomes. However, if one spouse itemizes deductions, the other must also itemize and cannot claim the standard deduction. The best idea is to make the decision about filing separately or jointly, if you are entitled to do so, after discussing with your tax advisor the best way to minimize the tax paid to the government. You and your spouse may agree to file jointly, if that is most advantageous, and then provide a method for sharing the tax savings (or dividing the liability).

2. Q. WHO GETS TO CLAIM THE KIDS?

   A. For parents who are divorced, separated under a written separation agreement, legally separated under a court order, or who lived apart at all times during the last six months of a calendar year, the parent who has custody of the children for the greater portion of the year (the custodial parent) is generally entitled to claim the dependency exemption. However, the non-custodial parent may claim this exemption if there is a court order or separation agreement that gives that parent the <u>unconditional</u> right to claim the exemption or if the custodial parent releases the exemption to the non-custodial parent by completing IRS Form 8332 and attaching it to his or her tax return. Where parents are in different tax brackets, it often makes sense to transfer the exemption to the parent in the higher tax bracket (although individuals in the highest income bracket have all exemptions phased out and disallowed). This can be a good bargaining chip in the hands of a custodial parent in a lower tax bracket. In addition, a provision in a separation agreement which provides that the custodial parent will transfer the dependency exemption to the non-custodial parent if that parent is current in all child support and related obligations by the end of each year can be a good incentive for the non-custodial parent to stay current with his or her child support obligations.

3. **Q.** WHAT'S SO IMPORTANT ABOUT THE DEPENDENCY EXEMPTION ANYWAY?

A. The dependency exemption reduces your taxable income and consequently decreases the amount of taxes you pay. For the 2013 tax year, the amount of the dependency exemption is $3,900 for each dependent. The ability to claim at least one dependent is also important in determining whether you can claim "head of household" status which results in a lower amount of tax owed and a higher standard deduction than if your filing status is "single." In addition, until 2018, there is a child tax credit of $1,000 for each child under the age of 17, and this important credit is linked to the dependency exemption. Only the parent eligible to claim the child as a dependent can take the tax credit for that child. This tax credit is subtracted directly from the amount of taxes you have to pay. The dependency exemption is also important in determining which parent can claim the new education credits which may be available for expenses paid for a child's post-secondary education. Caution: the dependency exemption, child tax credit and education credits all have high-income phase-out provisions which must be considered in determining whether you are eligible for these tax benefits.

4. **Q.** WILL I HAVE TO PAY TAXES ON THE CHILD SUPPORT I RECEIVE?

A. No. Child support is not taxable to the person receiving it and is not tax-deductible to the person paying it. Therefore, if you get $600 a month in child support, then this is actually $600 "in your pocket" which you will be able to spend on expenses without having to worry about taxes.

5. **Q.** I AM A DEPENDENT SPOUSE AND I HAVE FIGURED OUT THAT I WILL NEED AN EXTRA **$1,000** PER MONTH IN ORDER TO PAY MY MONTHLY EXPENSES. IF I GET **$1,000** A MONTH IN ALIMONY, I'LL BE ABLE TO PAY ALL MY BILLS, RIGHT?

A. Wrong. Don't forget that alimony, unlike child support, is taxable as income to the recipient and tax-deductible for the payor. In order to determine how many "real dollars" you'll have to pay expenses each month, you need to consider your tax liability on the alimony you receive. For example, if you are in a 15 percent tax bracket, you will need to receive $1,176.47 in alimony to have $1,000 available after taxes (since you would pay $176.47 in taxes on that sum of alimony). On the other hand, if you are the person paying alimony, you will want to consider the tax benefit you'll get from the payments of alimony in determining the "out-of-pocket" effect of such a payment. For example, if you are paying $1,000 per month in alimony and you are in a 31% tax bracket, you will in effect be "out-of-pocket" $690 per month because you will get a tax deduction of $310. Caution: the tax effect of alimony described here depends on the payments meeting the IRS definition of alimony. This means that the payments:

- Must be in cash;
- Must be made pursuant a divorce or separation instrument, i.e., a court order for spousal support or a written separation agreement;
- Must not be made while the spouses are members of the same household;
- Must end upon the recipient's death;
- Must not be disguised property division or child support payments; and
- Must not be designated as a payment which is "not includable in the gross income of the recipient and not allowable as a deduction by the payor."

6. Q. My spouse and I have agreed to sell our home so that we can each get our share of the equity in it. What will I have to pay in capital gain taxes?

A. Probably nothing. The Taxpayer Relief Act of 1997 changed the law drastically as to capital gains on the sale of a home. No longer do taxpayers need to roll over the sale proceeds into another home to avoid capital gain taxes. Under the new law, regardless of age, each taxpayer can exclude up to $250,000 in capital gains ($500,000 for joint return) on the sale of the marital residence which has been owned and used by the taxpayer as his or her principal residence for two out of the five years prior to the sale. The spouse who acquires ownership of the house related to the divorce or separation can tack on the transferring spouse's period of ownership to his or her own. This is good news for a taxpayer who didn't qualify for the exclusion under prior law because he or she moved out of the marital residence leaving the other spouse in possession.

7. Q. Now that I've read your client information letter on tax considerations, I don't need to consult a tax specialist, right?

A. Wrong. The tax laws are extremely complicated and have implications far beyond what can be addressed in this client information letter. The general information set out here is not a substitute for consulting with a tax professional. We recommend that you discuss the tax implications of your divorce with your tax adviser as early as possible in your divorce proceedings.

■ ■ ■

Index